Character Building

A guide for parents and teachers

DAVID ISAACS

Character Building

A guide for parents and teachers

FOUR COURTS PRESS

FOUR COURTS PRESS LTD
7 Malpas Street, Dublin 8, Ireland
e-mail: info@four-courts-press.ie

In North America by:
Scepter Publishers, Inc.
info@scepterpublishers.org
www.scepterpublishers.org
212-354-0670

It is a translation of *La educación de las virtudes humanasy su evaluación*, 23rd edition, 2000 (Ediciones Universidad de Navarra, S.A., Barañain, Navarra).

First published in English 1983 and
reprinted many times
Second edition 2001; reprinted 2006

A catalogue record for this title
is available from the British Library.

ISBN 13: 978-1-59417-376-9

Contents

Prologue: The permanent value of the family

'The family is in crisis' is a commonly heard phrase these days. The family, we are led to believe, is in danger of becoming obsolete. Its mission has been completed and society now has better ways of fulfilling the role traditionally assumed by the family. However, our ordinary powers of observation show that the person is born into a family, that the first physical and emotional contacts are established in the family, and that the basic security of the person depends on the family until he or she leaves home.

Of course, it would be easy to reason, from the other point of view, that a person might indeed be born outside the family. His first physical and emotional contacts could be organised outside the family and he could find a certain security in a different type of organisation. So, we must ask ourselves: Is it correct to hold that certain values specific to the family actually do exist? Or, at least: Can we discover and live certain values in a particularly effective way because of the specific characteristics of the family?

These questions can be answered from different points of view. Some may reply basing their answers on an emotional, almost instinctive, reaction which is the result of their own very positive experience of family life: for them, no other explanation is needed. That sort of response may be perfectly valid for these people. However, many people may feel, at some point, the need for a rational explanation of this conviction. The realities of life need to be discovered by the whole person if he or she is to have a truly 'integrated' development. This implies that the value of the family, which we may have experienced from childhood on, should be considered intellectually to judge its validity, to see if there is any real foundation for this conviction.

To be able to judge adequately, information is needed and information in general is seldom 'objective'. It is influenced, for example, by the motives of the people who give it, by their emotional state, and by their real knowledge of the subject. It is always a problem to gather enough data, and it is also difficult to distinguish between facts and opinions, between what is important and what is secondary. In other words, to be able to judge adequately, guidelines are needed to help us recognize what is most valuable, what is less valuable, what has no value and even what may involve a negative value.

Referring to the possible value of the family, a Christian would do well to take into account explicit declarations of the Church hierarchy. Relevant to this we find, in paragraph 3 the Declaration on Education of the second Vatican Council:

> Because parents have given life to their children, they are seriously obliged to educate them and, therefore, they are the first and primary educators. This duty, that is, educating the members of the family, is so important that, when it is lacking, it can hardly be substituted. It is, then, an obligation of the parents to create an atmosphere in the family inspired by love, by piety towards God and towards man, and which favours an integrated personal and social education. The family, for that reason, is the first school for social human virtues, which all societies need. Above all, in the Christian family, enriched by grace through the sacrament and the duties of marriage, the children should learn from their early years to know, to feel and to worship God and to love their neighbours according to the faith received in baptism. In the family they feel the first experience of a sound and healthy society of people and of the Church. Through the family, the children can be introduced easily into civil society and into the Church of God. The parents should consider carefully, therefore, the importance that a truly Christian family has for the life and progress of all God's creation.

To know that the Church has made such a clear statement may be sufficient information for many Christians. However, on this occasion, we are going to endeavour to offer a pragmatic justification of the family and prove its usefulness by appealing to its efficiency.

The family is so efficient

I would like to stress, first, three aspects of efficiency:

- performance: That is, getting the same results with less effort; getting the same results in less time; getting better results for the same effort, etc.
- personal satisfaction: Efficiency also implies that there be results for the doer of the action; it is not just a matter of mechanical efficiency. It is possible to give a good performance but without its being efficient because no personal satisfaction is found which can contribute to future efforts.
- personal development: Efficiency should focus on the future; the situation must not remain static. An important part of the situation is the doer; he needs to develop in the same way as the object of his action: personal development should result from an action for it to be considered really efficient.

If it does not produce better performance, greater personal satisfaction and more personal development, family life as a form of organisation cannot be rationally justified.

We must consider, therefore, some distinctive features of the family.

The family: a group of persons who share

The members of a family live in one and the same place, sharing space, food, utensils and so on. In the relationships between the members, the behaviour of each person is largely unforeseeable. The members of a family do not usually perform specific functions, and for that reason one has to think of each person more for what he is than what he does.

On the other hand, in social life we can observe a tendency to classify people, for example, according to their profession, or within a profession according to their speciality. Also, we can see how people like to know where others come from, whether they are married or not, and other pertinent details. However, all these characteristics are repeatable. To begin with, we accept others because of the way they dress, their schooling, their nationality and so on. Only after a prolonged period of living together with another person can we get to know and accept him or her for what he or she is and no one else can be – that is to say, for personal traits which are not repeatable.

In the family, however, the acceptance of the person's function coincides with the acceptance of the person himself. A mother accepts a child, for example, but at the same time she is accepting *her* child. This child, in this relationship, need be nothing more than that: child.

In this way, one may consider the family as a group of relationships, in which what is related and shared is the most profound and the most specific part of the person, that is, his intimacy.

To the degree that the parents pay more attention to what their children are worth in relation to external social functions, the family has less meaning. In fact there are some families where we can find only a conditional acceptance of the children – acceptance conditional on the marks the children bring home from school, on their obedience to a series of superficial rules of conduct, or on their submissive attitude towards parental authority. However, the family is really a basis for interrelationships where mutual acceptance is unconditional, because these relationships are not under people's control. No one chooses his children, and the child does not choose his parents nor his brothers and sisters. Of course, it is possible that there could be unconditional rejection, but this is unnatural and at the moment we are not considering pathological cases.

What we have just said has particular relevance in the context of a fundamentally competitive world where one of the values most highly revered is functional value to society. In the family the person has the assurance of being accepted and loved for what he or she is – a unique individual. In other organisations within society this is not the case.

Security and permanence

We have said that relationships in the family are fundamentally natural, and therefore the acceptance of one member by another should be based on the personal characteristics of each. But this acceptance, because of its very nature, is permanent. This is so because what has been accepted and what one accepts in others is not transitory. The radical part of the person does not change but rather develops, discovering its own values.

The child, we have said, will be accepted for his or her uniqueness; this unconditional acceptance is what produces the sense of security a person needs for developing and improving. If it weren't for the family, the person could only believe in himself and want to improve so that others might recognise his worth to society or to the organisation for which he works. The value of the person in the family rests on what he is. For that reason the acceptance of the person is unlimited, although in practice this does not mean that we should accept everything a child says or does.

With reference to marriage, the Second Vatican Council said in its document on 'The Church in the Modern World': 'as a mutual gift of two people, this intimate union, as well as for the good of the children, requires complete fidelity between husband and wife and argues for an unbreakable oneness between them'. Notice that the reason given for this indissolubility is that of mutual giving, not for being a sacrament, for example. Mutual giving supposes that the husband has given himself to his wife and vice-versa. Therefore each no longer belongs to himself, but belongs to each other. Something similar occurs with the children: the parents give themselves to their children and the result of this is permanence and security. This produces in the children a sense of confidence because they know that their parents are theirs.

One can understand that this fact, in practice, produces what we call 'optimists' if we consider an optimist to be someone who first and foremost sees the positive side of things and the scope for improvement, and only then the difficulties that oppose this improvement; he uses all the resources at his disposal and faces up to difficulties sportingly and with good humour. A child cannot do this without reasonably believing in his own abilities and without trusting in his parents' permanent love and acceptance.

The family, we are saying, because of its very nature, offers a situation of trust based on the permanence of the relationships which permit the growth of the person as he or she is, with personal freedom.

Personal style

Logically, a person who has not found stability in his relationships with others, ends up being unstable in other aspects of life as well. To grow, the person needs roots – emotional roots and historical roots – and he needs to know that he belongs to a process which began a long time ago and will continue in the future. The family allows us to put down these roots. Although trust and confidence are the characteristics which most help to create the right conditions, many other factors also contribute. For example, the person may be influenced considerably by the physical layout of different objects in the house. The photograph of grandfather or grandmother's china makes the members of the family feel that they are part of a continuous process. On the other hand, the children go out into the world and find disappointments and upsets of every kind. When they return home, although they complain about it, what they need is to find the security of their parents' acceptance and of the permanence of family relationships which can be felt and seen in small details of decor in the house. These objects help to create the specific atmosphere and style of the family which cannot be repeated in other homes. For this reason we can say that in the family every member has the possibility of growing within his or her own style instead of being influenced capriciously by external influences. This style will be based on the discovery of different values which will transfer themselves into standards and virtues.

Because it is a *natural* organisation, the family makes it possible to practice, in one's own way, a series of values which become part of the inner core of each person. These values are, for example, generosity, sincerity, loyalty and respect.

The family as first school of human virtues

We have already mentioned the Vatican II document in which the following sentence is found: 'The family is, therefore, the first school for social human virtues, which all societies need.' Is that really true?

The family, being a natural organisation, is not a cultural organisation; therefore, in the process of the growth and development of its members, it needs to use a system which suits its own nature. The acquisition of culture, for example, is a process involving the learning of facts which helps the individual to better understand reality and manage it sensibly. This broad cultural development is not principally the task of the family.

In the family it is a question of educating what is most natural – the inner core of the person.

To develop the different aspects of one's inner core and personality (and, as a result, our personal freedom), first of all one needs to know oneself. We need to know each person's qualities in order to be able to discover the best way for him to improve and develop. Development involves three stages – (1) self-knowledge, leading to (2) self-discipline leading to (3) self-surrender, that is, the service of others. This overall development is achieved through growth in human virtues: in other words, a person's human maturity is the result of well-balanced development of human virtues.

Society clearly needs these virtues to develop in each of its members, but it is difficult to imagine how this could be achieved without the family.

A virtue may be developed in relation to two aspects: the intensity with which it is practised and the rightness of the motivation underlying its practice. In society, generally, the interest shown in virtues is motivated by a desire to achieve better performance. That is, people tend to develop a series of human virtues partially because they need to perform better. However, in the family, *efficiency* should be understood in the sense that we have already explained. In the family it is possible to stimulate the members to develop virtues out of love, knowing that all the members of the family have the duty to help the others to improve, because as long as one is living so close to other people in a natural organisation, what grows strong or becomes ill is one body, one entity – the family.

It is the family, in this sense, that helps its members to make the outside cultural and social influences personally significant for each member. Within the family, external data can be translated into something meaningful for each person.

The unity of the family

However, we might ask how justifiable it is to develop and protect a family so that its members benefit at the expense of other members of society. Undoubtedly, if we have a scale of values, each person should protect and look after his own family first, because there he can find the peace and interior strength necessary to help others efficiently. However, he must reach these others as well. For this reason one should not understand the unity of the family as a closed system without exterior contacts. The family is, because of its very nature, an open system that can influence and be influenced by those around it. The unity of the family is not achieved by separating it from other organisations, but neither is it a result of stereotypical behaviour by its members. The family is not a factory. What one does in the family context should result from deeply-held convictions.

We might be able to create a family where all the members behave in a uniform way: probably it would look like a united family from outside. However, a family's unity is not the result of planning on the parents' part. Neither is it the result of doing things together. Unity consists in all the members of the family sharing and respecting a series of correct and true values. If there is agreement about these values and about what they mean, each member can then behave whatever way he likes, with personal style and initiative but asking for advice. It is clear that the unity which produces the best results is that in which the members are in agreement as to their duty – each one with his own particular style – to develop a series of virtues.

This can be corroborated by observation. Families which have a particular style of their own are those whose members are developing a series of virtues. Families without style are those in which there is no such unity of purpose.

One value which one finds in the family is a desire for personal improvement in order to serve others. But this will only be so if the parents do not stifle the real living together of a group of persons, each seeking his or her own human maturity.

The easiest way of stifling growth is to centre attention on trivial aspects of behaviour. In some families we find a mean and poor view of life, and when the members are only worried about their own welfare, for example, the result is a wilderness of envy, complaints, contempt and humiliation. But in the family it is possible – because each trusts the other, and all trust in the future and in the potentialities of the others since they are unique and valuable – it is possible, we say, to saturate every act with love and thus come to love the world passionately.

Perhaps, now, we can return to our concept of efficiency and consider from this point of view what are the lasting values the family should discover in itself.

Conclusion

Efficiency, we have said, requires good performance, personal satisfaction, and personal development and growth. We have mentioned a series of specific characteristics of the family while discussing the following themes – the family, a group of persons who share; security and permanence; personal style; the family considered as the first school of human values; the unity of the family. Is better performance to be found anywhere else? The individual and society in general: can they obtain the same results with less effort or in less time without counting on the family? Or better results for the same effort?

Everyone has qualities and characteristics, and potentialities which are sometimes dormant. But the person best equipped to serve others is he who has managed to develop his talents, that is, someone with an all-round education. The family, because of its natural ties, favours the development of the unique dimension of the person, the development of his inner core and of the human virtues which all societies need.

Man, a being endowed with freedom, needs the family in order to become aware of his own personal limitations and of his abilities, so as to be able to overcome the first and take advantage of the second. This is the way to develop self-control and be able to serve others better. If we consider society to be a grouping of free human beings, the family is also needed to enable society to reach its own perfection by the input of the individual richness of each member.

Obviously, if society is not seen as a group of human beings, every individual is a nuisance and so is the family; and the logical thing to do is stifle any organisation which tries to encourage personal style and replace it with an organisational set-up where each member is regarded as useful because of the function he performs and not because of what he is in himself.

The second question we have to answer is: To what degree does the human person find personal satisfaction through the family? By satisfaction we don't mean a passive state of well-being. Everyone has a certain number of basic needs (a minimum income, light, food etc.) but satisfaction is something which does not operate at the level of elementary needs of the body and its appetites; it has to do with what a person's potential is and the work he has put into realising that potential. A deep sense of personal satisfaction derives from natural things (not artificial things) once a person discovers the purpose for which he has been created and makes an effort to overcome the obstacles he meets in pursuing that purpose.

The family is a natural organisation, made up of different relationships between people who can discover the purpose of their lives – to help others to improve and to love them – in a natural way. In the family we can find a first circle of people in which it is reasonably easy for us to develop the virtue of generosity and derive the deep sense of satisfaction that comes from having made an effort to help others. At the same time we receive the attention and the love of the others directed towards the most profound aspects of our own being.

Undoubtedly the relationships within the family are not sufficient for us to find complete satisfaction. It will also be necessary for us to engage in work: man was made to work. And also he needs friends and companions. Each person can develop himself through all these relationships. And he needs, especially, to develop relationships with God. (We have already mentioned the Vatican II statement stressing the importance of the family for spiritual growth.) However, the family is still the place where a person can find an initial basic satisfaction, because the family accepts him unconditionally, loving the unique aspects of his being.

A person also needs to derive satisfaction from doing work well, from being appreciated by his friends, from having done something for them. But the satisfaction which allows the person to look after the wellbeing of others instead of his own derives from being at ease with oneself; and this sense of ease and wellbeing is a result of having pursued the purpose which we have discovered in life. This purpose can be discovered, as we have said, in the most natural aspects of life – in relationships with other people; in work; in nature; feeling small and insignificant in the immensity of creation, but knowing at the same time that one has an untransferable mission to glorify God.

And, to end, our third question: To what degree can we find personal development and growth in the family? The family, we have said, is the first school for the education of human virtues. From all we have said about this education, it is quite clear that without the family it would be immensely difficult to achieve the proper development of these good operative habits.

However, in real life many families do not have the basic features we have been describing. So, we should stress that the family as an organisation, by its very nature, has certain structural characteristics which exactly suit the human person. These characteristics are neutral to begin with, but, once the family starts to operate, its actual character depends a great deal on the inputs, the behaviour and attitudes, of its members. Therefore, from the point of view of education, the family only really begins to make practical sense when the people involved realise the opportunities for development open to them. There will always be actual families whose members are happy, united, satisfied and improving, and there will always be others whose members are in a personal state of crisis, who are dissatisfied, unhappy and useless. But it is wrong to say that, because of this, the family, as such, is in crisis. Many individual families may be in crisis because their members have not discovered the real meaning of the family as an institution, and do not wish to think seriously about the purpose of their lives. But there are also a lot of families which are united and happy.

We have been examining the efficiency of the family as an organisation, referring to specific values which can be practised there in a special way. But, perhaps this appeal to reason is not necessary. Perhaps it is sufficient to remember the trusting smile of a small child, to remember misfortunes, dreams and projects shared with a loved one, to remember the peace and satisfaction of being able to refer to 'my home', to be able to state categorically that the family has permanent value, the family is going to last.

Introduction: Training children in human virtues

A word about terminology

Before we begin I should like to say something about the terminology used in this book. The whole subject of virtues – of character and qualities – is a complex one: people speak of the theological virtues, cardinal virtues and so on, often without knowing the differences involved. I want at this point just to clarify two or three points.

There are three theological virtues – faith, hope and charity. Following Thomas Aquinas, these can be considered as 'operative habits' infused by God into a person's soul to equip him to act in keeping with the dictates of reason illuminated by faith; God is their object. These are infused virtues, that is to say they are received directly from God. However, there is another series of virtues which are also infused – the *supernatural* moral virtues. These do not have God as their direct object but they orientate human actions to an ultimate *supernatural* goal. And then there are the natural moral virtues; these are *acquired*, that is to say that man can through his efforts develop these virtues. Acquired virtue differs from infused virtue in that the latter is oriented towards man's *supernatural* final goal, whereas acquired virtue improves a person on the *natural* level.

In this book I am dealing with acquired virtues – 'natural' or 'human' moral virtues. Four of these are called cardinal virtues – prudence, justice, temperance and fortitude; around them hinge all the others: they are necessary to the proper development of a cardinal virtue, they are a subdivision of a cardinal virtue or one related to a cardinal virtue.

You will notice that I have not used the term 'social' virtue. In the strict sense there is no such thing. This term is used to emphasise the role which certain virtues play in enabling a person the better to serve others and society at large. However, I feel that it is quite confusing to make a distinction between individual and society, because society exists only in function of the people who go to make it up, and a person is a social being who needs others. Therefore, it is right to regard all virtues as social virtues, even though some of them sound more 'social' than others. Accordingly, we will be dealing with a whole series of virtues which help a person to have more self-mastery so that he can better serve and contribute to others.

I think all parents would like their children to be orderly, generous, sincere, responsible, loyal etc.; but there is a big difference between a vague wish and a planned goal which is, to some extent at least, achievable (that is what an objective involves). If training children in human virtues is going to get off the ground, parents have to make a genuine purposeful commitment to it. And if they are to do that, they need to be convinced of the importance of the whole exercise.

Why parents should be concerned about virtues

In the foreword I said that the family is a natural organisation in which what is related and shared is the most profound and the most specific part of the person – his intimacy. This is precisely why in the family a person can be accepted just as he is – largely for what he is and not for what he does. If we think of other organisations in society we will notice that people are accepted for their *usefulness*, their functionality. For example, a soccer forward is accepted as long as he keeps scoring goals. Once he stops, he is rejected. In school, for example, each pupil is accepted in function of being a student. If he doesn't study he is rejected. But in the family each person has the opportunity of being accepted for what he is – a unique individual.

A school is not a natural organisation: it is a man-made cultural organisation; by providing culture it supports parents in the training of their children. But parents, since they are the primary educators of their children and live with them in the natural institution of the family, ought to look after those educational things which are the natural responsibility of the family – things for which the family was instituted. To be specific, it is for parents to look after their children's development in human virtues – the development of good habits and qualities. They should not make the mistake of thinking that it is valid for them to delegate this job to the schools their children attend.

This is one very good reason for coming to grips with, for being committed to, the development of human virtues: the fact, that is, that it is a part of the family's basic role. But we should also realise that human maturity at the natural level is a result of the harmonious, balanced development of these virtues: as Vatican II's decree *Optatam totius* puts it, 'human maturity ... will be chiefly attested by a certain stability of character, the ability to make carefully weighed decisions, and a sound judgment of people and events' (no. 11).

To put it another way, we could say that it would be 'ideal' (but unrealistic) to expect a child to arrive at school-going age with all his virtues so well developed that all he has to do at school is appropriate culture. But since that is not the way things are, the school should help the parents: but the parents make the main contribution.

If I have referred to 'objectives', it might seem that the whole approach of this book is going to be very technical. But that is not the case. The important thing about objectives is not formulating them in written form or planning out some activities as methods to achieve them; the important thing is, rather, the will to make an effort to pursue those objectives. If the will is missing, the objective immediately stops being an objective and we enter the world of dreams and nice ideas. Sometimes, of course, it is good to use the technique of actually writing down objectives or planning ways of achieving them, but the whole thing is really dependent on the degree of commitment there is to achieving the objectives.

What I want to underline is that parents in trying to train their children to develop human virtues, are going to make use of the daily events of family life – rather than to plan specific activities. But they do need to be committed clearly in their minds to developing these virtues; in this connection they could usefully give attention to two aspects of virtue – *the intensity with which it is practised and the rightness of the motivation underlying the practice.*

How to increase commitment to developing virtue

If we look at any good habit, we can notice that it can be put into practice more or less intensely. You can act generously towards your friends only, or you can be generous towards those people who most need help. You can act generously only when you feel 'in good form' or you can do so even when you are tired, etc. If we parents realise the scope of each virtue, it will undoubtedly be easier to act in keeping with what we want to achieve. However, it is not just a matter of the intensity with which children practise virtues: also important is the right motivation behind their effort. An example: two boys are giving some money to a companion. The first is doing so because he knows the boy's father is ill and his family needs money to buy food. The second gives it because his companion has told him if he doesn't produce he will force him. The difference in motivation turns the action into something completely different. And parents also should give some thought to the kind of motivation best suited to the age of the child.

If parents get clear in their own minds what each of the virtues mean which they want to see developing in their children, it will be much easier for them to improve their own commitment to this task. That is why we will go on, later, to define or describe a number of virtues, showing how they operate.

Another way of improving your commitment to training children in virtue is by being aware of the various ways you can help your child to be better. We know very well that one of the most important ways of training people is by example. In fact, it has been said that one educates more by what one is than by what one does – but I don't think that is quite true. As I see it, we educate through the intrinsic relationship of being and doing. Therefore, the kind of example which educates is not necessarily 'perfect' example, but the example of a person who is really striving to do better. This struggle with oneself means that one must be demanding on one's will and try to see things even clearer with one's mind. One's aim is to educate one's children in both these areas – will-power and clearmindedness.

For a habit – a virtue – to be acquired, you have to repeat an act many times. And it is repeated only if, in some way, repetition is demanded. Parents can require their children to do certain things (this is a positive demand) or not to do certain things (a preventive demand). The latter calls on a child not to go near danger unless it is necessary, or not to develop some bad habit, for example.

If certain virtues are to be acquired, it seems logical that children should be actually required to do certain things. They should be required to do things and often to think about what they are doing and why they are doing it. Guidance always involves this; a good guide gets information and gives out information. In doing so he gets the learner to think and then he gives him help and support. This way of making demands – explaining, asking why, exploring motives – is more suited to some virtues than to others (it works with the virtue of loyalty, for example) and its usefulness also varies with the child's age.

Two problems

All this talk about being demanding with children could cause some parents to be a little wary. For example, there is the danger of taking away a child's spontaneity and creativity: in other words, we are not letting him be free. Or there is the risk of these habits just becoming meaningless routine.

As far as freedom goes, one thing must be made very clear. One of the components of freedom is scope to choose between a series of options. Imagine having to choose between playing tennis and not playing tennis. If a person knows how to play, he has scope for choosing. If he doesn't know, he is not free to choose at that particular time. The same holds good for virtues. At sixteen a young man wants to be generous but he has never learned to be generous. What will happen? He won't be generous: he has no real option. He can't acquire a habit in a flash; it's only by repeating actions that a habit is acquired.

As far as the second problem is concerned, routine can be understood as performing some aimless activity. Undoubtedly, there will be routine if we approach virtue as an end in itself and not as a means to achieving the Good. It's not a matter of order for order's sake: one wants to be orderly so as to make social life more pleasant, or to be really more efficient, for example. Now, there are actions which, depending on the degree a virtue is developed and therefore on the age of the child, will be more explicitly related to some goal. For example, a small child improves in the virtue of perseverance by tying his shoelaces. To the child, his purpose is quite clear. Yet we grown-ups tie our shoes almost without realising it – maybe even thinking of other things. But we wouldn't therefore say that the action had lost its meaning and purpose. What has happened is that we have acquired an ability: we can now make efforts in the direction of more important goals or things more suited to us. In other words, we can use what we have achieved to help us continue to improve.

Virtues, ages and motivations

There are two virtues necessary for developing all the others – prudence and fortitude. If they are missing, virtue is impossible. 'Prudence consists in choosing the good; fortitude, temperance and justice are, respectively, what counter obstacles, passions and pride – all of which would have us desert goodness'.[1] These are the four cardinal virtues.

As far as the way these virtues work is concerned, prudence implies that you do not lose sight of the purpose of what you do. If prudence is missing, a virtue can end up being an end in itself. Take, for example, the virtue of order. A person who sets out to be orderly as an end rather than as a means, can end up having a mania about tidiness. Sincerity, without prudence, can result in complete inability to keep one's mouth shut. Every virtue, except justice, has two opposite vices, 'one which is obviously its opposite and the other which looks quite like the virtue itself'.[2] For example: order – disorder, excess of order; diligence – laziness, working non-stop.

In practice, it is more reasonable to develop the virtue of prudence in relation to other virtues and, therefore, it will have to find a place at all age levels. The same is true of fortitude; this involves both positive action and resistance; it allows one to make the effort of will to acquire habits. In any event, we will keep stressing each of these virtues in a series of different situations.

In order to decide which virtues are most important at any particular time, various factors have to be borne in mind; these are:

- the key features of the age level in question,
- the nature of each virtue,
- the actual characteristics and the potential of the young person whom we are training,
- the characteristics and needs of the family and of the society in which the young person is living,
- the parents' personal preferences and capabilities.

We will go on to suggest a distribution of virtues bearing in mind the first two of these five factors – without reference to the other three. Before doing so, I want, therefore, to say something about these latter factors. No scheme of virtues, no matter what theory it is based on, should be used as a rigid basis for fixing how parents should approach this question of training. But it can always be used as a flexible basis, one used by parents to help them decide what are the best steps to take in their own particular situation.

Among the factors to be borne in mind are the actual characteristics and potential of the young person, on the one hand, and his parents' personal preferences and capabilities on the other. I am posing the question of how to balance what one ought to do (in keeping with the young person's needs) with what one *wants* to do and what one *can* do (what one's personal preferences and abilities permit). It is easy to think that our sole concern is for what the young person needs, but in fact very often we are doing what we like, what we *want*.

So we need to establish some sort of criterion for working out which factor should prevail in the event of a clash (e.g. in a case where the parents see that their child is particularly irresponsible; and at the same time are particularly keen on getting him to be generous; the question would arise: 'which virtue should come first, responsibility or generosity?'). It is impossible to give a concrete solution. All we can do is give some ideas to take into account.

Parents should not have in mind some preconceived model of behaviour to which their child should aspire. But they do need to know those basic criteria, basic standards or values, they should try to share with their children. If they manage to share these, the result is a united family in which each member acts with his own style. In this sense, the development of virtues in a family does not involve people behaving in the same way but rather in all of them having a basic unity of purpose.

You could say that this means cultivating in a preferential way that virtue which gives more scope for each child to develop his strong points in the line of serving others and which tends to support him in those areas where he is weak. In this sense, virtue is subordinate to effectiveness; its role is to get each person to function properly. The virtue which needs to be most pushed at any particular time can be considered that which produces best results, personal satisfaction and personal development.

Therefore parents could usefully concentrate on finding out what their children's positive points are – what virtues they have got pretty well developed already – and what their shortcomings are. Then also, the family is a natural organisation which has a right to be supported by all its members. To get on well together, learning from the others and each helping the rest to improve (this is a duty of all the members), you have to practise certain virtues which foster this mutual help. And finally, since virtues support one another, we could give some thought to joy, which is the outcome of the harmonious development of the virtues and which can be used as a test of whether genuine virtue exists. Which virtues should parents emphasise? Those which are likely to produce most joy for all the family. If a family lacks this cheerfulness, the reason is it is not doing much to cultivate virtue – or there is no reasonable balance in the virtues being developed. In a word, it is a matter of getting personal tastes to coincide with the needs and tastes of others, precisely through sharing certain basic standards or values. Here we have suggested two standards – the duty of each member of the family to help the others to improve; and joy/happiness.

Bearing in mind that each family is different and that each child and each parent needs different attention, we will now take a brief look at a layout of virtues by age level, keeping in mind the basic features of each age level and the nature of the virtues themselves.

Up to seven years old

- Obedience
- Sincerity
- Order

Until they are seven, children scarcely have the use of reason and therefore the best they can do is obey their educators and try to fulfil this duty with affection. But by emphasising this virtue for little children, we do not wish to imply that it is not important for older people. This simply means that, as the years go by, a person's grasp should improve in such a way that each acts correctly on his own initiative without having to receive a whole series of instructions from others. In any event, at all ages the merit lies in obeying whoever is in charge – provided that one is not asked to do something wrong. Obedience is produced by parents making reasonable demands. They will have to be very demanding – but only on a very limited number of points, giving very clear, precise instructions.

Children could obey because they are afraid or because there is no way out. These are very lowgrade motives. They should be encouraged to obey out of love, to help their parents: this is the first step towards developing the virtue of generosity.

At the same time we should develop in them the virtue of sincerity, because this requirement to do certain things (to obey) gradually has to be turned into a requirement to think (a form of guidance), and this guidance by parents only makes sense if it is based on the child's real situation. Sincerity has also a lot to do with modesty and we will come back to this virtue at the teenage stage.

We also include the virtue of order – for a number of reasons: 1) if it is not developed early on, it is much more difficult to develop it later; 2) it is a virtue necessary for people to get on well together; 3) it is good for mothers' peace of mind: and that, quite seriously, is something important.

Children can be asked to be orderly and tidy on the grounds that this makes sense; but it often makes more sense to appeal to their affection rather than their intelligence. A sense of duty is another reason for being orderly – for example, when being tidy is linked in with carrying one's weight by doing one's chores.

These three virtues will form a solid basis for moving on to other virtues at the next stage.

From eight to twelve years old

- Fortitude
- Perseverance
- Industriousness
- Patience
- Responsibility
- Justice
- Generosity

As we will see, we now come to four virtues connected with the cardinal virtue of fortitude; two connected with justice and one with the theological virtue of charity.

Children at these ages undergo a series of biological changes with the arrival of puberty, and it is very desirable for them to develop their will, so as to strengthen their character. They now begin to take more personal decisions but they need criteria in order to know whether their efforts are going in the right dircction. We complement the virtues connected with fortitude by including some virtues directly concerned with other people – responsibility, justice and generosity.

Anyway, it is logical for children of this age to focus more on what they are doing, on the action itself, than on the person at the receiving end of the action. They are not yet very aware of their own intimacy. This is a stage when we should try to get children to keep at things not out of obedience, but rather for the satisfaction of managing to overcome some obstacle. This is the age for challenging targets (but reasonable targets). Just as the small child is very aware of the rules of the game when playing with his companions and in general in his relationships with others, it is surely good to stimulate children to develop virtues out of a sense of duty towards their companions, for example, but without forgetting to enthuse them with a worthwhile ideal. In this way they will get the satisfaction that comes from making an effort to overcome themselves.

All these virtues call for the use of the will. When we come to the descriptions of the virtues we will see that they have to do with 'putting up with annoying things', with 'continually making an effort to give to others', to 'attain what they set out to achieve', to 'resist evil influences', etc. To do all these things they need to set their sights high and not to be content with mean ideals.

This is a crucial time for 'aiming high'. By this I mean raising children's sights up towards God and getting these human virtues to build up their developing faith.

It might seem that this is rather a lot of virtues to be developing all at the same time; but they are interconnected. Where a child focuses on one or two of them, he is very likely to improve also in the others.

As the years go by, young people come to need more explanations, better reasons for keeping up the effort entailed by trying to acquire a good habit.

As their intimacy begins to awake, we enter the period of adolescence, a period when the young person has to do things on his own initiative, things he did previously by invitation or simply because he was required to do them by outside influence. Now he makes a commitment on his own and everything acquires a new dimension.

From thirteen to fifteen years old

- Modesty
- Moderation
- Simplicity
- Sociability
- Friendship
- Respect
- Patriotism

From eight to twelve years of age, approximately, we have emphasised virtues connected with fortitude and justice, in so far as they involve a child adapting his behaviour to certain concrete instructions. From the age of thirteen to fifteen, it seems desirable, in view of the young person's greater awareness of his own intimacy, to insist especially on virtues linked with temperance, in the first place. The purpose behind this is to help him keep goodness in sight and not let his passions get out of control.

Parents are well aware how common it is nowadays for young people to be given bad example by others who indulge in all sorts of extreme behaviour in search of some superficial pleasure.

If we emphasised fortitude earlier on, we now come to harnessing that virtue to protect what is everyone's precious possession – his intimacy. By this I mean soul, sentiments, thoughts – not just physical intimacy. The virtues of modesty and moderation involve recognising the value of what one possesses, so as then to make better use of it – in accordance with standards which are right and true.

What kinds of motivation can we offer children at this stage? I think we have to give them reasons. We ourselves generally learned to behave by imitating our educators; but nowadays our children are not inclined to imitate us. They ask for reasons. And we have no reasons to give them. Or, at least, we don't give them in a way that they can readily grasp them. We know well that there are no standard recipes for bringing up children. But, in connection with giving information to young people, I would dare to offer a recipe: information should be given by the three C's – clearly, concisely, and then changing the subject.

Apart from those virtues connected with temperance, it is good also to emphasise others which have to do with the person's privacy and with his relationships with others. That is why I stress sociability, friendship, respect and patriotism. These four virtues presuppose being interested in one's own privacy and in the good of other people in a practical way. And it is here that the parents can make their biggest contribution. I refer to the guidance they give their children about how to channel their concern for others into practical acts of service. We should realise that the adolescent by his very nature is idealistic and also needs to have new experiences. If we parents fail to help him, then it is likely that outside influences will misguide him.

We have included one other virtue for this age bracket. Simplicity, because an adolescent needs it if he is to act in accordance with his ideals and to be accepted for what he is.

From sixteen to eighteen years old

- Prudence
- Flexibility
- Understanding
- Loyalty
- Audacity
- Humility
- Optimism

The first virtues we emphasise for this age level are based on the ability to reason things out intelligently; in other words, it is almost impossible to develop virtues fully without a certain intellectual capacity. I am referring to the virtues of prudence, flexibility, understanding, and also loyalty and humility. When we come to describing how these virtues work, the reader will be able to see why I say this. For example, I speak about: 'continually gathering information'; 'thinking out the consequences'; 'protecting a series of values'; 'recognising various factors influencing a situation'; 'recognising one's own shortcomings'; etc. Therefore, it seems good to emphasise these virtues at the stage when young people are more intellectually developed. In the previous age level we stressed that young people should be given information about how to approach virtues. The same applies here, only more so. In the earlier stage dangers arose out of letting their passions 'do their own thing'; in this later stage the main danger is mistaken *ideas*. Hence the need for flexibility so that they can learn from different situations without saying goodbye to the standards governing their personal behaviour. Prudence is important also: it implies that the young person keep his eyes open to what is happening around him and seek to know what's what, thinking about the consequences of possible actions before he makes a move. Parents should realise that already at these ages it is very difficult to require children to *do* things: nor is it such a good idea, anyway. Rather, what they should be doing is really requiring the children to think things out before taking decisions; they should be reminding them of the importance of adopting standards which can form a basis for acting reasonably. Young people should be obliged really to face up to what their lives are all about so that they can act in a coherent way, consistent with certain standards. Hence the importance of loyalty.

The reader will notice that, after the three virtues connected with prudence, we stress one connected with justice, one with fortitude and one with temperance. We are already at a more mature age level and, as far as the development of virtues is concerned, we are trying to achieve a certain balance between solid grounding on something permanent, a realistic assessment of one's potentialities as a person, and bold action to achieve a genuine good. In other words, loyalty, humility and audacity.

Before we finish I should like to refer to one other virtue, one which is very important for a society characterised by hatred and despair. I am referring to optimism. This is a virtue which needs to be developed in small children and at all ages; but I would give it a preferential place here, because it is possible, by applying one's will, to acquire the habit of always looking at things positively, of seeing the best in others and thereby being able to help them to improve. At these ages the young person should really make an effort to serve others, inspired by supernatural hope, realising that it is worth all the effort.

Conclusion

To finish this introduction to teaching children human virtues, I should like to emphasise once more that family life is something spontaneous, full of love and joy. The sort of thing I have been saying does not aim to be a plan or method; it is just a series of suggestions to help parents decide more prudently what is best for them and for their children. But sometimes it is useful to try to impose some structure on spontaneous life, just to get to understand it better and appreciate it more. That is why, at the end of the book, I give a schedule of virtues by age group – and a summary description of how each virtue works.

Stressing one virtue or another is not the important thing. What matters is that the *whole ensemble* of virtues develop. That's why I would ask parents to make an effort themselves to practise those virtues which they want to see developing in their children.

I'm sure that everyone will have his own favourite arrangement of virtues. Which virtues would I especially recommend to parents? Perseverance, patience and optimism.

1 Generosity

Generous people act unselfishly and cheerfully for the benefit of others, conscious of the value of their help and despite the fact that it may cost them an effort.

Generosity is a virtue which it is difficult to appreciate objectively in others. When judging other people's actions, we are normally more interested in what they have to offer than in their generosity as such. For instance, if we hear that some well-off person has given a large sum of money to a poorer relative, naturally we think of him as 'generous'. Nevertheless, such a gesture may have cost very little. What we do not know is the person's motive: has he genuinely seen his relation's need or does he just not want to feel guilty. In other words, there are different ways and means of being generous, and one and the same action may be a sign of generosity or not, according to how well we practise virtue and the integrity of our motives.

To do something for the benefit of others may take many different forms: for example, to give things, to lend things, to forgive, to give up our time, to listen to people, to greet people, to invite them home etc.; and all such actions presuppose a decision on our part. Generosity means using our will deliberately for something worthwhile. It involves a free decision to give something up, something which we have a right to retain. It does not mean simply getting rid of something, or walking away from it.

Appreciating what we have

One of the fundamental aspects of generosity, therefore, is that we appreciate and value what we have. Sometimes we may find it difficult or may be unclear in our minds about the true nature of what we actually possess or what we are capable of doing. We see this in expressions like: 'I couldn't do that, I haven't enough time to ... I am not able to ... , even though, very often, the problem has nothing to do with our ability, our time or our knowledge, but simply means that we lack confidence in our own capabilities and are unaware of what we are really able to do. Another very common difficulty is that we are unaware of the true value of the things we have. Which is better, an expensive toy or two hours of my time? To answer a question like this we need to have criteria for evaluating things. If the criterion in this case were 'a child' s happiness', then 'a few hours of my time' would be more valuable.

Precisely because the evaluation of what we possess is often a problem, we will look at some aspects of this question in more detail. As far as physical, tangible, possessions are concerned – money and things – obviously we can give them and lend them and so forth. However, there is a tendency to give what is left over, what one does not need, instead of giving in keeping with the needs of others. Of course, it is not a question of going to the other extreme – giving away everything one has in such a way that one' s family is deprived. A father' s first responsibility is to his wife and children; then he should look after other people.

Another danger is that of giving away physical objects because that is the lesser of two evils: an example would be the father who gives lots of things to his children to compensate for not spending time with them.

One's time is indeed something that can be given. We could call this the 'generosity of giving one's time' and it means being willing to sacrifice for the benefit of others something which we could use for our own benefit. For instance, it means being willing to put down the newspaper when a child wants us to listen to him; it means organising oneself better so as to be able to spend a quiet period with one' s husband or wife; it means helping a friend. People tend to assess the value of time by what can be done in a given period, by the results that can be produced in the short term and, consequently, they set up criteria of little intrinsic value. In other words, they assess their time according to the amount of money they can earn in a given period or the number of 'useful' contacts they can make, instead of realising that the best use of their time might be to produce a smile on the face of a child who is sad or unhappy, for instance.

We can be generous with our time by doing lots of things or simply by creating an atmosphere that will make the home happier, more peaceful, more restful, more secure or more united; on this point we could mention especially the importance or the desirability of a father's presence in the house. A person is generous if he is willing to make an effort to make life more pleasant for others, greeting someone whom he basically dislikes or doing little things which he knows will please somebody.

However, generosity is not only giving. Someone may be ungenerous if he is unwilling to accept things from others, if he is unwilling to let others be generous to him. In this regard, some mothers spoil their children by not allowing them to make an effort for the good of the family but stressing only their own personal success and comfort. Such a person's motives might at first sight appear to be genuine, yet when we realise that every one has to think about others and act for their good, we see that in fact she is doing harm. Still on the same problem we know that it is often much easier to do a job ourselves than to help the children to do it for us. To take over from them in these circumstances is not advisable because it means restricting the opportunities they have for practising the virtue of generosity.

We have been discussing various acts of generosity which parents and children can carry out within the family, and they all involve some effort. There is another type of generosity, however, which is even more difficult than those already mentioned. This is the case of forgiving. To forgive requires great personal sense of security and a willingness to serve others. It does not mean belittling the seriousness of what others have done to us or being naive about it, but simply to recognise the need that others have of receiving our love, our generosity, in response to whatever they have done to offend us; we have to make an effort to show them that we have not rejected them because of their actions. It means showing them that, despite what they have done, we accept them and have confidence in their ability to improve.

Motives for generosity

It is clear, then, that we need motives if we are to make the effort necessary to be generous. Our will has to be really brought into play guided by our reason. Let us now consider some further aspects of the definition we gave at the start. We said we must 'act unselfishly for the benefit of others'.

The spirit of generosity is seldom highly developed in young children, because they are unable to recognise the value of what they have or the needs of others. Neither are they good at trying very hard, and the result is they become over-possessive and are unwilling to let others use their things. Sometimes, on the contrary, they can be very detached and give everything away at random without thinking of what others actually need. Typical cases, which we find not only in children but also in older people are:

- those acts of false generosity toward people whom we like very much;
- those equally false gestures made in the hope of repayment in kind;
- 'generous' things done for our own benefit.

Let us take these one by one.

It is, of course, easier to do something for a person whom we like. This is why children and even adults tend to be kind to their brothers and sisters or friends, but not to others. We find this in very young children, but even more in teenagers, the difference being that teenagers tend to see everything in black and white; they judge people in over-simple terms as either good or bad, nice or nasty, and they are deliberately kind only to those whom they judge favourably.

Obviously a person is not genuinely generous if he makes an effort only for the benefit of those he likes; he must have his priorities right and help those most in need. It is equally obvious that a very young child cannot be expected to have this attitude. He has to learn to make an effort to please those he likes. We can conclude, therefore, that one of the genuine motives for generosity is to see a positive reaction in the other person. If parents smile or are effusive in their expression of thanks for any efforts made by their children, this will encourage them to continue and to behave similarly towards others.

Some falsely generous acts are done with a view to repayment. A child who has something that a playmate needs may lend it to him but in the knowledge that, the following day, when he wants something in return he will have good grounds for demanding it. The motive in this case, is 'repayment' ; there is nothing wrong in this for a young child. We cannot expect young children to do more than is within their capabilities. Indeed, we should often try to create situations which will allow children to do good deeds for motives which may be far from perfect. This will help them to acquire a habit of giving, lending, forgiving etc. and later they can be encouraged to practise the virtue for better motives.

Let us give an example to explain what we mean. A seven-year-old child is given a box of chocolates at Christmas. On Christmas day a dozen friends and relatives come to visit and her mother says to her, 'Why don't you hand around the sweets?' The child knows that she has fifteen chocolates left and a quick calculation tells her that she will have only three for herself. This result is far from her liking and she answers with a simple 'No' . Her mother gets cross, takes the box of sweets and offers them around, saying to the child, 'You must learn to be generous' , whereas the child thinks to herself, 'If this is generosity, I want none of it. It is not for me.'

In this situation the mother might well have suggested that the child offer a sweet to each of her five cousins, and if this is still too much to ask then she should accept the situation calmly, perhaps explaining why it would have been good to share the chocolates. She could then return to the subject on another occasion.

Giving something in order to obtain some benefit is very different; it seldom helps to develop the virtue of generosity. Rather, it means that one is thinking, in the first place, of the consequences for oneself and, in the second place, if at all, of the consequences for others. This kind of giving leads, rather, to selfishness. Of course, children do tend naturally to be self-centred; they see the world as revolving around them. This kind of self-centredness seldom constitutes a problem, provided that they can snap out of it when they see that others need them.

Generosity, then, is often motivated by a desire to please someone we like or by the hope of repayment. Nevertheless, parents can open up new horizons for their children by suggesting truly generous acts for them to perform or by explaining to them somebody' s genuine need of their help, thus encouraging them to develop the habit of acting for the benefit of others. There is little doubt that it will be easier for parents to encourage their children in this way if they themselves give good example and if they have created an atmosphere of cooperation and helpfulness within the family. This is why it is useful to give children regular jobs to do in the house. Parents should always teach them the value of their possessions (such as money or toys), the importance of giving, of being generous with their time etc. In this way children will acquire the habit of giving, based on a true understanding of things they own and their abilities to help others. Nevertheless, they must also learn to appreciate what 'the needs of others' really means.

The needs of others

True generosity must never induce us to satisfy the mere whims of others. This is where prudence comes into play and we know that virtue is meaningless without the support of prudence. What is involved here is an attitude of service, but service performed by means of prudent decisions. We need a proper assessment of our own situation and that of the other person so as to understand what we are trying to achieve; we will then be in a position to decide and act accordingly.

This point is particularly relevant to teenagers, since children aged thirteen and upwards can be expected to know from their own experience how to act for the benefit of others, even if their parents have never helped them in a systematic way. Nevertheless, their motives may be mistaken or confused.

One of the main problems with teenagers is that they may set no limits to their ability to be generous; they are concerned about others, for instance about people who are dying of hunger in India, but they are unable to relate their own limited capabilities to the reality of the situation. They recognise the needs of others in general, in abstract, but sometimes they fail to see that their parents and the people around them need them too. As we have said, they tend to classify people, thus neglecting to give practical help to their parents and relatives, while talking about helping the world at large.

On the other hand, teenagers do need experience and they need to feel they are capable of acting on their own. If their parents fail to find channels in which they can express these concerns, they may lose their way in searching for a 'solution', for instance, in drugs, sexual behaviour etc. Therefore, it is important to realise that the main task for parents is to instill into their children a good understanding of the principles on which they should base their lives and then let them carry on, intervening only to give guidance when necessary.

On the question of generosity, children need guidance before they start so that, on their own initiative, they can be helpful to others. Consequently, true generosity needs fortitude – a capacity to undertake and strive for something that we know is worthwhile.

Another problem is the ease with which teenagers confuse the needs of others with their own whims. That is, they find it easier to recognise the needs of others when they coincide with their own tastes, while neglecting to give genuine help to those who have most right to expect it, namely their own family and friends. Teenagers need to be given reasons, not exhaustive arguments but clear and precise information. Since the development of this virtue depends on the depth of our life and the rightness of our motives, it is clear that reason has an important function to perform.

Giving

Acts of generosity should not be allowed to become isolated from our intentions. That is to say, there is no point in getting into a routine of performing superficially 'generous' actions; we can avoid this danger only by striving to improve every day. Any generosity which is not deeply and firmly rooted in a genuine conviction that others have a right to be helped and served, that God has created each one of us to serve others, will never become a permanent and ongoing virtue.

Consequently, it is more important to give ourselves than to give things. It is quite possible to give without putting anything of ourselves into the gift, without feeling anything for the other person. Our action then becomes a mere outward sign for others, but a deceptive sign. What we must try to achieve is something unconditional: in other words, a giving of ourselves. To attain this, we must know what we are and, in a way, take possession of ourselves. To give ourselves does not mean abandoning ourselves; it does not mean giving everything to everyone all the time. That, indeed, would mean abandoning ourselves, indiscriminately; it would be equivalent to letting ourselves be robbed, as if what we have is of no significance or value. Our body is a good example of this: if we do not understand the value and dignity of our body, it is easy to abandon it, and even justify our attitude by saying: 'This gives pleasure to another.' A skilled worker would not give up his job to an untrained beggar, even though it might certainly please the beggar. How much more important it is to keep our body so as to be able to give it generously in a relationship blessed by God, in marriage, when the other person will recognise and respect the greatness of the gift.

Generosity and love

Although we are not discussing the question of love, it will be clear that, in speaking of generosity, we have been touching upon an expression of love. Love can be seen as a radical vibration of one' s being towards what is good. As J. Hervada says: 'While it is true that all love has certain common features, nevertheless not all love is the same. There is not simply one type of love which applies to all objects, for love derives from a pre-existing relationship between the person and the object of his love; objects of different value and which affect the person differently presuppose different relationships and, consequently, different types of love.'

Generosity, as a virtue, allows one to translate the basic possibility of loving into specific acts of service. A person's motives may differ at any given moment but, since God is Love, the ultimate motive must logically be the Love of God. In our everyday lives, we and our children need help if we are to act in accordance with what we fundamentally know to be our final goal. Such help will allow us to capture that radical vibration of our being towards what is good, and put it into action.

We have no choice in the matter of teaching the virtue of generosity in this sense. It is essential if our children are to mature, take control of themselves and advance in the service of God and man. The selfishness which is encouraged by the consumer society, the easy life and self-abandonment must be counteracted by fortitude and unconditional self-giving on the part of everyone who wishes to act responsibly and generously as a child of God.

SELF-ASSESSMENT

Briefing Note: Readers can use the twenty statements listed below to check on:

- the degree in which they are practising the virtue themselves,
- the degree in which they are educating the children in the same virtue.

The reader can mark himself/herself against each statement using the following scale:

5 I completely agree with the statement. It reflects my personal situation.
4 The statement reflects my situation to a large degree although I have some reservations.
3 The statement reflects my situation partially. I think 'in part yes and in part no'.
2 The statement doesn't really reflect my situation although there may be something in it.
1 I don't think the statement reflects my situation at all.

Then each person can discuss his or her reflections with spouse/friend/colleague and think about aspects to try to improve, personally and as educator. Probably there will be a number of aspects to improve, but only one or two should be chosen in order concentrate one's efforts.

Am I generous myself?

1. *I make an effort to meet other people's real needs.* (We should do things for others when they have a real need. It's not a question of satisfying their whims or only giving what we have left over.)
2. *I recognise what my talents are (capacities, qualities, knowledge) and I put them at the service of others.* (Sometimes we have 'hidden' capacities or qualities which we have never utilised because it means making an effort or because we are timid, for example.)
3. *I understand what my own possessions, my time and my efforts are really worth.* (There are many things we possess that we do not really appreciate. We don't give them due importance because we have gotten used to them – for example, our faith, our home, or our money – things others don't have.)
4. *I often do things for others.* (Sometimes we feel generous because we have carried out a special act of generosity. But the virtue requires us to carry out these acts frequently.)
5. *I carry out the following actions quite frequently: lend things, give things away, am available, listen to others, make reasonable demands on people.* (Each person will probably find that it does not take an effort to be generous in some ways. But there are other ways which require far more effort. For example, it may not take much of an effort for one to give money to a just cause but they may not be prepared to sacrifice the time they spend on hobbies.)
6. *I let other people be generous to me.* (If we are self-sufficient or just impatient, we may not let other people do things for us. Thus we are not giving them the chance to be generous.)
7. *I forgive others.* (This is probably the most difficult way to be generous.)
8. *I make an effort to overcome tiredness, illness, or laziness in order to assist others.* (Some people are only prepared to help others if they have slept well, or when they feel relaxed and in a good temper. A useful exercise might be to think about what moments in the day, or in what circumstances, one tends to be more or less generous.)
9. *I try to help others, seeking their good rather than my own satisfaction and without thinking about what I can ask from them in return.* (Sometimes we act

thinking about the other's good but, at the same time, thinking about what we are going to ask for in return or that now they owe us a favour.)

10. *I make an effort to help those who most need my attention.* (More often than not, it is easier to be generous towards some people than towards others. For example, towards one's spouse and one's children but not so much towards the neighbours. Or more towards some colleague whom we get along well with, rather than another whom we find less likeable, even disagreeable, but who has greater needs.)

Teaching others to be generous

11. *I help the children do specific things for others.* (For example: visit a friend who is ill; forgive a brother for something he's done; help out at home or in the class.)
12. *I offer the children opportunities to decide freely if they are prepared to carry out actions to help others.* (The educator should not try to oblige children to do something for others. At any rate that will not help them learn to be generous. Rather, it is a question of inviting them. For example: 'Do you think your friend would like you to help him get up to date in his studies after being ill?')
13. *I help the children discover others' real needs.* (This means helping them to think – for example, with questions such as: 'Have you noticed that Mum looks very tired? What could you do to help her?')
14. *I help the children distinguish between people's whims and their real needs.* (When others ask for something, the first thing to do is to think if we should really give it to them or not. Is it a whim? Or do they really need it? Once again we need to help the children to think.)
15. *I help the children appreciate the value of their possessions, of their time etc.* (Frequently children do not recognise what value things have. They need help to discover their real scope for helping others.)
16. *I help them to discover what their reasons are for helping others.* (It is as simple as this: ask the child, 'Why are you doing this?' or 'Why are you going to do this?')
17. *I help the children not only learn to give but also learn to receive.* (It is also true that some children receive almost all the time and that they give very little. But with the 'good', more mature, children, we should help them to learn to receive.)
18. *I manage to get the children to do things for others for worthwhile reasons.* (We can never know what motives the children have for acting in one

way or another, but we can try to show concern for their doing things out of a true sense of duty, or better, for love.)

19. *I try to find ways of helping the children overcome their tendency to want to be easy-going, and to overcome their laziness or their lack of interest, in order to start worrying about others.* (This depends a great deal on the educator's enthusiastic example.)

20. *I talk to the children so that they learn to relate generosity to love and especially to love for God and to God's love for us.* (We should talk about these subjects naturally at home or at school. And more so the older the children get.)

2 Fortitude

In situations which make it difficult to improve, courageous people resist harmful influences, withstand difficulties and strive to act positively to overcome obstacles and undertake great deeds.

Courage or fortitude is 'the great virtue: the virtue of those in love; the virtue of those who are convinced, those who are willing to take great risks for an ideal which is worthwhile; the virtue of the knight errant who for love of his lady undertakes countless adventures; the virtue, in a word, of one who, well aware of the value of his life (for every life is unique), is willing to give it up cheerfully if necessary to attain a higher good'.[4]

These remarks might lead us to think that one seldom gets a chance these days to practise the virtue of courage. Somehow or other every 'higher good' seems to be smothered in petty 'needs' created by man. There are few opportunities to be adventurous, because everything is already done, discovered, organised. Well may we ask ourselves, what channels, if any, exist to satisfy our desire to do something great, to undertake some great ideal? Christians are seldom in the extreme situation of being able to give their life for their faith – martyrdom is the supreme act of fortitude – nor is such a position even probable, at least in countries where the faith is accepted and practised by many. In the normal course of events, there is little opportunity for doing great things for the Church of Christ. Nevertheless, it is characteristic of Christians that the little things they do each day become great because of love.

Here we have a solution to the problem mentioned. It is not a matter of performing superhuman actions, of discovering unexplored territory, of rescuing fifty children from a fire; things like this are only flights of fancy. What we can, and must do, is to transform the simple things of everyday into a chain of efforts, courageous acts which may indeed become great and heroic, an expression of love.

This implies that anyone with a mean or petty outlook on life cannot practise or develop the virtue of courage. It is worth reminding ourselves that children need to be convinced that their life has a purpose, that however insignificant and useless one's life may seem, each individual has an inalienable mission to glorify God. Each one of us can and must love, leave himself behind, serve others, surpass his personal 'best' in order to yield more. Anyone who is selfish and unwilling to improve, who seeks only pleasure, is not motivated to develop the virtue of fortitude, for he is indifferent to good.

For this very reason we can say that courage is a great virtue for teenagers because, by nature, they are people with great ideals, who want to change the world. If young people fail to find proper channels for their restlessness, if their parents fail to offer them proper objectives, true and genuine principles, their hidden energy may turn towards the destruction of the very things they have created. In particular, if we teach our children to make great efforts to overcome themselves, but fail to teach them what is right, they may in fact very successfully pursue wrong aims.

These remarks are basic to everything which we shall have to say throughout this chapter.

Endurance

It is usual to divide the virtue of fortitude into two parts – endurance and enterprise. Let us consider the first of these two elements, which, despite what is commonly believed, is the more difficult of the two because 'it is more laborious and heroic to resist an enemy who, by the very fact of attacking us, shows that he considers himself stronger and more powerful than we, than to attack an enemy who, precisely because we take the initiative against him, seems to us to be weaker than we are'.

To follow up our previous description of this virtue, perhaps we should consider what is meant by resisting harmful influences and withstanding difficulties. In our normal everyday life we find we have to resist certain difficulties and, when doing so, we know that this is for our own good. There are other difficulties too which, if left unchecked, prejudice our chances of improving. Obviously, it is easier to withstand the former kind of difficulty. I am referring to things like a visit to the dentist, where we know that if we accept a small discomfort we can avoid severe or prolonged pain. On another level, it is not difficult to put up with a boring conversation with a person who we know needs an audience. In other words, if there is a clear objective it is easier to put up with a passing difficulty. This is exactly where we can begin to teach the virtue of courage to our young children, but we must not forget that there is more to it than that.

The main problem we find in connection with this type of endurance is the tendency of most small children to live strictly in the present. By this we mean that it is not sufficient for them to know that the long-term outcome of a passing annoyance will make it all worthwhile: the six-year-old child cannot be expected to accept an injection quietly, simply because he knows it will cure his illness. It is not enough to seek a cause and effect type of motive; such reasoning will have to be backed up by other considerations more in keeping with the situation and the child's personality. Let us consider a few examples.

Two children want to play with a noisy toy just when the baby has, at last, got to sleep. Their mother says, 'Stop playing with that: the baby is asleep'. Here she is asking the children to cease something which may have unpleasant consequences to others. The alternative approach would be to suggest another specific toy with which they could play and explain that the baby will sleep better as a result. In the former case the mother's authority is reinforcing a cause and effect type of argument. In the second case, the motive offered is a combination of implicit obedience (the mother has no intention of letting them play with the noisy toy in any case) and the possible attraction of her alternative suggestion. More effort is required on the part of the children in the former case than in the latter: they are given an opportunity to develop the virtue of fortitude by giving up their toy and resisting the desire to continue something which they find enjoyable. If the children are shown something which they have done for the benefit of their little brother or to help their mother, then their effort is connected with love and with their ability to love.

Another example would be that of a child who wants to go out to play before doing his homework, when the opposite is the rule laid down in that particular family. Again, an impulse has to be resisted. The child knows that if he does his homework first he is obeying the rule and ensuring that the homework will not be forgotten, but at that moment the relation of cause and effect provides a rather weak motive. Fortitude consists of resisting the temptation, and it may require an effort, perhaps a big effort, on the child's part, or stern action on the part of the parents.

We see, then, that in ordinary family life there are many opportunities for children to resist an impulse or put up with discomfort, in the knowledge that the result will be to their benefit. In so far as these efforts are backed up by the parents' authority, they help to develop certain habits. However, these habits need to be understood by the children, and the earlier the better. If, on his own initative, a child decides not to go out with his friends in order to help his father or to study, if he resists temptation to leave his homework unfinished or badly done, then this virtue is advancing along the right lines.

Children must also be taught to resist influences and accept annoyances which, if left unchecked, will be harmful to them. The difference between this type of endurance and the former type is that here there is no clear or obvious beneficial result. The influences with which we are dealing now have to be resisted in order simply not to lose ground on the road to improvement. An example would be that of a child who has borrowed an unsavoury magazine from a friend. If he decides not to open it there is no obvious improvement except in the obvious sense of avoiding something which is wrong. No ground is gained or lost, whereas to read it would mean some harm would be done.

Another example might be that of a child who finds himself about to fight with other children. There is no obvious gain in deciding not to fight, but to fight would be a backward step. Cases such as these involve teaching children to say 'no', not out of fear but to avoid unnecessary danger. Courage overcomes fear but genuine courage has to be governed by prudence. If there is no prudence, there may be foolhardiness, which means ignoring the dictates of prudence and running into danger.

In the life of any family obviously there are many rules relating to this matter, connected with what we have called preventive obedience. Parents tell a five-year-old that he must never cross the street on his own because a car may knock him down. However, children have to learn for themselves what may harm them or be a dangerous influence on them and, consequently, they must establish their own rules for real situations. This is why they must be taught to be prudent, to control their foolhardiness as we have said, but also to control groundless fears.

Perhaps we should now consider a fews aspects of real life: for instance, fear of the dark. We are not concerned here with the causes of this fear, or whether it affects the child from birth or only at a later stage; we are considering its implications for a parent who wishes to teach children the virtue of fortitude so that they can overcome this sort of fear. In the first place, we can expect that the children will make some contribution to the learning process, but only according to their ability. There is no point, therefore, in protecting them from all contact with the object of their fear, but it is wise to control the extent of such contact and give whatever help may be necessary. There are two extremes: one would be that of a parent who forced a child to sleep in an isolated room of an old house without a light or to go on an errand to a lonely place after dark, in order to teach him not to be afraid; the other would be to leave a bright light on in the bedroom every night and never allow the child to experience darkness. To control the degree of the fear and give whatever help may be necessary involves showing confidence in the child, encouraging him with affection, explaining the situation to him truthfully and persuading him to make an effort gradually to overcome whatever fear he has. If a child is accustomed to sleeping with the light on, a suggestion could be made to switch off the bedroom light but to leave the door open and the landing light on; later, the landing light could be switched off but all doors left open so that the child could hear his parents talking and so on.

Children, like adults, are often afraid of the unknown and this is where parents should offer some reassurance or moral support; this may take the form of a full explanation of what is expected of them (they may be afraid because they are unsure of what they are supposed to do or what is going to happen to them) or it may mean staying with them for a time. Here common sense must be the guide, the objective being that the children should learn to overcome groundless fear and to be brave without being foolhardy.

We may also wish to teach this virtue after the event, so to speak, after the children have suffered some sad or even harmful experience. Perhaps the child comes home crying because someone has beaten him. One possible 'solution' is to ring up the parents of the other child. But that does not help the 'victim' to build up the virtue of courage. It might be better to give the child a good motive for overcoming his annoyance: you could say to him, 'Now, there's a good chance to offer something to God'. Sometimes we forget that one of the best things we can do to show our love, our love for God, is to offer him the things that annoy us and resist the temptation to think of ourselves as victims. Besides, if we complain or let the children complain we are creating an atmosphere which goes against fortitude. Fortitude means accepting what happens to us in sportsmanlike way (not passively), trying to get some advantage out of even the most disagreeable situations.

Indifference

The three vices which are opposed to fortitude are, as we have said: fear, foolhardiness and indifference. On the subject of 'enterprise' we will refer to foolhardiness and fear. Before saying what we mean by 'enterprise' however, we might look briefly at the consequences of indifference. This is caused by a total lack of fear (up to now we have been referring only to unreasonable or excessive fear). Indifference affects those who fail to acknowledge that they have a duty to improve or who do not recognise or identify harmful influences, adopting a passive, careless or lazy attitude. Such people simply accept what comes their way without making any effort and some parents tend to protect or even take the place of their children in the efforts which they themselves should be making; the net effect is that the children learn nothing but being on the receiving end. They probably are quite indifferent to everything they know; but if they come up against the unknown and don't have their parents at hand to help them they will not be able to develop and, due to a lack of prudence or proper fear, they do not stand much chance of living an upright life.

A comfortable life, a life without sobriety, ends up being an exercise in selfishness. A selfish person when he gets what he wants enjoys a superficial 'satisfaction'; when he does not get what he wants he just crumbles or seeks any kind of escape – whatever is to hand.

To prevent children from being indifferent in this sense, you have to be very demanding with them from a very early age; they must be made to make an effort to 'resist' (whether it is a baby who cries for no reason at all or the adolescent who is in the dumps because some friend has annoyed him). 'Strong men, sturdy men, who are not afraid of pain, who can suffer in silence, who do not ask for sympathy, who are not afraid of sacrifice, who do not shrink with fright, who are fearless in the face of difficulties. Men without fear, who are not shy or selfish, who are never shocked by anything they see or hear. Maturity is courage. Energy and determination are not pride, they are two qualities of true virility.'[6]

To be able to keep going and withstand whatever may come our way and not become indifferent, we also need patience. This is the virtue which helps us to take physical or moral sufferings without sadness of spirit or downheartedness. We may undertand this definition more easily when we remember that the opposing vices are impatience and insensitivity.

It is now time to consider what we mean by 'enterprise' which came into our definition of fortitude when we said that it helps a person to withstand difficulties and undertake great deeds.

Enterprise

If we are to attack, and not simply defend, if we are to undertake great deeds involving sustained effort, we need physical and moral strength. It is easy to see why sport always calls for this kind of strength or courage. If we can overcome fatigue, exhaustion or weakness, it prepares us to undertake activities which are of direct benefit to others and give glory to God. Sports are of particular relevance here because the motive behind them is clear and direct: we want to climb the mountain, win the match, finish the race, beat our own personal record, not let others down etc. If we are incapable of making an effort involving physical endurance, it is quite possible for us to fail also in our ascetical efforts. Nevertheless, sport is not the only type of activity which is relevant here. We could also mention things like camping, getting up without hesitation at the same time every morning, taking a cold shower, walking to work etc. We might also consider teaching our children to put up with discomfort and even deprivation without complaint. Mothers should take care not to overdress their children in winter (just the right amount of clothes); they should let them go out in the cold, let them feel thirsty for a while without complaining etc.

So far, we have been speaking about fortitude or courage from the point of view of strength in what we do. Now let us consider some aspects of the virtue from the point of view of our positive undertakings. First of all it implies an attempt to attain something which is difficult and arduous.

To achieve any such objective, whether it be to overcome some evil or to attempt something more positive, we must show initiative, deciding what we want to do and then doing it, however great the effort involved. To see the possibilities of the situation, we need a certain sensitivity, translatable into a spark of initiative. This will never happen if we are habitually indifferent, as we have said. The moment of initiative, of noticing an improvement that could be made, requires an attitude of life which parents do well to stimulate in their children from an early age. There is no point in solving problems for children which they themselves should resolve or even in pointing out the complications and difficulties in a situation which they themselves should be able to see. At most, we might merely hint that there is a problem requiring a solution. For example, if children repeatedly miss the school bus, parents may intervene directly by waking them, dressing them, taking them to the bus stop and putting them on the bus. For the children, however, who up to that point have had to solve the problem of getting to school after missing the bus, this reaction is of no help as regards teaching them initiative and how to solve problems. The parents are better employed encouraging them in the morning in such a way that they do reach the bus stop on time, and then checking to ensure that the problem has been solved.

In general, any attempt to take advantage of a positive situation in order to improve involves initiative and perseverance. Naturally, children find it easier to do something presented to them in these terms than merely taking steps to offset something that may be harmful. We shall consider the question of perseverance later. Here we wish only to mention briefly some of the conditions necessary if the difficulties which we have mentioned are to be combated and overcome.

In the first place, there has to be strong motivation. The effort to be made must be seen as necessary and worthwhile – not only intellectually understood, but also deeply felt, for spiritual strength is essential if difficulties are to be overcome. This is a case in which anger is legitimate and appropriate. 'The person who has fortitude can use his anger as an instrument of his act of fortitude in attacking; not indiscriminate anger, but only anger which is controlled and directed by reason'.[8] In other words, if the situation to be remedied is unjust, fraudulent, false, etc., we must recognise this without being scandalised or shocked, and at the same time allow the fire within us to increase provided we control it. If our enemies fight back violently we cannot just stand by idly and complain. On the other hand, any foolhardiness will also have to be controlled: whatever we do must be done prudently, without wasting our energy to no avail.

In other words, 'on the road of virtue there are many obstacles and difficulties which must be overcome courageously if we are to scale the heights. Therefore we need great will-power to follow the way of perfection whatever the cost, great courage in order not to be frightened in the presence of the enemy, great bravery to attack and overcome him, and great constancy and perseverance to continue struggling right to the end, without laying down our arms before the end of the fight. This strength and energy must come from the virtue of fortitude'.

Difficulties in teaching fortitude

It is not unusual for parents to insist that their children do certain things which call for an effort. Children normally play some kind of sport and their physical strength increases little by little. Yet there are certain important areas which frequently escape the attention of parents.

- We must mention the importance of providing children with opportunities not only to do things requiring an effort, but also to learn to stand firm.
- Children must be encouraged to undertake, on their own initiative, activities that will improve them and that require continuous effort.
- They must be taught things that are really worthwhile and that they see to be important.
- They must be taught to take up a position, to accept certain principles, to be individuals capable of practising what they preach and what they think, that is, to be consistent. Parents must be aware of the need for improvement in themselves, as an example for the children as well as for its own sake.

As we have said, this virtue has certain special consequences for teenagers. When a youngster begins to take his own decisions, he may become careless; he may reject the opinions and attitudes of his parents without being able to replace them by anything personal. Thus any strongwilled person will be able to influence him because of his weakness. If he has not developed the habits related to fortitude, even if he wishes to improve and undertake activities to achieve some specific and recognised good, he will be unable to withstand the difficulties that arise. Inner strength must be based on one's past life.

On the other hand, if teenagers are strong on this point, their age gives them many opportunities to be generous, just etc., apart from other things, because they are inspired by great idealism. As we have said, they can conquer the world or, rather, conquer their world, their own individual world.

The virtue of courage underlies the development of all the other virtues. In a world full of influences from outside the family, many of them prejudicial to the personal improvement of our children, the only way to be sure that they survive as human persons worthy of the name is to fill them with an inner strength so that they will be aware of their capabilities and of the real situation surrounding them, thus being able to resist what is wrong and undertake what is right and make of their lives something noble, valuable and complete.

SELF-ASSESSMENT

Briefing Note: see pages 29-30, above.

Do I practise fortitude?

1. *I usually try to discover what the 'right' thing to do in each situation is.* (We should not make decisions, much less react, without first thinking about what are the right criteria to apply. We should not let ourselves be carried away by the emotion of the moment.)

2. *I try to overcome laziness, routine and blind imitation of others, by thinking for myself about what is really 'right'.* (Getting to know what is 'right' requires an effort, an effort to overcome basic tendencies. For example, discovering what is 'right' requires study.)

3. *I do usually manage to focus on what is 'good' for others even if it takes an effort or I have to suffer for having done so.* (Some people often make 'peace' their top value. But they understand 'peace' only as absence of effort. They feel satisfied as long as there is no conflict and no fighting. 'Good' requires effort and therefore there is going to be some kind of suffering. This is not always compatible with 'absence of effort'.)

4. *I make an effort to carry out everyday chores carefully and lovingly.* (Although we may understand fortitude as the virtue of the chivalrous knight who, for love of his fair lady, is prepared to take any risk, normally fortitude is expressed in little efforts to do everyday things as well as we can.)

5. *I resist temptations which the consumer society pushes at me.* (This means overcoming whims, not being influenced by what others do, not reading or buying everything we can, or not watching everything we can on television.)

6. *I put up with physical discomfort without complaining.* (Being comfortable and not suffering are seen as two important values in modern-day living. But fortitude means using one's will-power to avoid that approach.)

7. *I make decisions, with real initiative, to do worthwhile things for the children or for others.* (Being enthusiastic about life helps to get us out of the rut and help others to think, organise and do interesting things.)

8. *I make an effort not to get used to what is evil just because there seems to be so much of it around.* (It is so easy to get used to evil, and in that way fail to strive for good. We need to aim high.)

9. *I try not to complain the whole time about the bad things I see around and about. On the contrary, I try to do something positive to resist negative influences.* (An interesting exercise is to try to remember the occasions when we complained in the last week, for example. The more complaints, the less fortitude.)

10. *I overcome fear, indifference or my need for security, in order to carry out really worthwhile activities.* (Fortitude means taking risks, being magnanimous, thinking about worthwhile values, being enthusiastic about life. It is incompatible with the mediocrity which is a result of an exaggerated desire for security.)

Teaching others to practise fortitude

11. *I reason with the children to help them discover what 'good' means in each circumstance.* (If a youngster has a lot of will-power but doesn't know what is good, she/he can end up doing evil with great efficiency.)

12. *I try to look for situations which give the children the chance to become enthusiastic about something really worthwhile.* (Education in fortitude requires initiative from educators in order to be able to create or organise these situations. Often they will relate to actions where help is given to the needy.)

13. *I try to get the children to solve their own problems.* (A common tendency is to want to shield children from pain. For this reason the educators are often over-protective towards children and don't let them assume responsibility for their own lives.)

14. *I encourage the smaller children to cope with various kinds of difficulties.* (For example: not to stop running when they are not going to win the race, to climb to the top of the mountain although they are hot and tired, not to ask for water immediately the car trip begins.)

15. *I try to get the children to gradually face up to things that scare them.* (For example: fear of the dark, fear of being alone, fear of some bully at school.)

16. *I regularly organise or promote activities which require physical effort from the children.* (For example: walks in the hills, organised games, helping in jobs around the house.)

17. *I make sure the children keep the rules of the house/school, to help them develop their willpower.* (If the children repeat actions related to simple rules, they will soon take them in their stride. And, in that way, they will be able to concentrate on other more demanding objectives.)

18. *I look for ways for the children to have initiative, to become enthusiastic about some project, and to carry out what is necessary until they achieve their aim.* (One can't expect educators to carry out actions such as these everyday. But if we want youngsters to develop fortitude, we will have to set up things of this kind now and again.)

19. *I help the children learn to have their own opinions about things in life and be able to defend them when they are with their companions, in spite of what 'people' may say or think.* (It is not only a question of having personal standards but also of influencing others.)

20. *I help the children learn to say 'yes' and to say 'no' bravely.* (Peer pressure is immense and we need to help the children develop this capacity from an early age.)

3 Optimism

Optimists have confidence (based on reason) in their own abilities, in the help which they can get from others and in the ability of others; thus in every situation, they can identify, first of all, positive elements and opportunities for improvement and, secondly, difficulties and obstacles in the way of such improvement; they take advantage of everything favourable and face up to the rest in a sportsmanlike and cheerful manner.

Let us begin by considering what we understand by optimism as a virtue, since in normal use it means many different things. For instance, on a rainy day, with the sky completely overcast, someone says, 'Soon the sun will come out, you'll see, and we shall be able to go for that walk'. Another says, 'Let us light the fire and play a game. We shall enjoy ourselves, you'll see. Which of these two is the optimist, in the positive sense? The former is ignoring the facts, while the latter is facing up to reality; one tries to change the facts to fit in with his specific object in view, namely the walk, while the other concentrates on a higher object, namely enjoyment, and he realises that both the walk and the game are only means to that end.

Optimism can therefore be regarded as a personal quality which allows an individual to see the bright side of a situation, either realistically or unrealistically. Optimism as a virtue involves being realistic and consciously seeking the positive aspects of a situation before looking for the difficulties. Or it may mean trying to see what can be gained from the difficulties in themselves.

The degree to which we practise this virtue will depend on our ability to identify positive elements in situations which clearly present some difficulties. Some people are optimists only when the situation is completely favourable, but others manage to break free from the immediate state of affairs and fix on whatever goal they have. The latter, if they are really to develop this virtue – that is, if they are to develop their capacity to see the positive element in many situations even though there are serious obstacles – need to be properly motivated. This motivation comes from their self-confidence and their trust in the help others give them – and if they have faith, it comes especially from their trust in God's help. In other words, you cannot be optimistic unless you trust someone.

Optimism based on confidence

Confidence implies a recognition of each individual situation as it is our own qualities and abilities as well as those of others. It presupposes reliance on our own well-developed fortitude and the security and knowledge that others are willing to act in our favour. If it is to be meaningful, confidence must be based on reality, but always allowing for the possibility that we and others may improve.

On this basis, we can see that most people know themselves sufficiently well to be optimistic much of the time. Nevertheless, there are times when one cannot rely on one's own resources to solve difficulties or cannot see how any good can be derived from a particular situation which appears totally bleak. When one can no longer rely on oneself as the only person interested in one's welfare, then there is no alternative but to seek help to continue being optimistic; otherwise the optimism disappears. In other words, optimism which is not based on confidence in God, on the conviction that he always helps us and acts for our good, is fragile and indeed may lead to either naivety or pride.

Perhaps an example will clarify this point. Let us suppose we are faced with failure connected with our work, but we react naively, pretending that nothing is going wrong and that the crisis will pass. This is self-deception. Or perhaps we genuinely believe that, never having failed before, we can resolve the problem: this kind of 'optimism' is unrealistic and based on pride. If we have trust in nobody but ourselves, someday we are bound to find ourselves in a situation which we are incapable of facing. Only confidence in God and the belief that he has willed it so can give us true optimism.

Perhaps we should stress that optimism does not invariably lead to outward jubilation. Precisely because it involves confidence in God, in others and in one's self, what optimism gives us is inner peace. Expression of that peace may, but does not necessarily, take the form of behaviour or expressions normally associated with joy. For instance: when a near relative dies, we may be optimistic yet sad at the same time; optimism overcomes depression and downheartedness but it is fortitude that conquers sadness.

How are we to teach a child to have confidence in God, in others and in himself without being naive? To avoid being naive, as we have said, we should teach children to be realistic; they should be aware of the type of confidence which they can place in each particular individual. Their confidence should be rationally based. They must realise that they have to take personal responsibility for their own lives. Their parents may spoil them, spare them things which they should do themselves and allow them to be optimistic for a time by solving all their problems for them. Obviously, however, the day will come when the children will have to stand on their own feet, and therefore it is important to teach them to make good use of their own abilities and qualities and to look for help in a rational manner when they need it. Young children need to know that their parents are always willing to help them, but such help means doing whatever is best in the circumstances. This applies also to others. For example, there is little point in telling children that the doctor will always be able to cure them; we should simply say that he will do whatever is best so that they may recover. There is nothing wrong in always expecting the best, provided we are willing to accept something less than perfect with good grace.

It is right to tell children that they can ask of God anything they wish but that, since we are his children and he loves us, he will not give us anything that is not good for us. Trusting God means a belief that he will do what is best for us, not that he will satisfy every desire we have for things which seem good but in fact are not. It is not easy for a child to understand these distinctions because he is concerned only with the present moment; it is difficult for him to understand why he has to suffer now in order to attain human and spiritual maturity later. The problem is that he fails to grasp the importance of the end while concentrating on the means. Consequently, we should help our children, not by trying to solve their problems, but by getting them to make an effort themselves and supporting them with our affection and love. This will encourage them to be optimistic, not because things happen to go well, but because, even when they go badly, their parents' love is assured. If optimism is based on, for example, repeated personal success, it can lull us into a false sense of security. We may think we are optimistic simply because we have never failed, but that is not optimism, because we have not learned to relate everything that happens, pleasant or unpleasant, to high and worthy objectives.

To be more specific on this point, there are some children who, by nature, tend to rely on themselves; others, who are more hesitant, tend to wait to see what their parents will do in a particular situation. If a child is intelligent, good at games and sociable, he has every reason to be optimistic, because everything he does works out well and he find satisfaction, however superficial, in it all. Yet if he has not learned to rely on others and even need them, especially God, this satisfaction will certainly not last, because it is unrelated to the importance of personal effort and a recognition of the fact that he is a child of God. This kind of child should be made face difficulties, to enter into undertakings requiring more effort but which can be achieved, so that he will learn to accept defeat cheerfully and to discover the positive aspects of situations which at first seem hopeless. It is not a question of teaching children simply to be successful, but rather to make the best of every situation, relying on their own abilities, the love of their parents and the love of God.

There are other problems in the case of children who lack self-confidence, especially if this is caused by continual failure or having no one to support them in moments of need. People who have become insecure because of personal experience will find it very difficult to develop the virtue of optimism. It is precisely in cases like these that the theological virtue of hope comes into its own; a person without religion feels lost when things get extremely difficult, unless he manages to deceive himself, and this, as we have said, has nothing to do with the virtue of optimism.

A child who repeatedly fails needs often to be shown he is loved. Nevertheless, his parents should not try to persuade him that he is successful if the opposite is true. Rather, they should try to create situations where he can succeed and, consequently, gain confidence in himself and in them. What we are really suggesting is that parents have to encourage the virtue of fortitude, for the child needs the experience of having tried hard and actually achieved what he set out to do: this will teach him self-confidence. He needs to have benefited from the help of his parents in order to gain confidence in them. However, if children concentrate merely on achieving certain unimportant objectives, they will not gain that total confidence which fosters the love of God. The important thing is to combine success in trivial matters, with help and support at times of failure and a gradual realisation that every individual, however limited, has an inalienable mission to glorify God.

Here we come to an approach which gives meaning to the whole question: children who learn to realise that they have a mission of service in life always manage to find ways of helping others and, consequently, they become optimists. Those who seek only their own satisfaction are continually disappointed and this leads to sadness and pessimism; if disappointment is seen merely as an inevitable step on the way to improvement, it can lead us to that practical, realistic optimism which is our goal.

We have not mentioned older children in speaking of this aspect of confidence, because optimism is something which increases naturally on a human level from an early age, becoming more significant when it begins to include supernatural hope. The considerations we have mentioned apply equally to teenagers, although if a child lacks confidence early on it will be difficult for him to improve. Nevertheless, a teenager who feels that he is loved has at least preliminary motive to begin to develop this virtue. This means that a teenager who, up to now, has been pessimistic may change course and try to become an optimist at any moment, if he feels that he is loved or that someone needs him, or if he opens his heart to God and God, who never refuses what is good for us, gives him a new outlook on the course his life could take. It is never too late to make a new start and once a person realises this, in the knowledge that he can succeed because God will help him, he is an optimist. If his parents or a friend are willing to help him the process will work more quickly.

Realism and improvement

We have said that optimism consists of having confidence 'so that in any situation we can distinguish, first of all, the positive elements and chances of improvement and, then all the obstacles and difficulties, so that we can take advantage of anything that may be of benefit to us and face up to the rest in a sportsmanlike and cheerful manner.

In practice, this is far from easy, for we have to know what criteria can be used to decide which elements are favourable, what can be used positively and what has to be strongly resisted. We have just mentioned the possibility of a new start and this may be necessary if we have not done things properly from the beginning. At the moment of pessimism two points stand out: the genuine difficulties in the problems to be solved and the individual's personal difficulty in seeing the situation clearly. For instance, if an adult is disappointed or let down by a colleague he is unlikely to become pessimistic regarding what he can expect from people in general. If he has developed the virtue of optimism, he will continue to accept the other person and regard the situation as a chance to help him improve or, at the very least, an occasion to practise the virtue of fortitude. However, a child may be very depressed and upset by momentary disappointment, whether it be that someone has not invited him to his birthday party or that he has been falsely accused of doing something wrong. Only age teaches us to realise the relative importance of things that happen to us; children find these distinctions hard to make. Children have to be taught what is very important and what is less so, what is signficant and what is trivial. This involves getting them to concentrate, not on the action, but on its purpose and being realistic at all times.

In particular we must teach children to analyse their vague opinions and feelings. For instance, a child may say to his mother, 'I have nothing to do', or 'There is nothing to do around here', thus showing that he has failed to understand the situation. The mother must try to grasp what he is getting at if she is to find a solution within the actual circumstances. Another example might be that of a teenager who complains that all the other children have more money than he has. Here, again, a parent should ask questions so that the child begins to realise what is, in fact, worrying him. Then he can be helped to see more clearly what he should be trying to achieve and that his parents are confident that he will attempt it.

Up to now, we have been considering difficulties of a subjective type, but perhaps we should ask how to approach a situation where, objectively, there is good reason to be pessimistic. A realist sees all the aspects of a situation and he weighs them up objectively, or at least as objectively as possible, before deciding to act. Nevertheless, he may fail to realise that the 'objective view' does not necessarily fit the facts. One never has all the facts at one's disposal. 'Facts' have been provided, perhaps, by people who have gathered them in a rather unscientific way, or have added their own particular interpretation, and so on. Besides, in deciding what to do, one might simply judge what people actually do, not what they are capable of doing if properly motivated.

The optimist, on the other hand, sees beyond the 'facts'; therefore he concentrates on the positive aspect of things, the chances of improving the situation. Certainly he sees all the disadvantages, but he realises that frequently these can be overcome. In other words, he shows confidence in people's potential instead of judging them merely by the facts of the situation. This is not to say that he does not take the facts seriously.

For example, if a child fails an examination he may become very pessimistic. In this situation, even a realist might point to the facts and see little to give cause for optimism. Even here, an optimistic child will realise that the important thing is not the result, but the effort he actually made. He can then promise his parents that his mathematics will improve the following year. Even if his fortitude lets him down when it comes to the point, at least if there was some chance of an improvement in his mathematics, then his optimism was genuine and a virtue to be fostered.

A child with overstrict parents who never tried to understand or talk to him might think that they are useless. But, if he is an optimist he will concentrate on their good points and try to establish communication with them, at least from time to time. We are suggesting that children should acquire the habit of understanding the real circumstances in which they have to live. An unrealistic optimist might be ready to go out with companions who take drugs, overconfident of his own ability to resist temptation: this is exposing oneself to unnecessary danger.

Perhaps we could now examine more closely the type of help which parents could give their children to acquire this virtue as they grow up. Very young children need as cheerful an atmosphere as the older ones. This cheerfulness will derive, in part, from their parents' continually emphasising their childrens' strong points, encouraging them in accordance with their ability and potential. They will show their love at all times but they will not attempt to over-protect them from the trivial failures and disappointments that may occur. This is how children learn to have confidence in themselves and in their parents, a confidence based on reason. When there is confidence of this type based on love, the other things in life will fall into place and cease to be major disasters: the child will have solid roots to help him withstand difficulties.

In the various situations that arise, parents find ways of teaching their children to distinguish between what is important and what is not, as well as how to derive some positive advantage from almost anything that can happen.

For young children the main thing is to learn to have confidence. As they grow older, children have greater need of the virtue of fortitude in order to concentrate their efforts on feasible objectives. Dreams are good if they are recognised as such but, at this stage, optimism must be based on a realisation of one's mission in life. Not that a child should feel important; the point is that he is important. At the same time he continues to see how sensible it is to have confidence in others and to find a deep joy in placing his life at God's service. At this stage of their life, children should develop the virtue of generosity by trying to help others and accepting disappointments for love of God. This is how they make best use of their potential as children of God. When children reach adolescence, the world in general often seems so wretched to them that they do nothing but criticise. This kind of negative criticism is incompatible with true optimism: it is good to recognise the facts, certainly, but positive possibilities and potential must not be ignored.

One may become pessimistic about efforts to change the world, instead of serving the people close to one as best one can. Furthermore, adolescents need to feel that they are loved, even though they might reject such love outwardly. When they step outside their familiar territory, they need to feel sure that they can return home where their parents will accept them for what they are.

Optimism and fortitude lead to inner peace and joy. Optimism is much more than seeing the bottle half full instead of half empty. It means concentrating on the positive aspects of a situation rather than on its defects. We must stress, however, that permanent optimism is possible only when we realise that God expects from each one of us something that no other individual can do and, provided we ask his help, everything can work to our advantage.

SELF-ASSESSMENT

Briefing Note: see pages 29-30, above.

Am I optimistic myself?

1. *I am reasonably self-confident so I tend to make good use of my capacities, qualities and talents.* (Optimism is based on confidence. The person who has no confidence, in any sense of the word, tends not to take advantage of their abilities. They see only their limitations.)

2. *I trust others, within reason. I usually see their positive qualities.* (It is possible to be optimistic as regards oneself but not as regards others. There is always something positive to be found in the people around us.)

3. *I trust God so that, although I may find no sense in some specific event on a human level, I know that everything is for the good.* (Situations rise in most people's lives in which natural optimism doesn't make sense. For example, when a baby dies, a good friend has a serious illness or there is a personal financial disaster. Only supernatural faith can help us discover something positive in those situations.)

4. *In difficult situations, I make an effort to discover something positive and try not to complain.* (It is easy to be optimistic in positive situations. But when things don't go well, it is easy to start complaining, criticising and putting the blame on others.)

5. *In any kind of situation, I try to discover the positive points first.* (We should not falsify reality, in a desire not to see what is bad or untoward, but we should try to discover the positive elements first. This is a habit we can develop.)

6. *I am realistic and am usually able to face up to difficulties in a sportsmanlike way.* (Although one tries to discover the positive aspects of a situation, there may, in fact, be real problems. Optimism helps us face up to these difficulties in a sportsmanlike like way.)

7. *I am able to see what is feasible and what is not. Then I try to optimise the former.* (False optimism, or an excess of optimism, leads us to try to be and do everything and thus fall into a world of make-believe, and deceive ourselves and others.)

8. *In general, I face up to life with a good sense of humour.* (Good temper helps us accept responsibility for our own lives without feeling downcast or wretched.)

9. *I realise I should be optimistic in order to take advantage of all the talents God has given me, recognising that, in this way, I shall infect others with the joy of living and thus live as an authentic child of God.* (Some people may try to be optimistic just in order not to suffer, to feel better or to feel comfortable.)

10. *I usually feel at peace with myself, and this helps me overcome discouragement.* (This inner peace is not something we can develop as a virtue. It is rather an indicator that tells us we are living the virtue of optimism.)

Teaching others to be optimistic

11. *I create situations so that the children can live their lives joyfully.* (If there is a joyful atmosphere, the children will be more likely to discover what is positive around them.)

12. *I centre my attention on what is positive in each child so that they learn to develop self-confidence.* (Frequently, educators centre their attention on where each child needs to improve, or on what they do badly. This attitude does not help the child to be optimistic.)

13. *I help the children get to know themselves, to be realistic about their qualities and capacities, so that they can take best advantage of them.* (Children need help to get to know themselves. They may overestimate or underestimate themselves. We want them to be realistic.)

14. *I create or use situations where the children can learn to walk alone without my helping them unnecessarily.* (Unnecessary help is a limitation for the person

who receives it. If educators help too much, the youngsters' optimism may be false because it is based only on the help they receive.)

15. *I show love and trust to the children so that they can have enough self-confidence to accept responsibility for their own lives.* (Loving and trusting are not sufficient. They must be manifest. Only in this way will many youngsters launch themselves into worthwhile actions, taking advantage of all their talents.)

16. *When objective, negative things occur – for example, an illness, a lack of loyalty in some friend, failing an exam – I help the children look for something positive in the situation.* (There is no need to create situations of this kind. They will appear by themselves. But if some child seems always to triumph and never to fail, it may be useful to create some kind of problematic situation so that they can learn to overcome the problem. They will definitely find difficulties at some stage in their life, and it is better for them to learn to face up to them when they are young.)

17. *I talk to the children about what trusting in God means.* (Normally it is not a matter of long conversations but rather remarks and information given quickly and which help children to think.)

18. *I try to create situations so that those children who tend to fail most have the opportunity of succeeding in something.* (In this way their self-confidence can grow. If they fail in almost everything, their optimism will not grow nor will they take advantage of their qualities and capacities.)

19. *I organise activities in which the children are a crucial part.* (It is not a question of the children feeling important but rather of them really being important. When they start becoming responsible for actions and activities to aid others, for carrying out important jobs and so on, they will discover the satisfaction of a job well done and thus their optimism will grow too.)

20. *I teach the children to ask for the help needed to carry out their projects.* (Children need to learn when to ask for help from their parents, from teachers, or from their friends. They should also get used to asking for God's help, knowing that, in that way, everything will work out well.)

4 Perseverance

Once a decision is made, a persevering person takes the steps necessary to achieve his or her goal, in spite of internal or external difficulties, and despite anything which might weaken their resolve in the course of time.

Among the very many human virtues, there are several which have lost their true meaning in common parlance. Perseverance, however, seems to be one which is still understood and appreciated. At most one might have to clarify two preliminary points. Perseverance is incompatible with obstinacy: having taken a decision, it is not a question of taking the steps necessary to attain the desired goal if we realise that we have made a mistake in our decision, in selecting our objective or in choosing the means to attain it. Neither is there any point in going ahead if unforeseen circumstances arise which make it imprudent to continue. The second point is that perseverance should not be confused with mere routine. It is senseless to adopt a procedure and then maintain it meaninglessly, perhaps even defending it by pleading some non-existent relationship between what we are doing and some worthy goal.

Of special interest here is the notion of 'achieving the goal one has set oneself' and looking for solutions to problems which may arise, if we are to teach our children this virtue. This is a virtue upon which we should concentrate especially after the age of reason, that is, around the age of seven, and up to adolescence, because its development is dependent to a great extent on the parents' ability to command obedience, although guidance and motivation are, as always, very important. Teenage children are usually unwilling to be told by their parents 'what to do' . At best, they are willing to be forced to think. Although thought is important with regard to what one intends to do, particular qualities are required to carry out decisions once made. As we have said, this is an area in which it difficult for parents to influence teenage children. On the other hand, they can certainly help their children when they need such guidance; but if they are to ask for this kind of help, children must be aware that their parents are really able and willing to give it. Parents must, therefore, be informed about the interests and activities of their children or at least be able to direct them to others who are so informed, and they must make it clear that they are available and anxious to help.

So let us consider this virtue especially in relation to the seven to thirteen year age group.

Developing habits

As with the other virtues, there are two aspects to the development of this virtue: the intensity with which we practise it and the importance of correct motivation. Depending on the person's age, perseverance can be practised in countless situations; after all, it is essential for the practice of all the other virtues, without exception. Usually when children are very young, they can see no good reason for sustaining any effort for long; they tire easily and then they consider it logical to stop what they are doing and go on to something else. This is logical for them because they cannot see far ahead or deal with any long-term problems. It follows that their main motive for perseverance is obedience.

It is clear that to the age of seven children can be encouraged to develop certain habits associated with perseverance by making sensible demands on them that is to say, being strict on a small number of points. We refer, for instance, to finishing any game they have started, to fulfilling their promises provided these are reasonable, to eating at mealtimes, to doing their homework properly and remembering their jobs in the house. In short, we mean that they should develop certain habits requiring an effort but these habits may relate directly to any of the virtues. At first they may make little sense to the children, but later their parents will be able to explain them carefully. If these demands are then to make sense, the children will have to see that what they are doing is useful and proper. It follows that it would be absurd to ask any child to do something without giving him a good reason. Depending on the seriousness and the difficulty of the effort required, the reasons will have to be understood to a greater or a lesser extent, just as the degree of insistence, help and guidance will also vary. Let us now see some of the difficulties that may arise on the question of perseverance in one' s efforts and perhaps draw some conclusions of relevance to our children' s upbringing.

As time passes

Strictly speaking, the virtue of perseverance refers to overcoming difficulties that arise when the effort is prolonged in time, while another virtue, constancy, is concerned with overcoming all the other difficulties. Here, we will deal with all these difficulties.

The fact that a plan may spread over a period of time constitutes a genuine difficulty for persons of any age, especially if it involves some activity which cannot be done in stints, allowing a little rest and renewed effort after each episode. Such is the type of perseverance implicit in the development of the life of faith; precisely because the final goal can be attained only at the hour of death, we need the gift, the gratuitous gift, of perseverance, for which we should prepare by positive daily response to the grace which allows us 'to will and work' (Philippians 2.13), which makes the fulfillment of duty easier and more pleasant.

The individual, however, must also play his part and, by developing any virtue on a human level, he is in a better position to develop his life of faith.

If the objective (we are now referring to attainments on a natural level) is distant and unclear, then this distance and lack of clarity will have a negative effect on our effort. Lack of clarity means mainly that it is not possible to establish a direct link between what we are doing now and the goal we are aiming at. All we have is a vague general idea that there may be some connection. Besides, if we don't have personal experience it is even more difficult: for example, we older people know that if we keep up a series of efforts we can reach a particular goal. We run the risk of thinking that our experience is quite enough to get our children to make an effort in exactly the same direction. The first time anyone, adult or child, has to make an effort so as to reach some goal, he must be sure to keep his purpose very clearly in mind so as to take the proper steps to achieve it.

It is a good idea to divide long-term objectives, in management terms, into various stages, each one leading to the next. This allows us to shorten the distance between one step and the next, thus closing the gap between our present activity and its immediate object, however partial that object may be. It is important to be aware that, in any activity with a purpose, there is an initial moment of enthusiasm when we are excited by the purpose we have in mind. This initial moment may be long or short, according to the circumstances, but then we may get tired or dispirited, when little progress seems to be made, things go wrong and there are only difficulties in sight. Then comes a third moment, towards the end, when once again the goal comes into view, almost within reach, and the initial enthusiasm returns with a new maturity which includes the satisfaction of having made a reasonable effort. These considerations lead us to certain conclusions for parents.

Young children should be guided towards objectives of a short-term nature. There is no point in saying in September, 'If you get a good report at the end of the year we shall take you to the seaside in the summer'. If we want the child to improve at school, it would be more sensible to suggest that he concentrate on one subject, say, until Christmas and help him with his work on that particular subject, showing a special interest in seeing what he has learned about it at school and in his homework; if possible, we could ask the teacher about the difficulties the child is experiencing and find out how much is expected of him; we could also try to ensure that the child fully understands what he has to do for his homework etc.

There is another difficulty which parents may experience: this consists of not knowing what goals or standards they can set for their children. We have said that they can insist that children finish what they have begun etc., but here they are only taking advantage of actual situations, usually not involving any longterm effort. Let us suggest a few possibilities.

- We may direct the child' s attention principally either to the goal itself, the means to be taken or the person involved, though without neglecting the other aspects of the matter. (a) We could suggest that he should try to develop certain aspects of a specific virtue for a particular period, for instance, a month. (b) We could get him to carry out some particular job, telling him clearly at the beginning what exactly is expected from him at the end. (c) We could suggest that he help some particular person in a practical way, again suggesting possible final results.
- We should not only clarify the goal to be attained but also relate the steps to be taken closely to that goal. Thus, for example, if the object is to make the child more orderly, we should explain to him that this means tidying his room before he goes to bed, being punctual for his meals, getting up at a particular time every morning and so on.
- If possible, we should find an objective, at least at the beginning, which is of genuine interest to the child. We should follow this up by being very willing to 'lend a hand' when the initial motivation begins to wane. As we have said, there are different types of motives but undoubtedly if parents show an interest in the child' s perseverance, this is bound to be useful, especially if backed up by sensible suggestions.
- Finally, we should ensure that the child is able to do what is necessary to achieve his objectives; otherwise, he will have to be taught to do whatever is necessary or else the goal will have to be modified. We repeat, therefore, that every goal should be closely related to the ability and character of the child.

Other difficulties

A main vice opposed to the virtues of perseverance and constancy, apart from obstinacy, is inconstancy. This comes from factors related to the length of time involved but also, and especially, from having to give up other more interesting activities in order to stick to one's plan. Inconstancy is found particularly in people who give up their plan at the first sign of difficulty or who change their mind easily and frequently, just for the sake of change. They sometimes try to justify such changes by alleging that the second thing is better or more interesting than what they were originally doing.

These problems can be overcome by fostering in the child a certain sense of pride, and by getting him to experience, to feel deeply, the importance of what he has set out to achieve. If he does not take pride in going ahead in order not to let himself down, he may end up simply by looking for excuses and these are always to be found. The trouble is that excuses not only 'fool' the parents, but also deceive the child himself. It may also be useful to present these plans of improvement as challenges, especially if the parents try to improve at something similar at the same time. When we suggest that the child should experience and feel the importance of his objective, we mean that he should keep it constantly in mind, for only in this way can he hope to overcome his weaknesses, his inconstancy, if other more interesting or more amusing things come along to tempt him.

It is not that we want the child's conscience to be unduly troubled by each and every failure; if he does fail, he should be told about it, the reason should be discussed and he should then continue as before.

It is not only other, more interesting things which make the process difficult; obstacles also arise along the way within the plan itself. The best answer to these genuine obstacles is to foresee them, if possible. If we are not prepared they may take us unaware and we may be afraid to continue or, on the other hand, we may seek some solution which may take us along the wrong paths. In particular, parents should teach their children to foresee possible difficulties by pointing out some and encouraging them to think about others themselves. If we know our enemies in advance, it is easier to conquer them. Thus, obstacles will be no more than that, mere obstacles, rather than a total barrier which stops the child in his tracks and throws him off course.

Finally, there is the implicit difficulty of trying to improve in too many areas at the same time. We have suggested that the goal should be realistic, that is, attainable with some effort; it will serve no purpose if it is only a dream. On the other hand, no one can advance significantly in several areas at once; he may jab here and there perhaps but he cannot strive forward towards any permanent improvement. It is much better for a child to try hard on a limited number of points, rather than try a little over a wide area (although the former, in a way, calls for more patience and stamina on the part of the parent). There is no point in trying to distract him from what he is doing. As we have said, a child may waste his energies by disseminating them uselessly over a wide area; of course, parents are capable of doing the same. When this happens, not only do they fail to bring about any improvement themselves but also they prejudice their children's chances of improving.

To overcome all difficulties and correct any wavering from the set course, a child should be able to ask for guidance and such guidance is essential for the proper development of the virtue of perseverance.

Necessary and unnecessary help

In most cases, anyone who wishes to persevere needs to be able to rely on help along the way. And if we add to the importance of perseverance the need for prudence, it is clear that some consultation is bound to be necessary. It is natural that young children should need a fair amount of guidance from their parents but always remembering that unnecessary help limits the receiver. Keeping this rule in mind, we can lay down three different levels on which parents may act:

- telling the child what he must do;
- discussing the situation so that the child may draw his own conclusions;
- refusing an appeal for guidance.

We should, in fact, refuse guidance if we think that the child is asking for help out of sheer laziness or disinterest. On the other hand, if we see that he really needs us, the best thing to do is to discuss the situation with him. If he still fails to see how the obstacle can be overcome, there is no alternative but to tell him what he should do. Naturally, the younger the child, the more help of this kind he may need, but as he grows older and gets more experience he should be left more to his own initiative.

But there are two aspects to this problem because it is not just a question of giving enough attention to the child but of teaching him to *ask* the right person for help. A child who wants to improve in his studies must know that it is his teacher, not his father, whom he should consult when he has technical difficulties; if it is a moral difficulty he should go to his spiritual adviser, not just some friend; and so on.

An important part of the parents' job is to teach their children to recognise the kind of help they need and where they can get it from. It could be that they are so efficient in locating help that they don't make any effort themselves and thereby fail to develop the virtue of perseverance. There are things in life which anyone can attain and it is not a question of concentrating effort on these. If I want to develop my abilities to the maximum in order to serve other people to the best of my ability I will have to establish objectives for myself which I can achieve.

Here there is one objective which is totally personal, and inalienable: we refer to the task of giving glory to God. Perseverance is so important in living one's personal faith that perhaps we should say a little about it before leaving this subject.

Perseverance in the Christian life

As we have said, there are two difficulties that beset our perseverance in living a Christian life. The first is that the goal is never achieved in this world, for the task is lifelong: we can never say 'I have done that, I can now go on to something else.' The second difficulty is that there are countless temptations to throw us off the right track. Yet the goal itself is perfectly clear – the sanctification of ourselves and of others – and there is abundant help available to us. Consequently we may concentrate here on the problems caused by our failure to take advantage of such help and by our being unwilling or unable to give up momentary pleasures for the sake of an objective set before us by God himself.

We have said that all kinds of help are available – but a person has to have initiative to use them. Otherwise, we would not be free agents. So, it is up to us to go to the sacraments to get an increase in grace, to receive spiritual guidance, to learn more about the truths of faith by studying them, and especially to continuously ask for God's help.

Not only do we have to strengthen our relationship with God. We must also develop strength to suit the circumstances we are living in. 'In those countries where a particular religion, over a period of time, becomes the majority one, so that its practitioners do not come up against any great difficulties, they run the serious danger of becoming spiritually bourgeois, with all that that involves in terms of doctrinal superficiality and an empty performance of rites. In countries like this, when there is a period of radical change you get absolute upheaval in the religious and moral spheres. The principles underlying people's faith and morals come under challenge, and they fail to rise to the challenge – they argue in a shallow sort of way that religion has no place in an evolving world' .

We must, therefore, try to foresee the difficulties that may assail us on the way and accept them in advance. The Christian is beset by many difficulties which can easily divert him from his true purpose. The continuous effort required of him involves considerable self-control and he must always be aware of positively accepting his own limitations, rectifying his mistakes and starting anew. He can adopt either an optimistic or a pessimistic approach to the difficulties and obstacles that he meets in his Christian life. The pessimist becomes downhearted and goes ahead in a purely mechanical, frigid, or automatic way, while the optimist accepts these difficulties with generosity, he puts up with them, shows initiative and uses the obstacles as a means of strengthening his faith: this he does cheerfully and with God's grace.

Some personal effort is essential for young children to advance in their relationships with God; there is no point in making things too easy for them. Here again, we should be careful not to offer unnecessary help. In practising the virtue of perseverance which, in turn, is the basis of all other virtues, if children do their best for love of God they have mastered the highest motive of all. The virtue will be meaningful for them and they will be in a position to receive that special grace from God which they need to practise all the other human virtues.

SELF-ASSESSMENT

Briefing Note: see pages 29-30, above.

Do I pursue my goals

1. *I set myself goals for the future.* (There is no scope for perseverance if there are no future goals. Personal improvement and education call for reasonably long-term objectives.)

2. *I fix stages towards these goals in order to check whether I am making progress.* (Experience shows us that we need to specify these stages on our way to the distant goal, to keep our spirits up.)

3. *When I think of future goals, I also try to foresee possible problems with a view to overcoming them if they do arise.* (Foresight is also part of the virtue of perseverance. Unforeseen problems are more difficult to overcome than those taken into account at the planning stage.)

4. *I use the means necessary to achieve goals, but I also recognise when to give up a project if it makes sense to do so.* (Giving up a project is not always a failure. For example, continuing with a project although one realises the goals are not right or one hasn't the resources to reach it would not be perseverance. It would be pig-headedness.)

5. *Once I have decided to achieve a goal, I do all I can to pursue it.* (Some people have a lot of goals but then give up after a first moment of enthusiasm. They change their objectives from one moment to another according to their every whim.)

6. *I ask for the right help, at the right time, to pursue my goals.* (Usually, one cannot achieve one's goals without help at some stage, and especially in those moments of low spirits which usually come after the initial enthusiasm.)

7. *I regularly think about why I am striving, to make sure that that effort makes sense and that it hasn't turned into empty routine.* (It is useful to think about one's everyday efforts. Some will make sense. But others will have lost their meaning. For example, with a teenager, it will probably be more worthwhile putting one's efforts into getting them to think before they make their decisions, than getting them to clear up their bedroom.)

8. *When I set up some new goal which is objectively important, I look for something I can jettison in order to concentrate my efforts and my time on the new, important goal.* (Most people who want to stick at things will almost certainly already have their time full, and there is no point in piling one

thing on top of the other. That is why one needs to think about what one is going to stop doing in order to dedicate that time to the new project. For example, one could stop reading the daily newspaper or watching the news on television in order to find time to study.)

9. *I frequent the Sacraments regularly to help me persevere in my life of faith.* (One's life of faith also calls for perseverance, and one most certainly needs help to grow as a child of God.)

10. *I ask for God's help constantly to lead a good life and so that those who depend on me may do the same.* (To persevere in one's life of faith, one also needs to study in order to know more and more about the faith, and to receive spiritual guidance to make sure that the goals we propose are the right ones.)

Teaching others to practise perseverance

11. *When I set goals for the children, I follow it up until I achieve the desired results.* (Probably one of the greatest difficulties for educators is to keep after those things they want the children to learn.)

12. *First of all, I insist on the children doing those things that are easiest for them to do.* (Usually it is wiser to start with those things which require less effort, perhaps related to one of the child's hobbies or to some capacity which they already have developed.)

13. *I select educational goals carefully, to be able to give them my full attention.* (If one has many goals, one ends up putting little effort into many things. This does not produce results.)

14. *I try to be demanding in areas of behaviour suited to the child's age.* (With the smaller children, one could insist on them keeping promises, finishing their meals, finishing a race, or reaching the top of the mountain. With older children one should insist on their thinking before they make their own decisions. That means that I should insist less on their doing specific things.)

15. *I clearly distinguish what kind of help each child needs for persevering in each action.* (According to the situation, one will have to tell them what they have got to do, make them think before they make their own decisions, or just let them do what they want without interfering.)

16. *I give clear-cut objectives to the children so that they get used to persevering.* (These objectives can relate directly to some virtue: they can refer to actions which have to be carried out regularly – pick up the towels in the

bathroom, tidy up their bedrooms, turn off the lights etc., or be related to some person – look after a grandparent or a younger sibling for a period of time.)

17. *I help the youngsters to foresee problems that can crop up and to learn whom they should ask for help in each case.* (If one foresees what sort of problems can arise, one can look for ways of dealing with them. For example, one youngster could think of using the holidays to study, without taking into account what usually goes on at that time. They also need to know when to go to the teacher, to their parents or to some friend or someone else to ask for help.)

18. *I help the youngsters choose objectives suited to their real capacities and qualities.* (Adolescents tend not be very realistic and they need help in this way.)

19. *I help the youngsters set up goals which are not too distant in time.* (One can encourage children to set up objectives which are closer or more distant in time, according to their age and character. In all cases, the overall objective should be split into parts.)

20. *I reason with the youngsters so that they recognise the importance of their goals and recognise the need to make the effort involved.* (It seems to be more and more difficult to get youngsters to stick at things. The environment does not at all encourage perseverance and effort. Youngsters need to understand why we are asking them to make an effort.)

5 Orderliness

Orderly people follow a logical procedure (essential for the achievement of any goal) when organising their things, using their time, carrying out activities on their own initiative, without having to be constantly reminded.

Like all the other virtues, orderliness has two aspects – the intensity with which it is practised and the right motives. Sometimes it becomes an end in itself and, from the outset, we should state that it is a virtue that must be governed by prudence. Our brief description has said where, when and how order is involved, but there is another point which we should clarify straight away: this is the question of the order of priorities within the goals we set for our personal improvement. Regarding order in the home as a necessary condition for proper family life and good relationships between all the members is very different from imposing it as a requirement based on parental obsession. Orderliness should never go so far as to smother a spontaneous and loving way of life. We are not suggesting that our life should be structured in every detail, but only sufficiently to make it possible to pursue certain important objectives. And this means being prudent.

If we are to behave in an orderly manner, we need order also in our mental makeup. However, it is very difficult for parents to observe this in their children and it is more practical to consider the results of such mental order, rather than the merely subjective aspects. We can see how they organise their belongings, how they schedule and get on with their activities of many different types. We can see this, for instance, in their work, their play, their relations with others and their relations with God. To go into it a little more deeply, we can observe how they express themselves in speech and in writing, the preparation they make before going out, the way they enter the house etc. Such observation allows us to have a good idea of what is going on inside our children but we should also take a good look at ourselves. Example is always important and perhaps we could consider what we mean by this with regard to the virtue of orderliness.

Good example

Parents sometimes think that they have little chance of teaching their children to be orderly, because they are so disorganized themselves. This, however, is not so. In practice, we educate our children most effectively in areas where we ourselves are attempting to improve or where we have to try hard to attain a passable standard. Besides, parents who are orderly by nature often find it impossible to understand why the other members of the family are not equally so. They think that order should exist spontaneously in everyone and, if it does not, the cause can be nothing but sheer laziness or carelessness. The fact is that we are all different and we must learn to accept our children as they are, before going on to encourage them to overcome their shortcomings.

Good example is very useful provided children understand why we insist so much and provided our insistence makes sense to them. As we have said, order for its own sake is hard to justify and parents must work out, at the outset, why they want order and what standard they would find acceptable. The example of our own efforts is certainly the most effective but it also helps to point to what has already been achieved, i.e. the order already established in the house. An orderly atmosphere in the house is very important to children: this has to do with tidiness and cleanliness: if the housewife does not bother to keep the house tidy, to give her children clean clothes etc., the children are unlikely to be tidy. Personal tidiness and cleanliness is, therefore, important, not only for reasons of hygiene, but also as a preliminary for any attempt to be orderly. If order is based on prudence, it will allow us to work out some logical rules which will not have to make our house either a shop-window or a museum. We want our children to have their own way of doing things, but they must also respect others and be able to get on with other people. They must learn the virtue of orderliness without going to excess, and it is up to us to teach them where, when and how to stop.

Proper use of time

One of the main problems related to the proper use of our time is to distinguish between what is important and what is merely urgent, so that we do not continually sacrifice the former to the latter. Parents may fully realise that it is extremely important to speak to their children, to get to know them, to show interest in what they are doing, and yet, countless little problems arise, things which have to be done urgently, making it impossible to get around to the important things. If this is difficult for parents, it is much more difficult for children. Nevertheless, we must teach our children to schedule their activities so as to do whatever has the highest priority at a given moment. In particular, they have to coordinate certain daily routines with other specific tasks which take a given amount of time. For instance, the evening meal is a daily event but the child may be doing his homework just when his mother calls him to the table. There are two approaches to this situation: either it is more important to have the meal when his mother calls him, for the sake of a proper family life and because she cannot be expected to make each child's meal just when he is ready for it, or else the homework is more important and the meal should be relegated to second place. Common sense tells us some logical rules must be laid down to reconcile these opposing attitudes, rules worked out after consideration of the type of activity involved. We may find it helpful to think of five different types of activity:

- things which have to be done regularly, always at the same time;
- things which require a certain amount of time to be carried out;
- things that take up a certain amount of time but need not be done all at once;
- things that require a varying amount of time but can be done whenever is convenient; and
- things which happen regularly, and things which happen occasionally on a specific date.

As far as the household is concerned, children should first be told about those things which have to be done at a specific time, though not necessarily according to the clock. For example, they can be told that they must drop everything and go to the table when the mother calls them or that they must put their toys away when they finish playing. Here, certain 'chains of events' can be especially helpful for the younger children: for instance, when they come home from school they know they must (1) say hello, (2) take off their coats and hang them up, (3) wash their hands, (4) go to the table, and (5) eat whatever their mother has laid out for them. A similar 'chain of events' could be established for bedtime. There could be a rule that these times must be respected provided some other ongoing activity is not thereby interrupted. As far as possible, the same things should be done at approximately the same time each day, although we realise that this may often be impossible and we must all try to be flexible.

Regarding the second type of activity, we should try to plan the best time and stick to it. Naturally, this would be easier if we placed such things at the top of the list. There are always unexpected interruptions, and activities requiring a certain amount of time may be in conflict with these urgent things. In bringing up our children, we must teach them to set aside periods for such activities. Every mother will remember seeing her children begin to tidy their room, with the best will in the world, and then realise that their favourite television programme is just about to start; they leave the job half done and, unless she is very strict, it will never be finished. What she should do is explain to them that certain jobs take a long time and that they should plan ahead before starting them. This would help them develop an ability to relate the time available with the task to be carried out and they would learn to judge how much time each task is likely to require. This is orderliness.

The third type of activity involves remembering and taking care of whatever they are doing so that they can return to continue it when convenient. If they are reading a book, they must remember that they are reading it and where they have put it. Order in this sense is closely related to perseverance, because such activities can extend over a long period. Stamp collecting involves not only sticking stamps properly in an album, but also finding time to do so; learning the guitar involves laying aside some time for practice.

It is often difficult to plan those activities which take a variable amount of time, even though they can be done in any spare moment. A letter which can be written in twenty minutes may worry us for weeks; if no time is fixed for children to polish their shoes, it may never be done except when the parents get angry. We tend to use our 'spare' time by doing whatever is most pleasant or most urgent and, of these two, the most pleasant usually prevails. It is therefore helpful to realise that the virtue of orderliness demands that we place the things that are least pleasant, and necessary, at the top of the list, to be done first. Otherwise, they may be 'forgotten'.

Finally, we have the difficulty of actually remembering those regular, though infrequent, things, or those occasional things which have to be done on a specific date. We refer to such things as sending a birthday card, keeping an appointment, handing in an essay or ringing a friend. Very few of us have such a good memory that we can do these things without help. The simple solution is to use a diary. We say 'simple', although some people find it very difficult to jot things down in the first place and even more difficult to look them up afterwards. This habit, like all others, is more easily learned when one is young and, therefore, it is advisable to teach children to use a diary.

Children can be instructed and encouraged on all the points we have so far mentioned concerning the best use of one's time. Habits are learned mainly 'under orders' in the first place, but if teenagers are to continue making the efforts necessary and if parents are to give fewer orders, they must reach an understanding of why it is important to plan their time rationally, both for the sake of efficiency and to avoid disappointing or annoying others.

It is worth remembering, furthermore, that any of the things we do spontaneously in the normal course of events can be used to build up human virtues. Despite this, it will sometimes be necessary, not only deliberately to take advantage of the normal things that happen, but also to plan and carry out particular activities, which should have a high priority in the use we make of our time.

Tidiness

Another aspect of order is that we should put things in some logical place, which means keeping them somewhere that fits in with their nature and purpose. There are two reasons for this type of order; to look after things properly so that they function properly and to keep them somewhere reasonable, so that we can find them when we need them and so that we know that they are exactly where we want them. On the question of tidiness, there are two important points. Parents should get their children to put the things that 'belong to everyone' back in their place and they should insist that they tidy their own things in a reasonable manner, even though they may not affect the other members of the family.

How can we get them to keep things in their proper place without constantly having to nag? First of all, although it may seem obvious, everything should have 'a proper place'. We should be very patient but very persevering on this point. There are no instant solutions in matters affecting children and, on the subject of tidiness, which is often very annoying, we can only insist and insist again. At best, one might suggest certain aids, which might be helpful for a particular child but have no affect on another.

As we have said, children should know where everything is kept, and they should be told exactly when something should be returned to its place. Usually we would say, 'Put it back when you have finished'; but the word 'finish' is far from clear to a child. It would be better to ask what exactly he wants to do with the scissors, for instance, and when he answers, tell him, 'When you have cut out the picture, before you stick it into your book, put the scissors back in their place'.

Another solution is some form of punishment. For instance, if a child has not put something back in its place, he could be forbidden to use it the next time. This is a dangerous weapon, however, because it may be that he needs the object in question for some good reason, perhaps to do his homework. The best solution of all is to establish a general pattern whereby all the members of the family put things in their proper place. If everyone feels responsible for seeing that things are where they should be, irrespective of who has actually taken them in the first place, we are on the way to a tidy house and the development of a sense of responsibility for the whole family in each of its members. This is where the system of giving each child his own jobs can break down: jobs may be well done but only because they are a strict obligation and not out of any sense of responsibility to the family as a whole. If, instead of jobs, we expect everyone to be constantly helpful, we should achieve a situation in which everyone feels responsible even to the extent of reminding one another if something is left undone. In any case, as always happens in deciding how best to achieve something, each family will have to devise its own methods.

When it comes to finding a place for each child's things, this should be decided in accordance with the type and purpose of the objects in question. For a very young child, for instance, tidiness may consist of throwing everything into the wardrobe and closing the door. Of course when his mother opens the wardrobe, everything falls out. In practice, children quickly develop a logical sense and suddenly we notice that they put all the cars together, all the dolls together or that they have put all the big books on one shelf and all the small books on another. It is best that children should learn to tidy things in their own way, or at most with a little guidance from their parents, rather than that they should blindly follow their parents' way of being tidy. We should therefore insist that they be tidy, but not according to our rules.

It may help children to be tidy if they are asked to help their parents when they are tidying something: books in a bookcase, the kitchen utensils or clothes in a suitcase. It may also help them if we ask them to explain the 'system' they use in tidying their things: this may arouse a certain interest in finding the most suitable place to keep a certain toy safe, to be able to find it easily and to have it where it is most likely to be needed.

Doing things

Orderliness involves not only putting things in their proper place but also using them properly. We can hardly say that a child who deliberately breaks his toys is orderly, even if he tidies up after the event. Neither do we want to go to extremes, however, and say that a child should play with a toy only strictly according to the rules envisaged by the manufacturer or that he should play with one thing at a time, for instance. If the main object is amusement, however 'educational' an activity may also be, there is no point in being overstrict concerning the use of an object. It is sufficient to avoid improper use of things, without hindering the child from developing his imagination as he goes along. So, to use an umbrella as a gun may be alright whereas to use it as a lever to open a drawer that has become jammed is found to be wrong, because it may be broken.

In teaching the virtue of orderliness, parents must distinguish between things which need rules if they are to be used in a reasonable manner and things which, of their very nature, allow a greater degree of freedom. In practice, teaching children how to use things properly may mean teaching them to type, to use the telephone, to stick photographs in an album, to use scissors, to mend an electric plug etc.; all these things need rules if the children are to use them properly; otherwise, they might get broken or be dangerous. This type of lesson involves, not only physical objects, but also certain aspects of the child itself; in other words, he has to learn to use his intelligence, his emotions and his body according to certain principles, certain rules, for otherwise he may use his intelligence to destroy something good, just as he might use a toy to break a window. If we are not careful in teaching the correct use of things their very advantages and all their potential may be overturned and dangerous situations may result.

Let us return now to the distinction we made between objects which need rules for their use and others which do not. Some people may consider it disorderly to use books to build a castle, whereas others might not mind, allowing the child to play with them in any way he likes provided he does not tear them. Obviously, there are two different criteria involved here: the danger that the object itself may be damaged and the danger that it may be harmful to the child or to others. Nevertheless, there is a third criterion which must be considered: benefit that can be derived from the object.

In the normal course of events, parents teach their children to use things properly especially if they realise the importance of moderation in everything. If they fail to understand that their children should learn the proper use of things, however much money they may have to replace anything which gets broken, it is only natural that orderliness and moderation mean nothing to the children.

The orderliness children should be asked for in regard to their things is very good training for later on when they are learning to use their abilities and qualities in line with the purpose for which they were made. It is very difficult for someone to have a tidy mind if he is not more or less tidy about external things. In fact, people who fail to practise external orderliness can often have a nagging feeling that there is a poor connection between their final purpose in life and the way they actually behave.

Final remarks

When children are small, parents must make lots of demands on them to be orderly. At first the children will just do what they are told but they will learn to see the sense of what they are doing if their parents are alert to the main purpose behind all this. In order to obey actively (i.e. not just obeying because there is no escape) children need to be quite clear on what is expected of them; so parents should demand obedience but at the same time explain everything systematically. Consequently, if parents are disorderly in demanding order, they are unlikely to achieve very positive results.

The danger is that parents may be disorderly in demanding somethings while letting others pass, or in being strict at some times and not at others. We all tend to be rather uneven on the question of order: we may write a very logical and well organised letter, but throw our clothes on the floor when we go to bed; or we may speak and argue very precisely but leave our desk in chaos; we may dress carefully and smartly while being slovenly in the way we handle books. We should try to improve in all aspects of orderliness and acknowledge our tendencies to forget, overlook or justify our lack of order that comes from laziness. On the other hand, people who are orderly and tidy should try to understand that others are different and accept them as they are. Orderly people might think again about the purpose of their good habits.

Orderliness as a habit should be made meaningful so that teenage children may learn to practise it in their own personal way. When they were younger, their parents had to remind them continually to do the minimum; naturally enough, their parents are now rather tired of this and, if the battle is not won before adolescence, parents will be unable to devote their time and attention to matters which are more appropriate and more pressing at that stage. It is not that order ceases to be important for teenagers; on the contrary, without such a basis, it will be much more difficult to practise any of the other virtues. The determination necessary to develop the other virtues will lack the systematic basis without which they cannot exist.

SELF-ASSESSMENT

Briefing Note: see pages 29-30, above.

Am I orderly myself?

1. *I have a clear hierarchy of values for my own life and for the education of the children.* (For example, one hierarchy is that a married man should first look after his wife, then his children and then others. It means giving adequate importance to one's family, one's work, one's friends, and one's hobbies.)
2. *I usually act according to some logical rules so that there's a clear consistency between what I think and what I do.* (Unpredictable behaviour which only obeys one's feelings at each moment, or pure reactions to a given situation without thinking or deciding, only confuses others and does not benefit anyone.)
3. *I know what I am looking for when I try to be orderly.* (It is a matter of being able to justify orderliness in everything.)
4. *I try to be orderly to facilitate living together in the group and also for efficiency's sake.* (An excess of orderliness occurs when a person insists on being orderly without knowing why. It produces tidiness maniacs - people who prefer orderliness to joyful family life, for example.)
5. *I usually know where to find my things. I keep them in sensible places and I put them back when I have finished using them.* (This kind of behaviour is necessary for personal efficiency and also for others be able to use common property.)
6. *I divide up my time well so that what is most important receives due attention.* (Misuse of time is very frequent. For example, some people spend too much time watching television and not enough on their spouses or their friends.)
7. *I am punctual when carrying out my duties. For example, getting to a meeting, arriving home, keeping a commitment.* (Some people are very

casual about punctuality. It does not worry them and they are prepared to give any excuse for being late. For them, being late is just part of life. But punctuality is necessary for efficiency and to respect others. That means that unpunctuality is a fault not only against efficiency but also against justice.)

8. *I use tools and appliances - computers, electrical equipment, and so on - as per instructions.* (Orderliness means *reading the instructions* and thus avoiding danger or breaking the instrument. It also means learning to make full use of all the instrument's capabilities.)

9. *I use systems to remember to be orderly in these various fields.* (Some people have good memories and they remember to put things back in their places, they remember other people's birthdays, they are punctual and they use all kinds of instruments correctly. But others need to learn to use a diary, make lists of things they have to do, and make a conscious effort to remember specific things.)

10. *I think about how I do things in order to see just how orderly I really am.* (Frequently, some people are orderly in some aspects and not in others. For example, a university professor may be very orderly in her way of thinking but very disorderly in the way she dresses or keeps her papers.)

Teaching others to be orderly

11. *I know each child's capacity for being orderly.* (Each child is different and it is not only a question of knowing each one's limitations. We also need to know in what aspects they tend to be more orderly – for example, in the way they keep their things.)

12. mksm *I try to give good example by striving to improve in some aspects of orderliness or trying to avoid being finicky in some aspect of order and thus damaging the family or the class atmosphere.* (Example in striving to improve is what most influences the children. The 'perfect' example can be the result of excessive orderliness and can promote a lack of understanding towards others.)

13. *I teach the children to schedule their activities, so that each activity receives adequate attention.* (To achieve the development of orderliness – in all aspects – there are two kinds of attention which educators need to give children. With the smaller ones they need to insist on them *doing* things, repeating actions in order to develop the habit, and with the older children, they need to insist on them *thinking* before they make their own decisions.)

14. *With the smaller children I do 'keep on', so that they develop habits as regards things which should be done in an orderly fashion.* (It is useful to develop

habits and routine as regards *things*, but routine should be avoided when related to *people*.)

15. *I help the children see that activities need a specific and perhaps ample time to carry them out.* (For example, to start clearing out a cupboard just before lunch is not prudent. Neither is starting a new job five minutes before the bus leaves for school.)

16. *I teach the children to remember the things they have got to do at specific times.* (This will very often mean using a diary. Educators tend to take over from the children in these small responsibilities, telling them when they've got to go to the dentist or when others celebrate their birthdays. Children need to learn to be responsible for their own actions.)

17. *I organise 'chains of events' with the smaller children with the idea of helping them remember the things they have to do at the same time everyday or, at any rate, frequently.* (Everyday, the children have to do more or less the same things when they get up in the morning, when they arrive at school or when they arrive home from school in the evening. It is useful to help them link actions to times and sequences.)

18. *I decide on what things should be kept in what places. And I make sure the children return things to those places after using them and at the right time.* (The criteria one can use for choosing the best place to keep each article are: so that they cannot get broken and so that it is easy to find them.)

19. *I invite the children to get involved in things I do which require orderliness, to help develop a sense of order.* (For example, so that they can see how mother keeps the kitchen utensils in specific places, how their parents pack their bags when they go away, or how the teacher arranges the books on the shelf at school.)

20. *I teach the children to use their things correctly in order to make the best use of them.* (This does not mean that one has to be rigid, because certain articles can be used for other purposes without damaging them or without there being any danger for the child. For example, there is nothing wrong with letting a small child make a hut with a table and a blanket although that is not the 'correct' use for those things.)

6 Responsibility

Responsible people accept the consequences of their actions, be they intentional or unintentional, so that others benefit as much as possible or, at least, do not suffer. They are also concerned that those over whom they have any influence should act similarly.

Young people tend to talk a lot about freedom and little about responsibility. Perhaps we should ask why this is so, before going on to consider this virtue. Responsibility involves admitting the consequences of our actions and it would seem that young people, however irresponsible we consider them, are perfectly willing to do this; they accept the consequences of their actions in the sense of putting up with criticism from their parents, abandoning the comfort of an easy life etc.

However, we are responsible not only to but for ourselves. As O. Dun has said, 'responsibility means responding, making a response, to another's call. That other calling for a response may be one's conscience, a fellow human being, our social selves or, ultimately, God. However, if we are to respond, we must have learned to listen and hear. The Latin words for hear and obey are etymologically related.'[9b] This is what annoys teenagers: responsibility means having to account for what they do and not simply to take the consequences.

It is the fashion nowadays for youngsters to want to regard their lives as divorced from any commitment – to have a good time. And as soon as we begin to consider ourselves as our own bosses we cease to be responsible, for responsibility means obedience: obedience to one's conscience, to authorities, to God, in the knowledge that such obedience is not the passive attitude of a slave, but a positive act of commitment, a duty.

The motives for our responsibility will differ according to the situation in which our need to respond arises. However, let us look at a few examples of these differences. What is the main motive that will stimulate a seven-year-old child to work responsibly at school? There are many motives which may get him to study well: he may like the subject, he may enjoy the work, he may have a good teacher who explains clearly what he has to do. These are all motives for working well, but not necessarily for working responsibly. Responsibility means that the child must be aware of his obligation or duty to respond to somebody. The teacher will undoubtedly get him to do many things and this pressure will teach the child to be responsible in his work, by being forced to respond to the teacher. If he were to begin to do some team work involving several of his friends, his motive would change; he would be involved in the work of the team and realise that the others expect something of him. He will then respond to his companions out of a sense of duty.

If the child understands that his parents are partly responsible for his studies he may make a greater effort out of his sense of duty and love for his parents. Later on, if he realises that his work is a way to personal sanctification, he may increase his efforts out of love of God as well as out of duty. He may occasionally be told directly by someone what he should do, but it is his conscience which has to work out the relationship between his commitment and what he actually does.

Children have many good reasons for being responsible but the parents main function in attempting to develop this virtue in their children is the proper exercise of their authority. As F. Otero says, 'the authority of parents is a positive influence which sustains and increases each child's independence and sense of responsibility; it is a service they offer their children in the process of their education, a service implying the power to decide and sanction; it is a help which consists in guiding the part played by the children in family life, directing their increasing independence and making them responsible; it is an essential element in the love for their children, which manifests itself in various ways in different circumstances'.[10]

Let us examine some points in the attitudes of parents to their children with regard to this virtue, taking account also of the motives to which children have to respond appropriately.

Responsibility for one's own deliberate actions

To acquire the virtue of responsibility means learning, not only to accept liability for decisions made by others but also to take decisions oneself. Nevertheless, it is only natural that young children should begin to acquire a sense of responsibility by faithfully doing what they are told to do: that is what we meant when we referred earlier to 'decisions taken or accepted'. A young child may simply do what his parents tell him, because he is afraid of being punished, because his parents ask him affectionately, because he loves them etc.

Obviously, there are high and not so high motives. Equally obvious, it is one thing to obey and another thing to obey well and this is where we begin to consider the significance of benefiting others as far as possible. By this we mean that if a child does what he is told or carries out an order just to get the job over and done with, it is unlikely that he will do it very well. If he is to act responsibly, in the true sense, he needs a motive for everything he is asked to do, a relationship with another person, for instance his father. The question is, however, whether he has really done what his father intended and wanted, or whether he has only done the minimum necessary to fulfil the letter of his father's instruction. Or a mother tells her daughter, 'Put your clothes in the wardrobe, please'. If the girl is only trying to fulfil the letter of her mother's instruction, she will simply throw her clothes into the wardrobe whereas a responsible child will consider what the mother actually intended and will hang up her clothes as she has been taught. A child may also respond to his own conscience or to other people, as we shall see.

In this regard, we should explain to our children the difference between 'having responsibilities' and 'being responsible'. A responsible person considers the intention and does not confine himself to doing the minimum whereas a person who simply 'has responsibility' may merely fulfil his obligations, but without any real sense of responsibility, without trying to benefit others. This is not a positive and active acceptance of another's decision or instruction, but merely the fulfillment of an obligation.

There are two other, and more serious deviations from responsibility, from which we judge immediately whether a person is genuinely practising that virtue or not. We refer to a habitual tendency to make excuses for not doing something which should be done and an unwillingness to commit oneself fully to something until one sees that it is going to be successful; then when there is no danger of failure, and most of the work has actually been done, the person commits himself to the outcome. The first of these attitudes is especially common in very young children. These should be told that it is better to take the consequences of one's faults and failures than to try to deceive oneself or others. Fortitude is necessary to practise the virtue of responsibility, because if we accept decisions and then prove unable to carry them out, even if we responsibly accept the situation and seek the most satisfactory solution possible so that at least no one will suffer, we need fortitude to fulfill our duty as best we can, and this is precisely the object of responsibility.

Perhaps an example will show what is meant when we say that no one should suffer. A group of teenagers undertake to do something and they divide the work up between them, each one taking responsibility for a particular chore. One of them gets careless and suddenly realises that time has run out and he will be unable to do his bit of the work. Undoubtedly he has been irresponsible in failing to make time for the various things he has to do but at least he can ensure that his friends do not suffer by calling on others for help in the chore he undertook.

So far, we have been speaking of the responsibility that arises when we accept another's decision and we have been referring mainly to young children, since they are more likely to have to accept decisions than to take them themselves. Yet throughout the whole of our lives, we shall have to accept decisions made by others, although teenagers often seem to think that freedom consists of being rid of this obligation. They think they can make decisions but need not accept them. However, we are limited beings, we live in a society and, as we have said before, we must respond to the call to fulfill the purpose for which we were created, namely, to follow our vocation. This is what is meant by taking responsibility for our own lives: it is not a decision we take, but an invitation we accept. Similarly, an adult has usually no say in whether or not to work but he can accept the situation responsibly or irresponsibly. Teenage children should realise the need to accept others' decisions and to take responsibility for them.

Strictly speaking, the distinction between a decision we take and a decision we accept is false, because we have to decide to accept a decision if we are to carry it out in a responsible manner. Yet we must consider the consequences of accepting a decision made by another. If a child responsibly accepts a decision made by one of his parents it means that he will not blame them if things go badly. If he responsibly accepts an instruction, he will not complain how it is given to him or about any difficulty that arises: he has personally accepted all the consequences and will answer for them.

Responsibility and decisions

As we have said, responsibility involves, not only accepting decisions made by others, but also taking decisions oneself on matters on which one is competent, in order to improve and help others to improve. It is only natural that children should begin to take personal decisions in an atmosphere where their parents are at their side to guide them, in other words, in the home. Here we are referring to the matter of carrying one's weight. This, as Otero tells us, means 'a willingness as well as an opportunity to make a personal contribution to the common tasks, in questions either of information, of decision-making or of doing things, but always acting with a sense of responsibility'.

A sense of responsibility requires an initial decision (we make no formal decision of any kind before doing or saying so many things). For instance, parents may ask their children for their opinions as to how a certain family problem should be resolved: one child answers frivolously as if it were a joke, while another makes a sensible suggestion, not because of any conscious decision concerning this particular matter but because he has decided previously, probably in an unconscious way, that he wants to be helpful to all the family. Here a formal decision may be replaced by practising something important in a permanent way.

Some children, by nature, have a highly developed sense of responsibility, not because of any conscious decision, but because they are serious and careful. It is important, therefore, that parents should know their children from this point of view. Otherwise they may try to force a highly responsible child to become even more responsible, when in fact they should be helping with problems of a different kind: for instance, he may not be cheerful, he may be unsociable or unenterprising.

It is right that all children should make decisions and, even if one shows a natural sense of responsibility in doing his jobs and so on, he should still be encouraged to take personal decisions just like others who may have greater difficulty in doing simply what they are told.

Let us now see how we can teach children to be responsible in taking their own decisions and putting them into practice. Normally it should not be necessary to create situations in which children can take decisions, but only to make them aware of those which, in fact, they are taking continually. This will teach them to accept the consequences personally. For example, if they get weekly pocket-money they should learn to use it sensibly and make it last the week, without getting cross if another child has bought something which they would have liked. They could decide which friends they would like to invite to their birthday party. They could decide what toys they wish to take on holiday with them or what present to buy for their mother on Mother's Day and so on.

In all these cases, parents may provide information which will give the children a basis for their decisions and allow them to choose wisely. For instance, in choosing a present for Mother's Day, they could be reminded that they should buy something which their mothers would like rather than one which they like themselves, and a few suggestions may be made to give them some ideas. In the case of young children, the best thing would be to present them with a few alternatives, so that they themselves can choose.

The object here is to teach them to accept one alternative positively and to choose from among several. At a later stage the field of decision-making will be wider and they will think up the alternatives themselves. The object is to get them to take decisions responsibly, based on the facts available and thinking of the possible consequences. After that stage, we can insist they bear the consequences of their decisions without complaining or blaming anyone else. As we have said before, responsibility should be reinforced by fortitude and especially by perseverance, so that whatever decision is taken may be of benefit to others and not simply to ensure that they are not actually harmed.

If one's decisions are not merely to be of benefit to oneself, it is advisable to relate one's efforts to the service of others, thus also practising the virtue of generosity and, in particular, keeping clearly in mind what is pleasing and what is displeasing to God so that one may come to understand what it means to behave as a responsible Christian. This does not consist only of avoiding sin, but also of developing one's conscience so as to act more positively.

Parents can always guide their children in making the right decisions and, if they keep in mind the need to encourage this process, they can take advantage of many opportunities that arise spontaneously. On the other hand, if they notice that children are failing on this point, it may be appropriate to give the matter a higher priority and to create opportunities for them to take their own decisions. When this is done, parents should be very careful not to accept liability for anything that is wrong. For instance, if a child decides to leave his homework until after playing with his friends, and for some reason stays out longer than he had intended, it would remove the responsibility for the consequences of his actions if we were to let him go to bed at the normal time and do the homework for him or, alternatively, allow him to do the homework when he should be in bed. Perhaps the best thing we could do in this case would be to lend him an alarm clock to wake up early so that the work can be done.

With teenage children, we should lay down clear indications as to what types of decisions they can take without informing us, what decisions they can take provided they tell us and what decisions can be taken only after consulting us. In general, we can say that they should consult us on everything related to schoolwork, except with regard to technical points or their way of doing the work itself; the same applies to any decision affecting the rest of the family: for example, if it involves repeatedly eating later than the rest of the family; the rule should apply also to any new situation in which they have no previous experience. From the parents' point of view, they have two direct duties: first, to tell the children when and how they can make their own decisions and second, to give them adequate information and insist that they think first so that the decision will be a responsible one.

There is one type of decision which presents particular problems with regard to the degree of responsibility with which they enter into it. We refer to decisions taken collectively. At any level, these tend to diminish the degree of personal responsibility involved, for each individual feels only partly responsible for what is decided. When this happens, the results are seldom very satisfactory. On the other hand, it shows a very high degree of responsibility if someone feels able to accept the consequences of a collective decision to the same extent as if it were a purely personal one. This is something which parents should keep in mind when discussing with their children collectively some problem to be solved or some goal to be achieved. After taking a collective decision, at least they should speak to each child to ensure that he acknowledges his personal responsibility and the importance of the matter in question. In any case, there can be collective responsibility only if each individual has first acquired a sense of personal responsibility.

Unintentional actions

As already mentioned, we are responsible not only for what we decide but also for what we do, deliberately or not. If a driver knocks down a pedestrian, obviously his action was unintentional, but he cannot on that account adopt an irresponsible attitude. He will have to give an account of the accident to the authorities and try to remedy any damage he has caused, even though no moral liability may be attached to him.

Where children are concerned, if one child breaks another's toy, the fact that it was an accident does not exempt him from the responsibility of repairing or replacing it or getting his parents to do so, and he should also say he is sorry. Obviously, this is a point which parents can explain to their children, for it is a matter of basic justice.

There are other situations where it would not be sufficient to accept liability after the event; I refer to the requirement that we foresee the natural consequences of our actions. If a child plays football in the front room and breaks an ornament, it does not show that he has a well-developed sense of responsibility simply by being apologetic. If he had been responsible, he would have thought about the consequences of what he was doing and then he would have stopped doing it. This approach is especially important for teenagers, because they continually find themselves in new situations which may be harmful. In the first place, they should learn to consult their parents or others whom they can trust before undertaking something new, in order to be aware of the difficulty and dangers that may be involved. In the second place, they should realise that it may be more courageous and more responsible to say no to that new experience.

We are responsible for all our actions, especially when they involve an act of our will, but also when they result from lack of foresight on our part. However, it is to be expected that we will sometimes act irresponsibly without intending to do any harm, and, when that happens, responsibility means trying to undo the harm, repairing the damage done and making every effort not to make the same mistake again. Parents could explain these points to their children if they are clear about them in their own mind. We frequently look for extraordinary or unusual ways of educating our children, and we fail to realise that the main thing is to have clear ideas, give good example, explain things in simple terms and keep in mind what we are attempting to achieve.

Concern for others

We have said at the beginning of this chapter that responsibility includes a concern to ensure that others also act responsibly. In other words, a responsible parent must try to ensure that his children are also responsible; hence the suggestion that we have just made on how to teach virtue. However, they should also educate their children so that they may help their brothers and sisters, friends and even the parents themselves to practise this virtue more intensely. Out of a false sense of respect for others, children may believe that they should make no demands on their friends in this regard, or else they just get cross and complain without making any positive attempt to get others to see where their duty lies.

Our children are bound to have some friends who behave irresponsibly and if they make no effort to help them they may be affected by the same attitude themselves, because it is always easier to act on the spur of the moment or do just what they feel like doing. In this sense, we expect our children to show responsibility even in their relationships with others and this will be reflected in the virtue of loyalty, which we shall consider later.

On a human level, we all have a responsibility to others. Certainly, we must respect others, but this respect involves stimulating them and making demands of them within the bounds of the friendship which exists between us. Our children should feel responsible, and take responsibility, for their own lives, but also pay due attention to others, on the human level and, if they are Christians, also on the supernatural level.

A responsible human being accepts the consequences of his own actions, intentional or not; he also takes responsibility for what he is, namely a child of God.

SELF-ASSESSMENT

Briefing Note: see pages 29-30, above.

Am I a responsible person?

1. *I have accepted full responsibility as an educator. I have a profound understanding of the importance of my role.* (Responsibility requires this first kind of decision – of consciously responding for what one is. It is not so much a question of being responsible for a number of tasks.)
2. *I realise that responsibility means responding to those who have authority over me.* (I need to respond to someone in order to be responsible, and we all have someone with authority over us.)
3. *I am committed to something of value which I then try to share with those for whom I am responsible.* (Commitment is a result of having made a decision. We need to think about what is important to us and then strive to protect and defend those values.)
4. *After making a decision, or starting some action, I accept the consequences if it doesn't work out well.* (Some people try to pass on their responsibility to others. For example, if a child fails at school – mainly because they have made little effort to study – some parents put the blame on the school.)
5. *I spend a certain amount of time trying to foresee the possible results of my decisions before actually deciding.* (In family life, it is common to find parents reacting to situations instead of studying the question and

making a serious decision. Responsibility requires us, not only to accept the consequences of our acts, but also to foresee the possible results.)

6. *I accept the negative consequences of my own mistakes.* (An indication that this is so will be, for example, that the educator says she is sorry when she has made a mistake, or tries to rectify it when she sees that she is wrong, instead of stubbornly carrying on.)
7. *I usually commit myself to projects after studying them seriously, thinking about possible consequences for myself and for others, and without depending too much on other people's opinions.* (Some people are prepared to commit themselves to projects only if the majority of the group have already done so, or when they see that the project is working out well.)
8. *Although there are a lot of reasons for being responsible, I understand that the main reason should be because one is responsible to someone else or one is responsible before God.* (Someone can act in an apparently reasonable way for financial reasons, or out of fear, or to be efficient. However, they do not understand the most profound reasons for being responsible.)
9. *When I take part in meetings where decisions are made, I accept the consequences of those decisions even if what was decided did not coincide with my own opinion.* (In fact, to accept as one's own, decisions made in a group is not easy. It requires a large dose of humility.)
10. *I try to be responsible for what I radically am, that is, a child of God.* (This means, for example, frequenting the Sacraments, studying the truths of the Faith, looking for adequate spiritual guidance, living one's faith in relationships with others, praying and recognising God as Father.)

Teaching others to be responsible

11. *I recognise what each child's tendency is as regards practising the virtue of responsibility so that I do not pressure a child who is, by their very nature, already responsible.* (Each child is born different, and we must remember that there are vices arising out of an excess of each virtue. Perhaps a child who is already responsible needs to develop other virtues – flexibility, sincerity or understanding, for example.)
12. *I give the children orders so that they can learn to obey and be responsible.* (One way of being responsible is accepting the decisions made by other people. That means obeying them. If educators never give orders, they are taking away the child's chance to be responsible in this way.)
13. *I help the children recognise what decisions they are in fact making so that they can then accept responsibility for them.* (For example, helping a child

to recognise how they have spent their allowance, or to recognise the consequences of inviting some friends to a birthday party and not others, or the consequences of having signed up for some complementary activity at school.)

14. *I offer alternatives to the children so that they can think about the advantages and disadvantages of each one.* (When they are older they can come up with their own alternatives, but when they are younger it will be best to help them see what the alternatives are.)

15. *I give the youngsters advance information, or I help them find it, so they make responsible decisions.* (Here we are talking about the stage when the youngster is not mature enough to follow the complete process by himself. In fact we can find a lot of children who are fourteen or fifteen years old who make decisions with virtually no information. They do not recognise possible dangers or they consider themselves capable of overcoming any difficulty. They need help to think matters through.)

16. *I try to establish autonomous decision-making areas for the children in which they may make their own decisions and learn to accept the consequences unless real physical or moral danger crops up.* (If things do not work out well, educators tend to want to intervene to protect the child from suffering, but if they do, they are depriving the child of a chance to learn or grow.)

17. *I help the children pay attention to their friends in order to help them be responsible too.* (To be responsible involves helping others to be responsible too. For example, a student could help another to accept the consequences of having disobeyed some rule, or to keep their word, to do their work well or to obey their parents.)

18. *I help the children discover whom they are responsible to, and for what things.* (Little by little they are able to recognise the different authorities to whom they should be responsible. For example, teachers, parents, civil authorities, and, of course, God.)

19. *I teach the children to consult before making decisions, and to learn whom to consult in each case.* (In fact this means recognising who are authorities in each matter. For example, it is not a question of going to the teacher to solve a medical problem; neither should one go to the doctor to solve a problem related to schoolwork.)

20. *I help the youngsters accept responsibility for mistakes they make although they did not mean them to happen.* (A lot of things happen through lack of foresight or through naivety, and it is difficult to assign any real personal blame. All the same, we have to accept the consequences of our actions. For example, a child gets ill because they fall into a river. Maybe they weren't to blame, but they have to accept the situation.)

7 Respect for others

People who have respect for others act or refrain from acting so as not to harm, and indeed to benefit themselves and others, in line with their rights, status and circumstances.

In speaking of respect for others, it is important to distinguish, first of all, that respect which we owe to every human being as a child of God and that other respect which we owe each individual because of his particular status or situation. The first of these involves a general attitude of understanding and acceptance while the second points us towards specific intentions according to the elements we find in each particular human relationship.

This is clear in the relationship between parents and children, for instance. Here, the parent's personal qualities 'are only of secondary importance as regards motives for respecting them.'[12] They deserve the respect of their children, mainly, because they brought them into this world, they educate them and they are their superiors by the will of God. We are going to consider the practice of this virtue in different types of relationships with friends, companions and people in general, as well as between parents and children.

Before doing so, however, let us mention the question of respect for inanimate objects, which was deliberately omitted from our description of this virtue. It is meaningless to speak of 'respecting' a thing, since it can have no rights and it is impossible to prejudice or encourage its 'improvement', at least if by this we mean an increase in human or spiritual stature. Nevertheless, we often speak of respecting nature, books, other people's property, the rules of the game and so on; so, without doubt, we must be using the word in a different sense.

For instance, when we speak of 'respecting nature' we really mean that we must take care of natural things, use them for the purpose for which they were created; when we speak of 'respecting the rules of the game', we simply mean that we must obey them if they are to serve their purpose. It makes sense to speak of respect for inanimate things only if we realise that they are at the service of human beings and that we only administer things given to us by God. Consequently, it makes sense to 'respect nature', if we understand the motives for doing so are, first of all, that nature comes from God and, second, that we can enjoy it and, third, that if we use it properly, we can come closer to God. We must never regard respect for objects as an end in itself. We do not respect other people's property as such but only use it appropriately and are grateful for the benefit of it; we also try not to damage it by improper use. This refers both to material and spiritual things.

It is clear, then, that every individual has a right to be treated and appreciated by others for what he is, namely, a child of God. We are all therefore basically equal. Apart from this, each individual has a status and a situation of his own and, consequently, others must respect him in a specific way.

Friends, companions and strangers

In describing this virtue, we said that we must act or refrain from acting so as not to harm others and indeed so as to benefit them. How does this maxim relate to the notion of respect which we find among teenagers today? For youngsters nowadays, respect seems to consist mainly of 'refraining from acting'. They consider it wrong to cause or provoke any change in another person deliberately. Yet, in practice, they admit influences which give superficial though alluring pleasure and they reject others which might encourage any efforts to improve. Let us take an example: a group of university students provoke in their companions a need to demonstrate against something; some professors begin to speak with the students individually in order to ascertain points of view and to discuss the problem; those who are stirring up the unrest get very angry and accuse the professors of pressurising their companions: in other words they accuse the professors of lacking respect, when, in fact, it was they themselves who showed lack of respect for their companions by not allowing them to make their own decisions.

We must not only refrain from acting, therefore, but we must also positively act. Nevertheless, this action must be firmly based on truth if it is not to degenerate into disrespect. To be more specific, others have a right to hear, as far as possible, objective information. Therefore sincerity is a basic element of respect for others; and sincerity must be governed by charity and prudence: this means that there are times when it is better to tell the whole truth courageously and other times when it is more respectful to remain silent. The criterion to be used is in accordance with the degree of improvement being sought.

The practice of this virtue, insofar as it affects relationships between our children, their friends, and people in general, will depend to a great extent on their age. Obviously, very young children, who know only certain aspects of their friends, will respect them differently from the way in which older children will, knowing other different aspects of their friends' personality.

Younger children will tend to respect their friends, brothers and sisters mainly because of the things they own and the way they treat them. Let us consider this point. People have a right to use their possessions and give others this right as and when they wish, although, of course, they should also practise the virtue of generosity. A child has no right to steal or to make use of things which belong to others without their permission. However, if he is to understand the reasons for the rules he should be allowed to see some of the annoyance which others can suffer. It is understandable that he be attracted by other people's things and even that he think it unjust that they should have something which he wants; after all his sense of justice is not highly developed. It requires the virtue of fortitude to refrain from using other people's property and overcome one's selfish impulses. Consequently, it would seem sensible that each household should hold a balance between things that 'belong to everyone' and things that belong to individuals. Parents sometimes act as if anything a child owns can be used by everyone else but in that case they are neglecting an excellent opportunity to teach their children the virtue of respect.

Children must learn, not only to understand what it means to own something, but also to appreciate the effect it may have on someone if they refuse to acknowledge that he is the owner. Depending on the individual child, parents should stress either the notion of property or the emotional effect that can be caused in others. What we are trying to teach our children is that they should consider the consequences of their actions before doing something, because they must realise that others may be affected.

Children should be taught, furthermore, to respect the feelings of others. They should not arouse a child to anger or provoke him to seek revenge; yet, children often regard this kind of thing as a game and fail to understand an argument of the type: 'Would you like it if someone did that to you?' It may restrain them for the moment but they soon return to their previous behaviour. The ability to put themselves in the place of others in order to see the effect of what they are doing tends to be very slight in very young children. It is easier for them to behave properly because of certain clear rules. Perhaps one suggestion we could make is that there is little point in trying to develop this kind of respect for others in very young children but it is better to help them simply to be obedient and strong-willed so that, later on, when the time comes for them to learn the virtue of respect, they have sufficient inner strength to be able to practise it. But children can begin to lay the foundations of respect for others by living in an atmosphere of respect and affection. They need to have certain principles to understand where respect begins and finishes. Let us see a few examples. They will have to see that people are treated differently depending on their circumstances. If someone is working in the house, for instance, they would see that their parents treat that person differently from the way in which they treat their children, precisely because the relationship between them is different. Nevertheless, the parents may treat that person concerned politely or impolitely and, if they show no respect for her, if they do not acknowledge her right to be treated properly and with due consideration, the children are unlikely to do any better. That is how they learn to deal with people. If they hear their parents indiscriminately criticise a certain type of person, because of his race, his ethnic origin, his occupation or his personal qualities, this intolerance and disrespect are likely to affect the child also, and he may begin to say the same things or classify people in the same way.

In the case of younger children, we are trying to lay a basis which will help them to recognise and understand everybody's genuine capacity for improvement. If we ever lose confidence in a person's ability to use his or her intelligence in order to improve, we are regarding him as equal to an animal.

We have suggested that it is advisable to lay down rules for very young children as a preparation for the virtue of respect and perhaps these rules could be summarised as follows:

- Everyone is different and therefore must be treated differently.
- Everyone is as he is, without having to be classified. From this it follows that: (a) children should behave so as not to upset others, taking their things without asking, being unkind to them etc.; (b) they should not criticise others; (c) they should act positively to help others; (d) they should look for the best in people; (e) they should thank others for trying to help them.

Once children reach adolescence, respect for others becomes more meaningful for them. Once they discover their own identity, they begin to understand what it means to respect others and to respect themselves. Indeed the virtue of modesty is based on a correct appreciation of one's own intimacy and that of others and respect for those others follows logically. Let us consider some aspects of this respect which may cause difficulties for teenage children. Teenagers want to be respected by others and they are very conscious of this respect. On the other hand, they may not be at all conscious of failing to show respect to others themselves. They become very upset when a friend fails to turn up for an appointment but they, in turn, may he very careless about such things. They are annoyed when a friend tells stories about them but they maybe perfectly ready to tell stories about their friends. The more intimately two people know one another – close friends or brothers and sisters, for instance – the greater the respect they will need for one another, because such a relationship presupposes a deep understanding which allows them to spend a lot of time together. Brothers and sisters will find it especially difficult to live with one another unless there is a great deal of mutual respect because, obviously, we cannot choose the members of our family according to our likes and dislikes. Everyone is different, has a different way of doing things and has a right to live in his home.

There is no reason why parents should not explain these things to their children, if possible creating an atmosphere where situations will not arise that might provoke unnecessary disrespect between them. They should certainly be taught that it would be wrong to speak of a person's private affairs when others are listening, and it should be emphasised that each member of the family has a right to behave as he thinks best, provided he does no harm to himself or anyone else.

Another problem with teenagers is that they tend to interpret respect as 'refraining from acting' so as not to harm others, thus neglecting their duty to help people. Since all others have an essential ability to improve, our respect for them should oblige us to help them attain higher personal standards. Of course, if we are to do this, we will have to know the other person and be familiar with many aspects of his personal situation; it would show lack of respect if we offered gratuitous suggestions to a complete stranger: it would also show little common sense. However, if we know the other person and have sufficient contact with him to be able to show our interest, then our respect for him demands that we should act positively and help him.

Respect, in this sense, is based on familiarity with the other person's character and circumstances. If we know him fairly well, it will be reasonably possible to foresee the consequences of any appropriate actions we might care to take, and respect demands that we should consider these consequences before taking any steps. This point will become clear when we think of the relationship between boys and girls. A boy might make a dishonourable suggestion to a girl and try to persuade her to accept it either by giving her false reasons or playing on her emotions. If she then accepts the suggestion, the boy might allege that she had made up her mind freely whereas, in fact, there has been obvious pressure and lack of respect on his part.

Respect is meaningful only if it is based on objective reality and the truth of the situation. We must distinguish between each person's right to his own opinion and the right of others to be told the truth and have whatever information they may need in order to improve. There is no lack of respect involved in showing another person that his opinion is mistaken; it is precisely our respect for the truth that obliges us to clarify matters. Teenagers, however, frequently fail to appreciate the situation of others when it comes to their own 'right' to have an opinion. Undoubtedly they have this right but it does not authorise them to exercise a bad influence on their younger brothers or sisters or on less mature friends by using skilful arguments to prove their point. Respect for others demands that if we are not totally sure of the accuracy of what we see we should, out of prudence as well as respect, refrain from exercising any influence that might prejudice them. On the other hand, as we have said, if we know something is true, we should try to exercise a positive influence for the benefit of others.

To be specific, with regard to teenage children, parents should explain to them the meaning of respect for others and discuss the difficulties that may arise when they try to exercise this virtue in a positive way. They should be encouraged to think of the consequences of their actions, to assess the intellectual capacity, the age and the temperament of the people with whom they come into contact so that they may have true appreciation of each situation and act or refrain from acting in such a way that they will not harm others, but rather benefit them as far as possible.

Relationships with parents

'Respect for others should be both internal and external',[13] as Mausbach and Ermecke explain. 'We fail in this duty by inner contempt, injurious words, and a contemptuous attitude, non-fulfilment of a person's 'last will', and, above all disrespect'.[14] In dealing with parents' duties and the importance of teaching their children the human virtues, we have referred several times to the respect which parents should have for their children. However, we have not yet considered how they should teach their children to respect them as parents. And this is an important matter because children have a duty to respect their parents throughout the whole of their lives, even though the duty to obey them ceases when they leave home. (Children under age have a duty to obey their parents while they are under their care even if they do not live with them.)

Parents have to teach their children how to respect them and perhaps we should consider here whether there is any distinction between respect based on justice and that based on love. Obviously, we would like our children to respect us out of love, but there is a difference between the respect which they may have for their friends based on love and that which they have for their parents. This difference is derived from the fact that their parents have brought them into this world and, consequently, have authority over them from the very fact of being their parents. Their children should love them principally because they are their parents, and not for their personal qualities, as is the case with mere friends. Therefore, one cannot make a distinction between respect based on justice and that based on love, for any respect based solely on justice is incomplete, while respect based solely on love of one's parents because of their personal qualities is even less complete.

There are two ways of proceeding in our efforts to ensure that our children respect us: each parent should take steps to see that he personally is respected or else he may use methods to get the children to respect the other parent. On certain matters it may be easier and more appropriate to help the children to understand the other parent's situation rather than to emphasise their relationship with one's self, although it is also important to demand respectful treatment of oneself in order to maintain one's own dignity. Take the example of parents who find that their unmarried daughter has become pregnant; this in itself causes great suffering but they are even more hurt when another daughter accuses them of being responsible for the situation because they had not taught her sister to use contraceptives. In this second situation, the suffering is caused by a tremendous lack of respect. Teenage children sometimes think they have a right to think and do what they like in the presence of their parents. But to deliberately say or do things so that they may suffer or react in temper shows a great lack of respect, and parents should insist that children respect them, at least to the extent of not hurting them. In situations where parents and teenagers collide, it may become necessary to tell a child clearly that while he is under his parents' roof he has a duty to respect and obey them whether he likes it or not, because they are still responsible for him. When they reach adulthood, the duty to obey them ceases but the duty to respect them continues.

Children will find it difficult to learn to control themselves and treat their parents properly, unless the parents have shown that they, for their part, respect their children and always seek their welfare. Of course, children frequently fail to realise that their parents are acting for their good. In these cases, one parent should explain clearly but briefly the other's motives for what he does. It is not a question of arguing or convincing them; it is simply that children have a right to be given sufficient information to understand that their parents are acting according to certain principles in order to improve and help them. Otherwise, they will find it impossible to believe that their parents' demands are fair and reasonable. Thereafter, they should respect their parents and if they disagree with their decision, even if they consider it an unfair and unreasonable decision, they should express their point of view politely, in a way that will not be hurtful, and explain how they have reached a different or opposite opinion. Here we see that, when there is genuine affection between parents and children, respect comes naturally because, usually even without knowing it, children appreciate their parents properly, just as their parents appreciate them.

To encourage this affection from an early age, the parents' role and position must be defended. Parents may undoubtedly be friends to their children, but the relationship should be much more than that. The child expects his parents to make demands of him and he will certainly not doubt his duty to respect and obey them if they do not sow the seeds of that doubt. I believe this to be absolutely true, even though certain opinions do not seem to favour it nowadays.

The child will notice that his parents are strict with him because they love him, not for revenge or to annoy him, and he, in turn, will make demands on them. This is also a form of respect because the objective is to get them to fulfil their duties. This is why it is sometimes said that parents educate their children but that children also educate their parents: they educate one another when there is mutual respect.

From what we have said, we may conclude that without love, it is impossible to practise the virtue of respect for others, and love cannot be put into effect or interpreted indiscriminately: we have to take into account the other person's status and circumstances. If we forget that respect involves a belief in the essential possibility of each person's improvement, we end up by classifying others, thus limiting and diminishing their opportunities to advance on the human or spiritual plane. We must act when we can do good for others and refrain from acting when we may prejudice their chances of improving.

Our respect for others can be genuine only if it is practised out of our acknowledgement that we are children of God. Children respect their parents because God has willed them to be in that position. Respect is not something to be shared out according to the personal qualities we find in those with whom we come into contact; rather, it is something to which others, all others, have a right. The way in which we interpret and practise this virtue will depend, in each case, on our recognition of the rights, status and circumstances of others and on our willingness to act, and to refrain from acting, out of love.

SELF-ASSESSMENT

Briefing Note: see pages 29–30, above.

Do I respect others?

1. *I usually manage to obtain an atmosphere of understanding and acceptance in the family or in the class.* (This atmosphere is based on a number of little things. For example, listening to others attentively, avoiding unfounded criticism, taking care with one's tone of voice or gestures so that they do not express scorn or contempt.)
2. *I recognise that everyone can improve.* (The contrary would be to put a label on a person and would also show that that judgment was final. For example, that one particular child cannot be trusted or that another will always be useless at his studies.)
3. *It is quite clear to me that 'things' do not have rights and are at man's service.* (We should look after things to make best use of them. For example, not allowing a youngster to use some machine because they could damage it (although they have received an adequate training in its use) is a way of not showing respect, not for the machine but rather for the youngster.)
4. *I normally act with the clear idea of wanting to help others.* (A false sense of respect for others leads people not to act in case others think that they are prying or because they don't want to risk receiving a rebuff.)

5. *I try not to do things which I think may harm others.* (There are occasions when it would not be prudent to try to do something specific for other people. The action could hurt them more than help them.)
6. *I understand that different people should be treated differently and therefore be shown respect in different ways.* (A weak and ill person needs to be shown respect in a different way to another who is strong, healthy and energetic. One needs to show respect for a teacher differently from the way one treats a member of the family.)
7. *Before acting to try to help another, I always try to ensure that I am well informed about their situation.* (In this way we shall be able to act in the most appropriate moment and according to the person's real needs.)
8. *I treat everyone with the respect they deserve.* (Everyone, as children of God, and one's own parents, one's friends, civil authorities, etc. according to the dignity of their position.)
9. *When talking to others, I try to avoid general judgments about people, indiscriminate criticism and any kind of prejudice.* (We can usually notice signs of disrespect for others in conversations. We can also notice people who prefer to keep quiet rather than talk badly about others.)
10. *I think about how best to serve each person, at the same time recognising that there are no magic formulae which are right for everyone.* (A 'formula' in fact means that we consider everyone to be the same.)

Teaching people to respect others

11. *I help the young children to respect other people's property and the rules of the game in general.* (This requires insistence by educators. Young children do not understand the abstract concept of 'respect for others', but they can develop habits related to the virtue.)
12. *I recognise the chidren's right to own possessions and I help them distinguish between what is private property and what is common property.* (In some families and schools there is a tendency to consider virtually everything as common property, thinking that this will develop solidarity. However, we all have the right to acquire and own possessions. We should look for a reasonable balance between private property and common property.)
13. *I teach the smaller children not to upset others, taking their things away from them, breaking or dirtying their possessions or treating them with lack of consideration.* (A small child can recognise that another is emotionally upset, and this, in itself, can be a good reason for them to be respectful.)

14. *I reason with the youngsters so that they realise that we are all different and therefore they should act in a different way with each person.* (This means telling them how they should act towards their parents, their teachers, their friends, people of the opposite sex, people they don't know.)

15. *I call the children's attention to the fact that criticising people, talking badly about them behind their backs, or despising them, is disrespectful.* (This is common behaviour but far less in those children who live in families where the parents give a good example as regards respect for others.)

16. *I help the youngsters recognise the respect that is due to their brothers and sisters and their friends; respect for each one's intimacy, for their property or for their good name.* (Respect for others is especially difficult in those groups where it is not possible to choose the other members - in the family or in the classroom, for example.)

17. *I help the youngsters see how they may be influencing other people negatively by playing on their emotions or because of an age difference.* (For example, some boy may take advantage of a girl's emotional state to get what he wants. Also, older brothers and sisters tend to take advantage of their age to get what they want out of younger ones.)

18. *I teach the youngsters to recognise the dangers involved when there is a lack of respect for others in different relationships.* (In educational matters we seldom find novel, worthwhile methods to achieve our goals. We need to reason with the youngsters, giving them a clear, concise and accurate information about the question in hand.)

19. *I explain to the youngsters how they should respect their parents all their lives.* (They should obey them while they live under the same roof or while they are not of age.)

20. *I manage to get the children not to use offensive language, not to have a disparaging attitude towards certain kinds of people and not to treat anyone badly.* (Although we wish to focus education positively, looking for situations in which the youngsters can really show their respect for others, it is also necessary to focus on specific kinds of behaviour which show serious lack of respect for others.)

8 Sincerity

Sincere people make full disclosure, where appropriate, to the right person and at the right time, of anything they have done, seen, thought or felt with regard to their own or another's situation.

On the subject of sincerity, Pedro Rodriguez remarks that 'nowadays everyone claims to be sincere and at least would like that claim to be justified. There is much talk of the sincerity of young people, of the contemporary theatre, of modern songs. The point about the prestige of this great virtue is that, basically, it comes from ignorance of what it genuinely involves.'[15]

If we look at the description of this virtue which we have just suggested, we realise that many people ignore the stipulations 'where appropriate' and 'to the right person and at the right time'. Yet, if sincerity is to be genuine, it cannot consist of saying everything at random. We have to recognise the truth about ourselves and others, we have to possess the truth so to speak, before we can disclose it in accordance with certain principles. In particular, sincerity should be governed by charity and prudence. The problem of 'going too far', however, is not the only distortion we find in young people, although it is probably one of the most prevalent in teenagers. There are other distortions, caused by a false understanding of reality or deliberately deceitful disclosure of the known truth: we refer here to lying, hypocrisy, flattery, slander, gossip etc. Before considering these two types of distortion, let us look at the situation of a person who sets out to practise the virtue of sincerity.

The author to whom we have just referred tells us that sincerity and humility are two forms of one and the same virtue, while St Thomas explains that humility regulates man's tendency to project himself as greater than he is. It is worth pointing out, therefore, that sincerity is not possible while a person is deceiving himself. Yet the difficulty of knowing ourselves comes from a tendency to compare our own position to that of others. 'The golden rule of my reality as a human being comes to me not from my relationship with others, but primarily from my relationship with the Creator'.[16] The fact that we are children of God is extremely important and it should inspire us to make every effort to know ourselves so that we can use everything we have in the service of God and of others, without unduly overestimating or underestimating ourselves. Here it is worth insisting on the importance of discovering our intimate selves, in the knowledge that we shall then be in a position to assess ourselves as we really are and be able to disclose whatever is appropriate to the right person at the right time. We must avoid falsifying any situation or interpreting it maliciously; we must avoid using what we have and what we are senselessly being carried away by our own or others' whims in such a way that we confuse sincerity with what is nothing but veritable intemperance.

Let us consider some of the difficulties involved in seeing things as they are and then go on to examine some of the distortions which may arise in disclosing what we see. We shall also mention some points connected with teaching our children to be sincere.

Seeing things as they are

If we are to see things in a way that will help us to improve, we must distinguish between what is important and what is unimportant. This distinction is irrelevant for someone who has no wish to improve, who regards life simply as a place where he finds nothing but pleasure and sees no need to make any effort to improve with a view to the ultimate purpose for which he was created. Of course it is easier to seek pleasure on the spur of the moment and then deceive oneself when things go badly, to escape or cover up unpleasant situations or one's basic dissatisfaction with other types of stimuli, such as the cinema, sex, drugs and so on. We should therefore make every effort to improve with a view to some objective, however unclearly understood as yet, so that sincerity, or indeed any other virtue, may be meaningful.

In the light of these considerations, we must try to teach our children to see the importance of this type of improvement, so that it may provide them with a principle by which to judge all other aspects of their personal situation. Undoubtedly, personal improvement makes more sense to an adult than to a child, at least when faced with a wide range of information presented to him. On the other hand, young children are unlikely to be faced with a large array of facts, which can so often cloud issues for grown-ups. When dealing with children perhaps what we should try to achieve is an awareness on their part of their abilities and qualities, so that they can be positively helpful to others. Children know they are doing the right things when they imitate something they have seen others do if that something has been useful or pleasant for themselves. For instance, a little girl decides to tidy the living room. This not only pleases her mother, but also shows that she is beginning to recognise her own ability to be helpful and undoubtedly she has found a certain satisfaction in what she has done. She is beginning to discover that fundamental aspect of herself, mainly that she has been created for a purpose. She is far from understanding this fully, of course, but at least she is beginning to distinguish between pleasure that gives satisfaction and pleasure for its own sake. If children seek pleasure alone they are neglecting part of themselves and, consequently, anything connected with the virtue of sincerity will have little meaning. Perhaps they do not tell lies or gossip, but only because it does not give them any of that pleasure which they have substituted for the true purpose of their lives; the pleasure is taken away, for example, because their parents punish them or someone is angry with them.

Small children need to be given adequate information at an early stage so that they begin to realise that life has a purpose and that this purpose can be achieved only through personal effort, based on their own abilities and qualities. If they are to be sincere with themselves, they need to know that one of the principles according to which they should judge the facts presented to them, important or not, is the relationship between these facts and their own possibility of improving.

We shall see the significance of this principle if we consider some of the distortions of sincerity. If an eight-year-old child tells lies, obviously his parents are not aware of the facts they need in order to guide him. If he believes he must tell the truth solely because his parents have laid this down as a rule, without properly explaining it, he may lie simply to avoid the punishment which he will regard as an act of revenge on the part of his parents for breaking their rules. If, on the other hand, he is aware that the purpose of sincerity is to allow him to improve, and if his parents present it in this way, at least he will have fewer reasons for being deceitful, even though he may still tell lies for other reasons.

We must now consider some difficulties related to the importance of being aware of one's responsibility and qualities as well as the efforts needed to use them for the welfare of others in order to improve personally. Even if we ourselves consistently follow the principles we have given to our children, youngsters may begin to abandon these when they come into contact with influences outside the family. The object of many people today, old and young alike, is simply the search for pleasure, freedom from any type of duty. In these circumstances, it is impossible to grasp important aspects of one's position, because, as we have said, there is no longer any criterion for action.

I believe that the solution lies in giving full explanations to teenage children. Many parents have a way of life based on a number of rules or modes of behaviour which they themselves accepted more or less passively at first, only later practising them in an active way because experience has shown that they help them improve. These parents are often unable to explain things to their children or to counteract dangerous influences and they sometimes put up illogical arguments.

To be sincere and recognise one's personal situation as a human being created by God for a purpose, for an end, means being just with oneself.

Other problems also arise in being aware of our own position and that of others, but our approach to them should always be the same: to stress the positive angle, those aspects that offer a chance of improvement, and consider the negative elements only in relation to those same chances of improvement.

One of the other problems that may arise is the difficulty of distinguishing between facts and opinions, interpretations,dreams or mere fantasy. If an eight-year old says that he cannot do something, it may be true, but if he means that he will never be able to learn to do it, then he is deceiving himself. His parents could explain things to him and teach him to do whatever is involved so that he can change his mind about being unable to do it. In other circumstances, the child's original statement might be false; in other words, he might have said it simply to avoid doing something unpleasant. In this case, the parents should show him how important it is to admit the truth and suggest that he might say, for instance, 'I am tired and I don't want to do it'. With great affection, parents should always help their children to see things as they really are and one of the things they should learn at an early age is that two people may see the same thing differently and may contradict one another without lying. For example, one child may accuse another of cheating at some game; the second child denies the charge and the conflict starts which has to be settled by a parent. What is important here, first of all, is to ascertain the truth by asking for facts rather than opinions and, secondly, to concentrate on finding a way of ensuring that a similar situation should not arise in the future.

Other situations which involve a distortion of reality are, for example, a little girl who has no brother or sister who invents a fictitous character to play with her or, on a different level, a boy who breaks something in the house and accuses someone else who was not even in the house at the time.

I choose these two examples because neither of them involves malice. If what we are trying to do is to get a child to improve, what we can do in the first example is to look for companions for the child and, if that is not possible, not to break up the make-believe world she has created – provided of course that she realises the difference between the real world and the make-believe world. She will grow out of this stage. In the second case, you have to show the boy that he has got it wrong. It is not a matter of breaking down the boy's insincerity by heavy reasoning: but of making him see that he is not telling the truth and that we are not going to punish him just because he has broken that thing.

So, in a way, the basis for training children to be sincere is a parent's awareness that sincerity is an absolute priority. If parents don't realise this, then they end up worrying about other aspects of the child's behaviour and not fostering sincerity. Imagine a situation where an adolescent has gone to a picture which his parents banned, just because all his friends decided to go one day when they all happened to be together; if the parents appreciate the importance of sincerity, they will probably prefer that he himself should tell them of his disobedience and the reason for it, rather than hear it from someone else and punish him for disobeying them. If they have actually explained to him why they think that film is unsuitable, the child himself will be in possession of the facts and will probably make a correct decision as to what he is to do; if he then gives in to the temptation, he will be likely to admit it afterwards.

This brings us to yet another problem regarding our assessment of the facts of a situation. Everyone tends to deceive himself with regard to his own capability of withstanding harmful influences; his intellect is so important for a teenager that he tends to forget his physical and emotional reactions: the intellect thinks it is in control, when in fact this is far from the case. Sincerity with oneself means admitting one's personal weaknesses and recognising certain dangers in subjecting oneself to influences which parents have identified as being harmful. The difficulty here is to get teenagers, who generally esteem the virtue of sincerity so highly, to take the next step of understanding it as a full and frank exchange of information. They tend not to interpret it as a recognition of their own situation as having anything to do with improvement. Consequently, their notion of sincerity is closer to pride than to humility and is more akin to lack of control than to frankness. It is clear, then, that there are various ways of deceiving oneself, many of them caused by a culpably deformed conscience.

Distortions of the truth

Going on to consider some distortion of the ways in which we express the truth, let us concentrate on the provision that we should make 'full disclosure, where appropriate, to the right person and at the right time', as expressed at the beginning of the chapter. What this provision really means is that sincerity should be governed by prudence and charity. If we are interested in improvement, the justification for sharing some part of our inner self with another person is precisely the hope that some improvement will result. There is no point in pouring out our ideas to everybody all the time: this would be to have handed over control to our whims, our basest passions and whatever we feel on the spur of the moment. As human beings, with a sense of purpose in life, we must exercise our will.

One of the difficulties that teenagers experience is that there seems to be a gap between this intentional view of sincerity and what they tend to call spontaneity. Even if this is not quite a gap, other people at least have difficulty in reconciling this notion with the idea of openness in general. Spontaneity is sometimes confused with self-abandon, throwing off inhabitions, acting on impulse – activities which are more instinctive and animal-like than human, making no use of reason or will. If we are to keep within the bounds of reality, there is no point in ignoring certain specific aspects of our nature, which are obvious to anyone: spontaneity is of no value in itself if it means self-abandonment; on the other hand, if it is associated with frankness and openness, conducive to our own and others' improvement, then it is meaningful.

Such spontaneity is related to frankness if that means genuineness, simplicity in our motives, openness and honesty. The opposite of this kind of spontaneity is deviousness, that is to say, speaking our minds to the right person at the opportune moment but as part of a plan of strategy, in an unnatural way, having little to do with personal genuineness. Neither would there be any sincerity in the 'strategy' of feigning emotions, concealing facts or having special sources of information, while deliberately adopting an attitude of innocence or natural simplicity, for instance.[17]

By all means, we should behave in a genuine and simple manner, but realising that every situation involving human relationships requires an effort of will to balance the help we are going to give with the needs of others so as to achieve improvement. It is not that we have to think about this improvement continually – indeed, our behaviour would be very artificial if we did – but rather to keep it in mind and act prudently.

If this is a problem for teenagers, what can we do to educate the younger children along these lines? Briefly, we should encourage them to talk to us about themselves. Without this basic communication, it will be impossible to guide them, but once this is achieved – and with some timid or shy children it may take a long time – we can try to direct them as follows:

- to distinguish between fact and opinions,
- to distinguish what is really important,
- to understand who should be told what,
- to decide what is an opportune moment, and
- to understand the reasoning behind the distinctions.

Children who are inclined to talk too much will have to learn to channel and control their exuberance. In the case of children who speak very little, we shall have to find a situation in which they feel at ease. Normally the problem of poor communication will not be resolved directly, at a particular moment, by insisting that the child tell us more, but rather by creating situations, seeing opportunities or taking advantage of certain circumstances to start the child talking. For some children, this will take the form of a parent showing interest in something they have done and asking directly, 'How did it go?'; with others, the situation may arise when going for a walk, washing the dishes, or cleaning the car or just when they are finishing something they have enjoyed.

We shall now consider some problems to do with falsifying the facts.

Falsifying the facts

One of the most frequent manifestations of insincerity is simply telling lies. This means trying to deceive one's listeners concerning the facts as one sees them. Therefore when a small child calls another a liar, he is generally not using the word in its proper sense; what he means is that the other person's understanding of the matter is different from his own. There is usually no intention to deceive one's listeners before the use of reason, that is about the age of seven. Before that, children often find it very difficult to distinguish reality from imagination and they do not realise the implications for others of what they say. In these early years, we should encourage their imagination, by constantly pointing out the difference between real and imagined situations. Consequently, it is not advisable to invent imaginary reasons in order to encourage real life behaviour; for instance, it is undesirable to say to someone, 'Don't go there or a wolf will eat you or to speak of the stork when a new baby is expected.

On the subject of genuine lies, we should keep in mind the following points:

- Lying comes from some need felt by the child; therefore such needs should be eliminated as far as possible and the child helped to face up to difficult situations;
- Lying is also contagious and, as always, parents' example is vital; and
- To avoid certain types of lies, the child must be able to express himself clearly: he should therefore be taught to grasp the reality of situations and express it.

Let us consider these causes and remedies.

A lie may indeed 'solve' many problems in the everyday life of a child, usually saving him from unpleasant experience. Thus, for instance, he may say that he is late from school because a teacher was talking to him, instead of telling the truth, namely that he has been playing on the way, because he knows that his parents will get cross or even punish him if he tells the truth. If we were not to punish children in instances of this type, unless absolutely necessary, we would eliminate the need to lie in such situations; we might even reward sincerity, but never becoming naive about it. Of course, if an isolated occurrence were to become an unacceptable habit, then some punishment would have to be imposed.

A child may sometimes feel the need to be equal or better than his friends and he may tell lies about his parents, his possessions, where he has been on holiday etc. These needs are not easy to obviate and perhaps the best one can do would be to point out, in a loving way, the good things he has and to discuss his desire to be different and to have different things.

Teenagers may lie in order to avoid trouble or to protect their privacy, in which case there is no point in forcing one's way into their confidence. It is better to create situations in which they themselves may feel the need to confide in their parents, while also keeping a watch from a distance, finding out from others what type of places they are frequenting and so on. It will not be conducive to any improvement if we force children into situations in which they are more or less obliged to tell lies. It is obvious, of course, that if children refuse to talk about their genuine problems to people that can help them, they are reducing their chances of improvement.

Parents' example may be vital because, almost without realising it, they can give the impression that lying is permissible. The typical example of lies that parents tell is to get whoever answers the phone to say that they are not at home if they find it inconvenient to speak to the caller, or to tell a policeman who stops them that they did not see the red light. Yet, perhaps, there are even more serious types of insincerity of which adults are guilty: we refer to hyprocrisy, flattery, slander, gossip and so on. Without going into detail on each of these faults, it is clear that sincerity must be governed, as we have said before, by prudence and charity. There is no point in giving an opinion if we have insufficient information and, if we have such information, we should not use it if it can damage someone else in a negative way: we say 'in a negative way', because occasionally it may be necessary to 'damage' them in order to achieve some improvement. This, as always, is the guiding principle. We are reminded by J.A. Galera[18] of St Augustine's saying that, although everyone who lies is attempting to conceal the truth, not everyone who conceals the truth is actually lying. It sometimes happens that someone knows the truth but neither may nor should disclose it. These are the well-known cases of professional secrecy, trade secrets and natural secrets.

There are some situations in which other virtues prevail over sincerity. For instance, someone makes a noise in the class and the teacher asks 'Who did it?'; the culprit does not answer. What should the others do? If silence is not going to prejudice the whole class they should remain loyal to their classmate, even though he has shown himself to be insincere. In other words, loyalty prevails over sincerity.

At the beginning of this chapter, we mentioned that the truth should be disclosed clearly: this involves clarity of expression and courage. There is no point in blurting out confused explanations intermingled with excuses; we should tell the truth in a simple way, in an orderly fashion and with a sense of responsibility. Here again, if parents wish their children to tell them everything of significance, they must give them guidance on what is and what is not important so that they will learn to be sincere.

Practising the virtue of sincerity

The degree to which one practises the virtue of sincerity will depend on each individual's ability to recognise facts as they really are. It is easy to tell the truth when there is no conflict of interest involved. What we must teach our children is to distinguish between facts and fantasy, between truth and mere opinion, between what is important and what is less important, both in straightforward situations and in emotional circumstances; this means insisting on the importance of telling the truth without embarassment so that they will be able to receive proper guidance as long as their parents are in a position to give it. By 'proper' we mean explaining what is prudent, what is meant by the opportune moment, the right person and so on; sincerity means being honest, fair in all our dealings with others and fair in our relationship with ourselves.

Sincerity should be based, primarily, on children's confidence that their parents love them and that they are willing to help rather than judge. We then realise that it allows them to know themselves as they are in comparison with what they should be, so that they can improve. Lastly, the highest motive for sincerity is to see ourselves as children of God with a specific purpose; we must certainly recognise our human limitations but also our greatness as God's children. Only thus can we love in a way appropriate to what we are and only thus can we advance each day humanly and spiritually.

SELF-ASSESSMENT

Briefing Note: see pages 29–30, above.

Am I sincere myself?

1. *I try to create an open atmosphere of communication and trust in the family or in the classroom so that the children get used to being sincere.* (In fact, to practise any particular virtue one needs an 'atmosphere of virtue'. All the virtues are interrelated, and we need to practise them in a natural rather than a programmed way.)

2. *I am conscious of my own real situation, my qualities, my capacities, my limitations and possible prejudices, and I know what is important.* (If one doesn't know what is important, and does not know oneself, it will not be possible to help the children do the same. And if they aren't conscious of what their real situation is, how are they going to tell others about it?)

3. *I understand that the most important thing is to recognise that I am a child of God and to strive to improve according to an objective notion of what is good.* (Some people recognise their real situation only partially, for example, being conscious only of their whims and caprices. In that case, they will only be able to manifest that reality, and little improvement will result.)

4. *I normally discuss my personal experience with the next person.* (It is not a question of telling everyone everything. For example, we share some things with our spouse, others with a friend and yet others with a companion at work.)

5. *I normally share personal experiences at the right time.* (One should not automatically share what one knows or what one thinks etc. The virtue of sincerity must be governed by prudence.)

6. *When I share information about ideas, feelings etc., I do so to help others or to look for help towards my own improvement.* (It is not a question of wanting to help or be helped all the time, but we should remember that that is the idea behind sincerity. We should not think that sincerity is telling everyone everything at any time.)

7. *When I talk about what I've seen, what I've heard etc., I do so prudently and charitably.* (Sincerity requires prudence but also charity, in order to do things for people's good. In fact all virtues should be expressions of love.)

8. *I base my sincerity on trust and naturalness.* (We should try to avoid turning on a 'sincerity mode' but rather speak with simplicity, frankness and honesty.)

9. *I make sure that I give good example to the children by neither lying, nor covering up the truth, or trying to mislead other people.* (For example, 'Tell them I'm not at home', or 'I'm going to the match but ring up work and tell them that I'm ill.')

10. *I am conscious of the times when I cannot and should not reveal some truth.* (For example, professional secrets; but also knowing how to keep a secret in general or not talking about some intimate family matter unnecessarily with others.)

Teaching others to be sincere

11. *I teach the children to be sincere with themselves, helping them to discover their personal capacities and qualities.* (It is impossible to make the truth known if one does not previously know what truth is.)

12. *I teach the children to recognise important values in life so that they can pay attention to what is important and downplay what is secondary.* (For example, if I don't tell the children that their feelings are important, it is possible that they won't pay them attention and therefore will not talk about them.)

13. *I try to reward sincerity in my everyday relations with the children.* (If one uses punishment when a child has not been sincere, he may not feel

motivated to try to be sincere in the future. In any case, fear of punishment is a very poor motivation.)

14. *I use the children's sincerity as a basis for counseling them.* (Helping children should be done personally. Therefore one needs to know what the situation of each child is. One cannot counsel a child well without having any specific information about him.)

15. *I prefer to trust the children and believe what they say, without being naive.* (Sincerity is stimulated through signs of trust. Lack of trust leads to lies and the falsification of reality.)

16. *I help the adolescents discover the most important aspects of their lives.* ('Important' means anything which can influence significantly the values one wants to live in life.)

17. *I help the children distinguish between reality and imagination.* (It is good for children to develop their imagination, but it is not good for them to mix up reality and fantasy.)

18. *I keep an eye on the children who talk too much, to help them learn that there is a right time and a right person.* (One may have to explain the possible negative consequences of talking about the wrong things to the wrong people.)

19. *I create activities so that those children who have problems in expressing themselves can do so with maximum confidence.* (Often this will mean doing things together. When we do things together, each person's attention is centred on the action rather than on the other, and thus we can informally bring up the subject and start communicating.)

20. *If a child tends to lie, I try to find out why and then take some action.* (For example, some children may feel a need to lie in order not to seem different from their friends, or to be more important, or for fear of some punishment.)

9 Modesty

Modest people recognise the value of their own privacy and respect that of others. They protect their privacy from the gaze of others; they reject anything which might encroach upon it and relax this practice only in circumstances which can be of benefit to themselves or others.

It is curious how the word 'modesty' may conjure up in our minds, before all else, a notion of restraint, of something practised in misguided ways in the past. As J. Choza says, 'modesty is a virtue and therefore a duty, but everyone feels relieved when he is exempt from it, in other words, if it is cast off simply as a social convention. That is why psycho-sociological literature – which, like all literature, sets up to please the public – tends to consider those habits which are virtues primarily as mere social conventions.'[19]

Yet modesty is very important for people living in a society which tends to destroy the individual's privacy and intimacy. 'Mass production' attitudes and disorder in social habits and morals can make the individual a mere accomplice in the general trend. Yet if human beings are to deserve that name, they must discover the meaning of their human dignity and they can do this only by closely relating what they are to the end for which they were created. In this context it is clear that we must take possession of ourselves to some extent and understand the purpose of our lives, in order to be worthy human beings.

The cardinal virtue of temperance differs from the other cardinal virtues in that 'it is verified and operates solely on the person practising it[20] and, as modesty is closely related to temperance, we find that this is a virtue that has very few repercussions that can be observed from the outside. Since it refers specifically to the individual's privacy, in teaching our children this virtue it will probably be easier to judge the extent to which it is being practised by what a child 'does wrong' rather than by what he 'does right'. For this reason, it is too easy to concentrate on the sixth commandment and neglect the practice of the virtue itself which is, as we have said, a good operational habit.

The importance of privacy

Perhaps we should now consider what it means to 'recognise the value of one's privacy' and how to know whether our children are capable of doing this.

When a young person discovers that he has a unique private life, comprising a reality composed of spirit, body and emotions but unknown to others, he may react in two different ways. He may try to share this intimate experience with others, perhaps with a special friend or even with everyone, or he may keep it in his heart, reflect on it and later either talk about it or not, as the circumstances dictate. He may realise that what he is thinking and feeling is so important that it should not be wasted by blurting it out to the first person he meets or, on the other hand, he may tell everyone about it. This causes a certain difficulty because some people consider that it is selfish to keep things to oneself.

We should therefore remind ourselves that everything we have is from and for God; we must administer whatever God has given us in such a way that we glorify him to the best of our ability. To keep things 'for' ourselves may be selfish but to keep them for God certainly is not. Furthermore, if we are to use everything we have in the service of God, by serving others, it follows that we should try to think clearly about what and when we should give to others, though without ever going to the extreme of being a squanderer.

Another point that should be explained is that openness is not opposed to modesty. Openness requires us to act in a way consistent with our purpose, without being devious; modesty does not conceal reality: reality is patent, though controlled by a personal decision.

If modesty is considered as a virtue, which begins with an appreciation of one's own privacy, we must ask what signs we must look for in order to see how well our children are practising it. We can start by noticing whether they are beginning to recognise aspects of their life to do with their privacy: this will be clear because they will keep a part of their life to themselves. This is why we find that very young children begin to protect the intimacy of their body, for instance, by allowing no one to be in the bathroom while they are having a bath. There seems to be a natural modesty of this kind. Similarly, older children begin to protect certain aspects of their lives from their parents' eyes, and parents with adolescent children sometimes get angry because they tell them little or nothing about themselves.

When he discovers his own intimacy, an adolescent may easily go to the extreme of shutting himself off in a private world of his own, rejecting parental influences as intrusions on his privacy. Yet, at the same time, he may become very communicative with his friends, in order to avoid sole responsibility for that world of his own.

It is a positive sign when teenage children begin to distinguish between information which they want to pass on to their parents and things which they prefer to tell others or keep to themselves. Modesty does not mean a breakdown in communication with others; this would only lead to loneliness. Rather, it means regarding oneself as reserved for the right situation later on. Consequently, another positive sign is the child's ability to be with himself without evading the responsibility for what he is. We refer to his ability to remain quiet, to be silent for a while, not to need noise, the television or the radio the moment he comes into the house and so on. As J. Pieper says, 'through contemplation, man establishes contact with the divine being and he assimilates pure truth, which is the supreme good.

The essence of the moral person consists in holding himself available for the real truth of things and living according to the truth which he has made part of himself. Only a person who is capable of seeing and accepting this will be able to understand the depths of destruction which an impure heart can unleash within him'.[21]

Privacy is therefore a valuable thing provided that what is being kept private is good. We must be able to emerge from our privacy to seek help, not in a random way but from a suitable person. And this is the third sign by which we can notice that a youngster appreciates his intimacy: we notice that he goes to an appropriate person, priest, a parent or a friend, so as to keep his privacy intact.

To sum up, the three signs that will help us to know whether our children value their privacy are:

- They begin to shut others out from certain spheres of their life, to do with their body or their emotions.
- They are capable of remaining silent and alone for certain periods.
- They keep their private matters safe by seeking guidance from an appropriate person.

Modesty in practice

Before discussing how we should teach our children the virtue of modesty, we should consider how 'respect for one's privacy' is expressed. Choza mentions three relevant areas – the home, one's dress and one's language. With regard to the home, he says that the primary reason why men build houses is not to protect themselves from the climate or from animals, but that they need to protect their intimacy in space: my home is my privacy, my private place, and when I invite a friend to my home I invite him to share that privacy, to be in my company in an intimate way. We therefore need a home which we have conceived and created personally, which provides us with an intimacy, not to be lonely, but to be in intimate contact with the privacy of other members of our family. For this reason, it would seem to follow that parents should allow their children, as far as possible, to establish a certain space of their own. If they create nothing of their own, but only share in the environment created by their parents, naturally they may feel out of place: their intimate self has nowhere to live or express itself. It has always been recognised that parents should give even very young children at least a drawer or some little place of their own which would not be invaded. This is much more important for adolescents.

Another point is that if children of this age communicate with their parents and play an active part in the household, they will probably wish to invite their friends home rather than always go out with them. To be more specific, some parents try to leave a room undecorated so that the teenager children can arrange it as they think best. It is also very important to teenagers to have a bedroom of their own if possible or, at least, not to have to share it with too many others.

If a teenager is to practise the virtue of modesty, he needs a suitable place, where he can have some privacy and be on his own. An example would clarify this point. If a teenage boy goes out with a girl for longer than that initial period during which it is normal to conceal the relationship from his parents – precisely because of a healthy sense of modesty – he will normally then require some appropriate place for the friendship to develop. If he feels identified with the atmosphere in the household, with his parents, brothers and sisters, he will have the courage to invite the girl home, perhaps with some other friend, to watch television, have a chat or any other healthy activity. On the other hand, if he feels uneasy in the atmosphere of the home, he may wish to replace it with some falsely 'intimate' place, a club, a discotheque, park or even a car. Such places may seem private to him because of their isolation, their darkness, the music or even the flashing lights – in other words, because of some purely external conditions which do not conduce to genuine intimacy. For instance, clubs and discos make it impossible to talk; they encourage a type of communication based solely on physical contact, vibration of the instincts stimulated by sound, by darkness or even by alcohol. This is opposed to modesty from the outset, because it encourages a distortion of true intimacy.

The proper sphere of intimacy for two young people who are still far from being able to think of marriage is an area involving discussion of ideas, thoughts and plans, sharing some kind of activity such as study, practising some hobby, going for a walk or to the cinema, for example. If the youngsters have developed a proper sense of modesty, they will see how far they should and should not go in this kind of intimacy and they will behave accordingly. Modesty will draw a veil of respect over any premature physical outbursts or over inappropriate revelations on matters affecting the deepest recesses of the human heart. Obviously, if the home circumstances are not such as to allow the children to maintain their privacy, they will go outside the home, with all the consequent risks: situations in which there is an abuse of intimacy or where modesty does not exist because the atmosphere is inappropriate. This can be seen clearly in the lives of the hippies who have no home and little interest in dress.

Modesty, we repeat, helps the individual to keep in control of himself so as to be in readiness for the proper moment. If we relate this point to the subject of clothes, we see that dress functions in this way. Once again Choza tells us: 'The modesty of covering our body means that it is kept under our control, that it is available to no one but ourselves, that we have no desire to share it with everybody and that, consequently, we are in a position to surrender it to one particular person or to nobody. This is the explanation of a husband's or fiance's insistence that his wife or fiancee should dress decently'.[23]

In this particular area, modesty is especially difficult when it even seems to come into conflict with 'fashion'. A wife's desire to please her husband or a young lady's wish to look her best on a social occasion is perfectly acceptable, provided it is done with elegance and decorum, but it is easy to degenerate into vanity or immodesty. Here we are concerned with possible immodesty and it would seem that there is only one valid criterion, namely to put oneself in the position of the man and ask oneself whether a particular dress will excite his instincts in such a way or to such an extent, even mentally, that he may take a share in one's intimacy or privacy. The point to bear in mind, therefore, is not only whether one covers much or little, but also how it is covered.

With regard to modesty in our language, there is plenty of scope for thought. 'The experience of "not knowing what came over me", with regard to one's emotions, and consequently being upset, is a very common one. The fact that we don't know 'what came over us' shows that we are not in control of our own emotions. The ability to express our frame of mind in words indicates the ability to control it objectively and, consequently, the ability to communicate or to surrender what is ours . . .' . When we say of a person that he has no sense of modesty because he speaks indiscriminately of intimate aspects of his emotional life, we mean that his intimacy is 'public property' (Choza).

One's intimacy should be made manifest only when it will be beneficial for one's own or another's improvement. We shall return to this point later but, for the moment, let us notice the dangers inherent in an over simplified notion of sincerity. This virtue is not practised by speaking of intimate subjects to all and sundry nor by revealing one's personal problems to anyone we happen to meet, but by discussing them properly and without embarassment with someone who is in a position to deal with them appropriately. It is a healthy sign of modesty to refrain from discussing one's intimate matters before strangers and to protect from the curiosity and inquisitiveness of others, not only one's problems, but also the feelings, sentiments and states of mind that make up the thread of one's emotional life. It is also a sign of modesty not to speak frivolously or without good reason of events or subjects which normally affect people's intimate lives. In this regard, it is obvious that certain types of expletive or interjection show a lack of modesty in anyone who uses them.

One's private life is not something that should be exhibited in public. It should only be disclosed in the appropriate circumstances to the right person at the right time: a true friend, one's spouse, one's confessor, a relative or other person who can be trusted.

External influences

Our attempts to practise the virtue of modesty may be seriously harmed by external influences. If we want our children to be full of strong passion which they are able to keep under control, we must obviously teach them to use their will-power, but also their ability to think, so that they will be aware of the effects of such influences on them. They will then be able to keep from certain dangers and vigorously resist others.

We have already mentioned the effect of certain atmospheres which play on the passions, based on a combination of certain types of music and lights. This can easily lead to self-abandon and lust. There are less obvious but equally harmful influences to be avoided in the cinema, the television and one's reading matter. Children often think that they are mature enough to distinguish between the artistic appreciation of a film, for instance, and its erotic subject matter, but one's passions are never neutral: they react to any kind of stimulus, and even if there is no immediate reaction, seeds of discord are very likely to have been sown within one, in one's heart. Without realising it, one begins to develop new attitudes characterised, not by true or correct principles, but by the elasticity of their makeup, so that one begins to be carried away by an outside influence and to lose one's own personality, which is based on the elements of one's intimacy and privacy.

It is also worth reminding ourselves that it is quite possible to allow people to abuse our privacy and we may even unintentionally abuse that of others. Modesty reminds us to be on our guard against the attempts of others, conscious or not, to pry into matters that do not concern them, and we should try to help our children in this regard also. Someone has said that we are not rational animals, but sentimental animals who try to rationalise our sentiments. Parents should be extremely vigilant concerning everything that may influence their children, especially of a sentimental nature, because there are relationships of this kind which can be particularly damaging to their modesty.

Although we have stressed that this virtue protects one's privacy from the gaze of others and rejects everything that may harm that privacy, neither should we forget that it is perfectly valid to discuss intimate matters in circumstances which may conduce to the improvement of oneself or others. There is a right time for everything we do and everything we say, and not only a right time, but also a right reason. By this we mean that our improvement may be helped by discussing our intimate problems with a suitable person. We have often seen the opposite of this happen in a film when a drunkard begins to blurt out his problems to a complete stranger in a bar: this is an example of loss of intimacy caused by drunkenness. On the other hand, this same person might have discussed his problem with a close friend at a well chosen moment provided he could be sure that he was not annoying the friend and that he would benefit as a result. It is not right to discuss one's own or other people's private matters either for fun or out of vanity.

It may also be useful to recount some experience from our personal life for the benefit of a friend or one's child, if it may help that person to understand his own situation better and to solve a problem. A human being should not be a recluse; we are not suggesting that anyone should protect his privacy falsely for his own enjoyment or to bemoan his lot in silence. What he should do is ensure that his reasons for sharing his privacy are of the highest, so that he will automatically be selective in the people he chooses to share his experience.

Teaching modesty

We have been considering certain aspects of this virtue which may be helpful to parents trying to teach their children. Let us now be a little more specific, dealing first with younger children and then with teenagers.

Since we are speaking of privacy, it might seem that this virtue has little application before adolescence, a stage which is characterised precisely by the discovery of one's privacy and intimacy. Yet we can prepare our children long before they reach this stage. There are certain habits which they can learn from a very young age. We refer to acts which help to develop the will, such as jobs in the house, keeping to a timetable, getting up quickly and so on, for all of these condition the children to be strong in matters which, later on, they will undoubtedly find difficult, even though at first they may seem unimportant. There are also habits connected with the privacy of the other members of the family, such as knocking before entering a bedroom, asking 'delicate' questions when the other children are not present or always having some clothes on when walking about the house.

All of these matters are closely related with the development of our conscience, by which we can see very clearly the importance of God in our lives. One aspect of modesty is what is sometimes called 'sex education', although it would be better if we could speak of giving information about sexual matters within a course of 'love education'. Referring to the friendship between parents and children, Blessed J. Escrivá says: 'this friendship, this knowing how to put oneself on the children's level, makes it easier for them to talk about their small problems; it also makes it possible for parents to be the ones who teach them gradually about the origin of life, in accordance with their mentality and capacity to understand, gently anticipating their natural curiosity. I consider this very important. There is no reason why children should associate sex with something sinful or find out about something that is in itself noble and holy in a vulgar conversation with a friend. It can also be an important step in strengthening the friendship between parents and children, preventing a separation in the early moments of their early life'.[25]

Respect for one's body is essential in learning and practising modesty. Similarly, parents should give their children sexual education in keeping not only with their actual age but also with their physical and mental maturity and with the environment of the place they live in. Parallel with this they should teach them the duties laid down by God's law in regard to sex, so that they can distinguish between what is sinful and what is not. Where the virtue of purity is concerned nothing is trivial: fault in itself (prescinding from subjective factors and particular circumstances) is either gravely sinful or else just bad manners or poor hygiene.

Apart from matters directly related to purity, an understanding of modesty requires that we keep in mind the importance of explaining to our children that, in everything they do, there is a question of what, where, when, how and to whom it is done; it involves consideration of the circumstances, the persons, deeds and words. They should be taught, for instance, that they should not tell outsiders about family matters, that they should not habitually use expressions referring to the private aspects of life and that they should not be curious about other people's intimate matters. Children should be taught these things from a very early age, so that they may become sensitive to them.

The home atmosphere is something that can help or hinder the practice of this virtue to a great extent. If parents treat one another in a refined way, they will ensure that the family life is such as to make things pleasant for everybody; if they are careful not to make unsavoury remarks about other people's private affairs and not to speak of intimate things relating to the children with outsiders while they are present, they will create an environment in which the children can develop their own private lives with open lines of communication connecting them to the other members of the family. This will be fundamental for the development of modesty during adolescence.

If we look carefully at family customs we will realise that many of them are linked to the protection of intimacy. For example, being home at a reasonable time, dressing properly, choosing entertainment and leisure activities, especially where films and shows are concerned. If children fail to realise the need to be self-possessed so that later on they can really give themselves, these rules will seem to them to be – when they reach adolescence – meaningless impositions. Whereas, if they recognise the need to develop modesty and if they have acquired the criteria for appreciating this virtue, then they will see the various rules for protecting this virtue in a more positive light.

We can help them in various ways. If they learn to reason things out and use the information their parents give them, adolescents can develop their strength of will. It is wrong to think that will on its own or intelligence on its own is enough. We have already mentioned the importance of reason, but up to now we have said little about the will, that is to say, that personal struggle involved in developing the virtue of modesty. Following V. Garcia Hoz, we can say that 'teaching alone does not provide a complete education; it has to be supplemented by personal effort, personal struggle. This is particularly true in matters relating to sex education. The Christian use of sexuality cannot be achieved without effort, an effort that at times has to be heroic. This applies especially to young people in whom the strength of the sexual tendencies combined with immaturity of personality make a more rigorous struggle necessary. Apart from this, youth is also the best time for seeing life as a struggle and for being disinterested in many ways. One of the firmest foundations for the sexual aspects of education is to strengthen an awareness in young people that human life can be fully lived only as a struggle'.[25a]

We must teach our children to avoid situations which may be harmful to them, to keep control of their senses and to be in command of themselves at all times by ensuring that their reason dominates their body. All of this must be done without forgetting the supernatural resources available to them, principally prayer and the sacraments.

M. Scheler says that 'modesty is the security area of the individual – the indivisible individual – and of his unique values, and it marks out the sphere of love by not allowing sex to break loose before the internal unity of love has come into being'.[26] If we teach the virtue of modesty at the same time as generosity, we are laying the foundations for the emergence of love. Every virtue is an expression of love but these two have a special significance. The understanding and practice of self-control and of self-giving are two of the most important points in the education of children.

SELF-ASSESSMENT

Briefing Note: see pages 29–30, above.

Do I practise modesty ?

1. *I appreciate what relates to my intimate self: my soul, parts of my body, my feelings, my thoughts.* (One can only make proper use of what one knows and appreciates. If one doesn't give importance to one's feeling or thoughts, for example, one may make bad use of them, sharing them unduly with anyone and at any time.)

2. *I understand that sometimes I should keep things to do with my intimate self private, and that sometimes I should share them with others. When I share these things, it is because I am looking for help from the other person or because I think that through sharing that intimate something, I may be able to help them.*

3. *I look after the intimate aspects of my life in order to make good use of what God has given me, and act for the glory of God.* (Sometimes people follow

rules related to modesty blindly, without thinking about why they should do so. This can cause people to be scrupulous or just selfish.)

4. *I can be alone, by myself, in silence, without doing anything; in fact, I actually look for these moments frequently*. (Silence creates the right environment for reflecting about oneself, for knowing oneself better. Modern day life tends to complicate things so much that we need to make a special effort to find these moments.)

5. *I try to find out what other people's real needs are before talking, before sharing something intimate. And when I recognise a need, I share my intimate self without worrying about what the other person will think of me.* (Clearly we need to think before sharing these intimate questions. But we should share them if the other person needs this kind of attention. Sometimes we don't do it because we don't want the other person to change the 'good impression' he or she has us.)

6. *I share matters related to my intimate self with someone in whom I can confide, to get help in my struggle to improve*. (This is especially evident as regards one's spiritual life, and it is one of the reasons for the sacrament of Confession. On the other hand, there are aspects of our lives which we should share with our spouse, with a good friend or with a colleague.)

7. *I try to allocate space in the home or at school so that each child can exercise their right to intimacy*. (What a good thing it would be if each family member had their own room! Or at any rate their own space for keeping things. We also need to look after those places where the children change clothes at home or at school.)

8. *I usually dress according to elemental rules of modesty.* (A useful criteria to apply is to consider whether one could be provoking a person of the opposite sex. It is not so much a question of square inches of the body being covered but rather of the way the clothing is worn and the way one walks or sits.)

9. *I try to be careful about what language I use in order not to be vulgar or crude. And even more so, as regards language that can offend God.* (Sometimes it may be useful to remember that God is our Father, and to think about how he would react to our language. If we are sensitive, we will be able to notice how other people suffer from our lack of tact or unsuitable language when we are talking about actions which are, in themselves, violations of intimacy.)

10. *I have strong passions but I control them with my will.* (Modesty does not mean that one should not have strong passions. We need strong passions but we have to be able to control them in order to express them at the right time and to the right person.)

Teaching others to practise modesty

11. *I help the younger children recognise those aspects of their intimacy they need to look after.* (In most cases the young children will not understand the abstract concept of intimacy. The children become conscious of their intimacy at eleven or twelve years old. All the same, we can teach them to develop habits related to intimacy from a very early age.)

12. *I help younger children get used to respecting other people's privacy.* (This is a sum of small details. For example, knocking on the door before going into someone's bedroom, not telling tales about intimate matters to do with family or friends, turning off the television when there is a programme which can damage their intimacy, not walking around the house without any clothes on.)

13. *I get the children used to asking questions related to intimate matters in private.* (Each child has different needs which have to be attended in a different way.)

14. *Parents: I give my children appropriate information about questions related to sex – to each one according to his/her needs, and in a relaxed, refined way.* (We need technical, scientific language to do this. It should be considered as a gradual process and be related to love and faith.)

    Teachers: I try to get the parents to look after the sex education of their children and, as a lesser evil, help those students individually whose parents do not want to get involved.

15. *I help the youngsters recognise the influences reaching them from television, from magazines, from films and which go against modesty; and I also help them to keep their senses under control.* (They need to recognise the importance of protecting their intimacy. If they don't, keeping their senses under control will not make sense.)

16. *I reason with the youngsters so that they understand that one should not pry into other people's privacy or encourage them to dress or to behave themselves in ways which go against modesty.* (This sometimes happens between members of the same sex, but more so with members of the opposite sex. To respect others means recognising their dignity as children of God.)

17. *I insist on the use of good language, trying to get the children to avoid vulgar or crude expressions which go against modesty.* (We need to insist on this right from the start when the children are young. Also, we should draw their attention to the bad use of language on television and so on.)

18. *I explain to the youngsters how to share their thoughts and their feelings with others when they think that, by doing so, they may help others.* (Modesty

helps to protect and look after the intimate aspects of our lives, but this does not mean that we do not have the duty to share intimate things when we think we can help others by so doing.)

19. *I help the children to get used to going to the right people to receive help in developing their intimate selves.* (This may mean introducing them to some priest so that they can receive spiritual guidance; encouraging them to talk to some young person, but older than them, who has solid criteria; or just talking to their father or their mother.)

20. *I help the youngsters recognise what places it is best to avoid if they want to protect their intimacy.* (There is a contagious effect of 'what others do' and it can be powerful even in the case of youngsters who appear to have solid criteria.)

Moderation

People who is moderate distinguish between what is reasonable and what is self-indulgent; and they make reasonable use of their senses, their time, their money, their efforts and so on, in accordance with true and upright principles.

The main reason why we should teach this virtue is to enable our children to live a genuinely Christian life. It is impossible to advance in the Christian life if we are attached to human pleasures, or if we make immoderate use of them, because the saturation of the senses makes it impossible to live a spiritual life. A non-Christian may be interested in practising this virtue in order to achieve a certain self-control and resist outside influences. Consequently, such a person will use his senses, time, money etc. in accordance with whatever principles he accepts, even if they are not based on truth.

In any case, moderation is one of the virtues which seems of least interest to youngsters, mainly because they regard any control of their appetites for pleasure as a constraint, failing to realise that if they are immoderate, they can easily fall prey to outside influences and be manipulated by others. For example, as Mausbach and Ermecke say, 'nowadays, thanks to the modern media, we are surrounded by advertising and the media often take unfair advantage of our impressionability for the benefit of their own financial advancement. They promise to satisfy all our desires and end up by making us slaves of our own inordinate appetites'.

Since the need for self-control does not seem to be accepted by young people, perhaps we should pause for a moment to consider how they justify their search for pleasure and their attempt to break away from control of themselves. In fact, their reasoning seldom goes very deep and tends to take the form of explanations like the following: 'There is no harm in having a good time, is there?' 'I work, so why shouldn't I spend my time and my money as I like?' 'I am only amusing myself without harming anyone' and 'It's no longer in fashion.' These explanations are meaningful only for someone who fails to realise that he is a being created with a purpose. If we reject this fact, then pleasure becomes an end in itself and everything else is justifiable on the basis of this criterion. If we admit that human existence has a purpose, then we must admit that pleasure is something which leads us to behave as we should provided we control it with our will. Thus, for instance, there is certain pleasure in eating, but the purpose of eating is to nourish the body; the pleasure involved encourages us to eat properly and this is quite acceptable so long as it does not become immoderate.

The explanations which we have just noted refer to partial aspects of the matter. We have no wish to imply that one should not have a good time, nor that a young person should follow outside instructions in spending his money or his time nor that it is not good to avoid harming others. This is not the point. The point is there is a higher purpose, which should regulate our mode of behaviour. Each individual should take responsibility for his own life, in such a way as to make good use of everything he possesses, in the service of God, and of others. He must not only avoid doing harm: he must also do positive good. There is no point in spending his money and time simply for his own pleasure, he must use them for his own benefit and the benefit of others. Lastly, the phrase 'It's no longer in fashion' is a meaningless explanation which puts pressure on people not to remain isolated or be different from others. Fashion is never a sufficient justification for any personal decision.

The consumer society

Even when we fully realise that our life has a purpose, it is not easy to practise moderation, because the consumer society makes it difficult to distinguish between genuine needs and mere tendencies or whims. If we compare what our grandparents had in their houses with what we have in ours, this point will become clear. How many of our possessions are necessary and how many are superfluous? A moderate person ought to know, in general, if he needs the things he actually acquires; in other words, he should have certain principles. To see what these principles might be, we could ask ourselves how a certain person actually spends his money. Apart from what we have said about the conscious search for pleasure, people also act instinctively and let themselves be carried away by mere impulses; the result is an action which responds to an appetite without any thought behind it. Besides this, some people acquire property in order to show off, to be in fashion, just for a change, to compensate for some inner dissatisfaction or to fill some kind of vacuum in their lives. Yet other people always want new things, interpreting 'new' as the latest product on the market, instead of realising that the genuinely new thing is the one that keeps on offering us something of value.

This rather pessimistic view of society is reinforced by the sales experts, who understand how people behave and take full advantage of it. It is therefore essential to be aware of what is happening in order to be able to use our will and our ability to reason, so that we can take our own decisions on the basis of some principle or criterion. What kind of principle? We could, for instance, ask ourselves the following questions:

- If I do not acquire this article, will there be negative repercussions on the objective I have in mind?
- Could the purchase I am about to make be considered by someone who knows me, and knows my circumstances, as an injustice towards others?
- Why am I really making this purchase?
- By living in this way, do I always end up creating a new need?

A moderate person does not deceive himself. He recognises the value things have and, therefore, he is a realist. He is in a position to use his resources for the benefit of others and has the assurance that that, in fact, is what he is doing. But moderation does not mean that a person should not spend money or eat or drink, etc. This is obvious, if we consider the case of a person who does not spend money unless it is absolutely necessary and even then spends it with a bad grace. The name for this is 'avaricious'.

But it is difficult to find the just mean between wasteful and reasonable expenditure. This is difficult because it is not simply a question of the amount we spend. We have said that an immoderate person seeks many pleasures immoderately, but yet it is legitimate to have good taste, to enjoy the things that God has given us, to rest and seek entertainment in order to work better. For instance, it might seem that someone who has been accustomed from an early age to works of art, good food and so on is less likely to be moderate than one who has not been brought up in such circumstances. The question involved in this example can be resolved by stating at the outset that there is no point in comparing one person's situation with that of another. The only relevant factor is how each individual's circumstances relate to his practice of this virtue. His moderation or his lack of it will be reflected in the importance which he attaches to his own personal pleasures as against other, higher ends. For instance, if he is wealthy, he may own a lot of property but he may have put little or no effort into acquiring it and, if he is not attached to his possessions; if he tries to live his life serving God and others; if he deliberately controls his desires, then he is practising the virtue of moderation. Apart from this, it might be unjust for such a person not to use his property for the benefit of others, by which we do not necessarily suggest that he should renounce the things he owns.

In short, good taste and an ability to use one's senses in order to enjoy life are extremely good qualities provided they are used as the basis of one's duty to glorify God and fulfill one's purpose. The question is how are we to teach our children to be moderate in using their money and, in general, in acquiring things which are related to superficial pleasures.

As we have said, the important thing is not to bring them up merely to know what is practical and useful, but also to ensure that they have good taste and are able to enjoy the things that God has provided.

Perhaps we could say a word here about whims. By a whim, we mean a superficial, passing desire produced by an unthinking and unjustified reaction. Once again, we are discussing motives. If a parent buys a toy simply because his child has seen it in a shop window and screams that he wants it there and then, he is showing little respect for the virtue of moderation and he is not training his child on the right lines. Yet, if a child sees an interesting toy in a shop window, there are ways of asking for it without becoming immoderate. Furthermore, it is important to develop the child's self control, so that he will not be unduly perturbed if some desire remains unsatisfied. Countless opportunities arise in the normal course of events which can be put to good use in this regard. For instance, there are not enough apples to go around the whole family, the favourite breakfast cereal has run out, the child sees something he wants after he has spent all his money for the week or, indeed, when there is plenty of his favourite food on the table. In cases like these, parents can teach their children not to get annoyed, or to make a special effort to leave something which they could actually have and, furthermore, to do so cheerfully. If children are not to regard moderation as something unpleasant and boring, the parents themselves must show that they are practising it joyfully. If a person gives up smoking for Lent, this is both a mortification to be offered to God and, at the same time, something which will help him to practise moderation. However, he must be very careful not to be bad-humoured and force the rest of the family to mortify themselves on his account, for this would encourage a view of moderation as something associated with long faces. On this point, it is often useful to motivate children by teaching them that these little efforts on their part can be offered up to God or to our Lady, for instance.

Another good reason for practising moderation includes a realistic assessment of the financial position of the household, for this will encourage the children to keep the good of the family in mind depending, of course, on their age and maturity so as not to worry them unduly. Here, it may help a child to acquire this virtue if it is suggested that he should get a job to bring some extra money into the home, if this is needed. Similarly, a mother may take her children shopping to let them see the price of food. In general, what we are suggesting is that children should know the value of things and be able to distinguish between what is necessary and what is pleasant but unnecessary, so that they will realise the difference between a mere whim and a justifiable desire on their part.

We have already emphasised the importance of the example that parents give their children, but perhaps we could discuss this point further because many of the conflicts between parents and teenage children have something to do with the virtue of moderation.

If parents give bad example, their children may acquire certain habits by imitating them before they understand the principle underlying what they are doing. Parents should therefore realise that their behaviour may not only be harmful to themselves but also have repercussions on their children. For instance, if parents go out every weekend with their children, and spend an inordinate amount of money on drink they can hardly expect the children to be careful about how they spend their money. If a parent thinks and talks about nothing but entertainment, films and shows, he can scarcely expect his children to take other aspects of life seriously, though we are not suggesting that, in itself, there is anything wrong in enjoying films or shows; on the contrary, they are extremely helpful if they allow the person to keep going in his ordinary life.

Parents should also be careful about the relationship between their work and their free time, because if they regard their work merely as a means to earn money, they are quite likely to think that the purpose of their free time is to allow them to spend it and, consequently, they would work simply in order to enjoy themselves and satisfy their whims. The main difference between what we do at work and what we do in our free time is that we have less freedom to decide what we want to do, depending on our mood. Yet everything we do should be directly or indirectly aimed at some important objectives – after all, we are human beings – and although the things we do may involve different degrees of effort and some may be more pleasant than others, they all form part of one and the same whole.

From what we have said so far, we may now stress the importance of teaching our children the following:

- To value what they have and what they might have.
- To control their whims and to do so cheerfully.
- To think about their reasons for spending money.
- Not to be attached to pleasure.
- To identify the appetites that should be controlled.
- To have high ideals that will give them deep satisfaction, rather than seeking superficial pleasures.

There is a further aspect of moderation which we have scarcely discussed up to now: we refer to the use we make of our time.

Using our time

One of the results of not being moderate is that we waste our time. If we are constantly seeking ways of satisfying our appetites, it follows that we will spend most of our time in that pursuit. The way we use our time may be a basic indication of how we envisage our personal life, showing a real and constant relationship between what we consider important and our normal everyday activities. It is quite possible to fill our life with so much activity that there is no time left over or, at least, no time to let us think about what we are actually doing. Consequently, we tend to enjoy the activity itself and lose sight of the goal towards which we are working.

Someone who is active in public life may undertake a course of action to achieve a certain good objective. Soon, however, he is caught up in public life itself, being involved in social relations, in knowing people, in fulfilling various functions and in being better known. If all this activity replaces or displaces the objective he had in mind, and becomes his only guiding principle, then he has left moderation behind.

Another example would be that of a mother who 'enjoys herself' when looking after the children and being with them, even spoiling them in many ways, to such an extent that she cannot bear to leave them in order to look after her husband. We constantly have to distinguish between what is necessary and what is merely desirable, between high priority matters and things which can be left aside. People say they have time only for important things, but in deciding what is important they are experts at deceiving themselves so that what they really want is to find excuses to do what they really like doing rather than what they should do. Just think of the perfectionist: this is a person who cannot leave something until it is almost perfect, not because it has to be done 'perfectly' but because he finds tremendous satisfaction going on with something even after the job is completed. We are by no means suggesting that we should not work well or do things properly; the important thing is to do what is necessary to achieve our object. In many human undertakings, we can be satisfied with an adequate standard, below the level of perfection, so as to go on to other things which are also important. There is only one area in which we must achieve the highest possible perfection, and that is in loving God and others. Love means many things and perfection involves learning to love through everything we do: putting love into all our actions and loving people continually. We can take a holiday and leave our work behind us for a certain period of time, or we can give up a hobby for a while, but we can never rest or take a holiday from our duty as children of God.

Precisely because of this natural tendency to find excuses that will justify doing things we like, we must find ways of checking our motives and teach our children to do the same. In particular, this means having our principles clear, taking time off to think about these principles and how they relate to the things we actually do so that we can proceed accordingly. We have already spoken about principles. As far as 'taking time off' is concerned, it is important to realise that human beings need inner peace to think about their situations seriously. This can be done in moments of silence when we are alone with our thoughts and we begin to take responsibility, not only for what we do, but also for what we are. We should also teach our children to think about their personal situation, not too much but sufficiently to know whether they are acting consistently in order to achieve the objectives they have in mind.

To 'act consistently' is not as easy as it sounds, unless we discover and intellectually admit that there is little moderation in our life. This defect which involves our appetites and our intellect needs the will to overcome our laziness and love of comfort. All the virtues need support from the virtue of fortitude, but moderation needs it in a special way.

Parents and teenage children

We have mentioned different views of moderation on the part of parents and teenage children as one of the basic causes of conflicts between them. It is inevitable at this stage that parents begin to notice that their children are immoderate, because they are in a position to make personal decisions more than ever before. Previously, if the parents noticed any immoderate behaviour, they were probably able to correct it without delay whereas, in adolescence, this is no longer quite so easy. Now they begin to criticise their children for spending their money unthinkingly, or wasting their time, or going to bed or getting up late and so on, and all of this is seen as immoderate behaviour. The teenagers, in turn, blame their parents for exactly the same things. They accuse them of being lazy, of spending their money on their own whims, of being in a rut as far as work is concerned and of being interested in nothing but entertainment, all of which is equivalent to accusing them of being immoderate.

Unless there are some genuine reasons for these conflicts, such as the case of parents who give bad example and yet demand that their children should behave properly, the reason for this kind of hostility is that the children have not been given clear and true principles on which to base their decisions. In the absence of such principles, they concentrate on isolated aspects of their behaviour, on mere details, without realising that the practice of moderation does not call for strict uniformity: each individual has to take his own personal decisions in his own particular way, but for this he needs clear and true criteria or principles to guide him

Parents will be unable to give proper guidance and even to maintain the unity of the family unless there is agreement between them and their children on the question of principles. It is interesting to see how easily we accept as valid our own ways of seeking the things that please us, and yet we are intolerant with others. If we concentrate on the search for principles, we will be able to put pleasure in its proper place and respect other people's valid interpretations of these same true and proper principles. The practice of moderation will allow our children to overcome their selfish impulses, even in their search for perfectly legitimate pleasure and will save them from being bewitched by material things. Thus, they will be in a position to love, to live a Christian life and to find inner peace and joy in the knowledge that, whatever they are doing, they are doing well.

SELF-ASSESSMENT

Briefing Note: see pages 29-30, above.

Do I practise moderation?

1. I *am usually conscious of the fact that I should put all that I own – my time, my possessions, my efforts, my money, my senses – to the best use, to help others and to serve God.* (A first requisite for living moderation is to recognise the different things that one owns and which can be put to different uses. The second thing is to realise that one can use them according to good or bad criteria, or just let oneself be swept along by the impulse of the moment.)

2. *I can firmly say that I have not set up 'pleasure' as the main goal of my life.* (In fact, it is one of the most common goals, but often in a rather unconscious way. To do things thinking about other people's good takes an effort. And making an effort is not very popular these days.)

3. *When I distribute my time, spend my money, or make an effort, I distinguish between what is really a whim and what is reasonable.* (The consumer society produces a lot of temptations. Following a whim means spending what is ours on anything which can produce pleasure, without thinking about how others may benefit from the action.)

4. *I am conscious of the power that advertising has over me, the effects of what others do or buy, or the effects of the way influential personalities use their time.* (An interesting exercise can be to make a list of how one has spent one's money, time or efforts recently and consider what the real motives were for each action.)

5. *When I eat or spend time on a hobby, I always try to finish wanting a bit more.* (Being satiated in any field usually indicates a lack of moderation. It is more evident in matters to do with food or drink, but it can be applied just as well to other kinds of actions.)

6. *I am convinced that what I spend cannot be interpreted as a lack of justice – to the poor, for example – by someone who knows me well.* (Moderation does not mean giving away all one's possessions but, rather, using them well. For this reason, immoderation can only be recognised realistically by someone who knows me well.)

7. *I look after my own possessions and common property in order to ensure that they are well used.* (It is a question of using those possessions in the service of others. Some people look after possessions as though they were an end in themselves. For example, insisting that the sitting room should always be neat and tidy, not thinking about the joyful living

together of family members which may require a certain untidiness, at any rate for a time.)

8. *I find a harmonious way for spending my time on the family, on my work, with my friends, on my duties as a citizen and as a child of God, without exaggeration and without falling short.* (The good use of time is an essential part of moderation. It would be useful to take note of how one has spent one's time at the end of each day, for a week or two, and then tot up the time spent on different things. This can be a good basis for seeing if the time was well spent.)

9. *I am not tied to any particular possession, or any particular routine, or any specific activity.* (One can judge how much one may be tied to something through the degree of bad temper that rises when we cannot make use of the possession (one's favourite arm chair), when the routine is broken (the need to read the newspaper before leaving for work), or when we cannot carry out some activity (the game of golf) because of a family obligation.)

10. *I live moderation joyfully, not falling into an easy life or becoming greedy.* (It is particularly important to live this virtue joyfully. What it avoids, principally, is becoming satiated with material goods; it keeps one's spirit lifted up to God.)

Teaching others to practise moderation

11. *I teach the children to value what they possess so that they can be conscious of their possibilities.* (Usually this means giving little bits of information from time to time, about how things can be used and how to use time etc.)

12. *I help them distinguish between what is necessary and what is superfluous, between what is reasonable and what is just a whim.* (A good exercise is to make a list of all things we have at home and that our grandparents didn't have.)

13. *I help the children have good taste, not necessarily to buy the cheapest thing but to spend money wisely, and to enjoy their possessions reasonably.* (Sometimes people put a very negative tone on this virtue. And this should not be so. Moderate people are elegant, make good use of their possessions, and enjoy the things God has given them.)

14. *I try to get the smaller children to control their basic appetites. I insist on self-control.* (It is not easy to act in this way because aspects of education nowadays are based on the opposite. Words such as 'self-esteem 'or 'tolerance' are understood incorrectly. For example, self esteem is often identified with not feeling bad; and tolerance is understood in the sense

that all ideas have the same value and therefore there is no need to make an effort to discover truth.)

15. *I teach the children what money is worth. I teach them how to earn, save and not just spend money.* (Money can be a good means for educating and it also has a very dynamic importance in society. But if one uses money badly, it will probably create more problems in the area of moderation than anything else.)

16. *I teach the children to distribute their time in a harmonious way, and I help the older children to make decisions about the use of their time.* (There is frequent lack of moderation in the way children use their time. Sometimes it will be spent in front of the television or on the computer, or on some hobby or on going out at night or just in sleeping.)

17. *I try to help the children avoid trying to become too perfect at certain things.* (Moderation is not only a question of not spending too much time on activities of little educational value, and of avoiding spending time on useless activities. It is also a question of not spending excessive time on activities that are very positive in themselves. For example, spending excessive time and attention on some homework.)

18. *I devote time to reasoning with the youngsters, to help them discover true and correct criteria for making their own decisions in relation to moderation.* (To think 'well' requires information. And we must make this information available to the youngsters – clear, specific, and concise information.)

19. *I try to help the youngsters act in line with their values.* (There are some youngsters who have mixed up ideas and strong wills, others who have mixed up ideas but little will-power, others who have clear ideas and a strong will and, finally, those who have clear ideas and little will-power. This last group is where educators have special problems. It is relatively easy to get over clear information about important matters, but getting the youngsters to live in an appropriate way is another thing.)

20. *I create a happy atmosphere in which the youngsters can live moderation without associating it with long faces, boredom or rigidity.* (The idea of superficial pleasure is usually packaged in a very attractive way. Moderation should be lived in an attractive way, too. People can then spend their resources on the right thing, at the right time. This produces an interior happiness which is hard to beat.)

11 Flexibility

People who are flexible adapt their behaviour readily to the particular circumstances of each person or situation, but without abandoning their own principles of behaviour.

Flexibility is a virtue which is widely accepted in today's society, but mainly because it is interpreted as being easily led and being willing to try anything. According to this definition, flexibility is meaningless. Spontaneity, with which it is often confused, is not an end in itself; at most, it is an appropriate condition for the practice of other virtues, especially sincerity. If spontaneity is to be of any value, it must be governed by the will in association with the intellect. Therefore the last part of the description we have just given is of special importance, namely, the provision that we must not abandon our personal principles of behaviour. Flexibility involves having such principles and thinking out how to relate them to our everyday activities. With this in mind, we mention two ways of behaving flexibly, according to the circumstances of the situation. If the circumstances in question are matters of opinion, flexibility means being willing and able to consider one's own point of view as provisional and therefore capable of being revised or modified.

On the other hand, there are circumstances which are not matters of opinion, and this fact will affect the way we behave in our relationships with others and in our work. When it is a question of objective truth, we cannot revise or change our opinion, although it may well be that we can find a better way of expressing it. Sometimes there is a radical difference between fact and the way in which a particular person has expressed that fact, because human limitations are involved here; in these cases the person should be flexible in his handling of fact in dealing with others. Here we refer to his way of listening, expressing his opinion, giving information and seeking points of mutual agreement. In this regard, an essential requirement for the practice of flexibility is to know what permanent criteria govern one's life and, on the other hand, what points are matters of opinion and provisional. It sometimes happens that an 'expert' on a subject which is a matter of opinion is unwilling to admit that anyone else can help him to revise or learn more about his speciality. Since this attitude is appropriate only on matters of objective truth, there may be serious discord in his dealings with others. For instance, if a parent discusses matters of faith, political questions or cultural affairs with his children and is equally certain in his views on them all or, on the other hand, if he treats all these subjects as equally debatable and open to argument, the children are unlikely to distinguish between what they can simply accept or reject and what is open to discussion. The result will be both confusion and a tendency to go either too far or not far enough in the virtue of flexibility.

We have mentioned the importance of true and proper principles; we must now consider how to act flexibly but firmly in matters of objective truth and how to be flexible on matters of personal opinion.

Flexibility and firmness

Like all other virtues, flexibility makes sense when it is used with the intention of seeking goodness and truth. Therefore it does not consist of a series of techniques, although there are certain specific points we must learn if we are not to behave in an intolerant manner, while trying to be flexible. We can apply these suggestions to our work and to our relationships with others.

Let us now consider, first of all, how we approach our work. Here, we find it necessary and beneficial to go on improving and learning all the time. We refer to learning and studying technical, cultural, doctrinal and religious matters. In any kind of study, we should adopt an attitude in keeping with the nature of the subject being studied. If this refers to a matter of objective truth, we should use our mental ability – part of the virtue of flexibility – to find a way of understanding what is involved, using our critical faculties only to go deeper into the subject, and not to call it into question. In dealing, necessarily or accidentally, with matters of opinion, we should first of all assess the level of our knowledge relating to the area in question. If our standard of education is sufficient to allow us to be certain, we can use our critical faculty to benefit from whatever is useful and reject the rest.

With regard to reading matter for ourselves and for our children, it is quite common to find that people consider themselves capable of remaining firm in their principles even when, in fact, they are easily influenced; and we find other people who believe it is right and virtuous never to be firm, but to have an open mind, on every subject under the sun. In practice, it is impossible to read any book, magazine or article without being influenced to some extent. Undoubtedly, someone with a high level of intellectual education will be in a better position to adapt his way of reading to the actual content, thus achieving genuine flexibility without being carried away by the author's reasoning. In the absence of this high standard of education, however, people are very easily influenced and a university student, for example, simply by reading the works of some philosopher, is readily convinced that they are totally correct; then, when he reads another, with contrary views, he finds himself convinced again by the second author. This is a danger to everyone, young and old, and we have to be very prudent in our reading because everything we read is so contagious.

Flexibility allows us to stop reading a book when we realise that we are not in a position to make a correct critical appraisal of its content; there will be other books which we can read with a critical attitude, taking advantage of some things in them that are useful and rejecting the rest; while yet other material can be read quite positively and its content fully assimilated. If we are unable to make these distinctions we are not flexible, because we are tied to a false criterion which consists in thinking it is good to read everything.

We have chosen the subject of reading matter as an example related to our work, but what we have said may be adapted to any other aspect of our occupation.

Firmness and flexibility in relationships

Up to this point, we have been discussing flexibility in our personal activity, where each individual has a duty to be loyal to himself and to the basic principles that govern his life. It is also important, however, to be loyal to the principles implicit in the bonds of friendship, although the difficulty in this case is to find the appropriate way of dealing with our acquaintances: we cannot betray our own permanent standards, yet we have no wish to destroy our friendship by being inflexible. People are free to accept or reject those permanent truths and values which we consider fundamental and we have no right to coerce them into submission. Indeed any attempt at such coercion might create a situation in which we could be accused of inflexibility and our attitude might seem to imply a lack of respect for others. How, then, are we to resolve this difficulty?

Respect for others requires that we never lose sight of people's basic ability to improve and neither must we forget our own suceptibility to dangerous influences. With regard to this second point, flexibility will ensure that we abandon conversation when we find that the other person is superior to us in his ability to argue and that he may exercise a harmful influence upon us. On the other hand, if we think that we can help that person to improve, then we should seek the best way of doing so. At the beginning of this chapter, we suggested that flexibility allows us to adapt our behaviour readily to the particular circumstances of each individual and situation. This means that we must be genuinely interested in the other person: it is not enough to pretend to be interested. In other words, if what really interests us is the matter we want to talk about, rather than the genuine needs of our listener, then we shall probably express that matter rather badly. Everyone has certain prejudices; we may be ignorant on some points and we may have a 'mental block' on others. Flexibility, therefore, means that we should listen, not just to the words, which may be inexpertly chosen, but rather to the person who is speaking, and try to understand what is going on in his mind. Otherwise we shall be unable to adapt our behaviour to that individual at that moment. For instance, if someone is worried about a particular problem, he will feel unable to discuss any other topic seriously, at least until he has first got the worry off his mind.

We have implied that there is no question of changing or falsifying the information we want to convey, but only of finding the best way of expressing what we want to say, taking account of the needs of others. However, the situation itself must also be kept in mind: there is a big difference between listening to a friend privately and giving a lecture to five hundred people. Naturally, in a formal situation we must think out the best way of communicating with others without being unfaithful to our permanent principles; in less formal situations it is much easier to give an opinion about various topics without having prepared what we are going to say, though we may run the risk of giving way on fundamental issues for social reasons.

If we have learned the virtue of flexibility, we shall be able to adapt to each individual and each situation, while still remaining faithful to our permanent principles, which we shall defend with great firmness.

Adapting our behaviour

If we consider the two aspects of improvement in any virtue, namely, the intensity with which it is practised and the rightness of our motives, we shall see that there are many such motives for practising the virtue of flexibility. These are, among others, the desire to learn from others, to learn from new situations, to get on well with people, to be able to adapt our behaviour continually to the principles that govern our life. Undoubtedly, this last motive is of great importance and it is directly connected with the rightness of our intentions. We cannot always adapt our behaviour to these principles in time, but if we are watchful of what we are doing and aware of what we have done, we can always rectify as we go along or, at the latest, after the event. We have a duty to be honest in this matter. It is not always easy to be flexible in new situations where we have no experience to guide us in adapting to the circumstances; consequently, we should try to learn from others. That is to say, a flexible person is one who has learned from his own experience and that of others. Hence the importance of observing and listening.

If we are to learn from others, we must believe that what they have to say may be interesting and worthy of our consideration. People are often willing to listen to certain topics but not to others, even when these are open to debate, because they consider themselves 'experts' on these subjects or at least they are convinced that they know more than others. This attitude makes it impossible to learn. Of course, we are not suggesting that one should listen to every kind of nonsense; we have every right to expect that others will put forward their best ideas and, if appropriate, in a proper form.

Besides, if the subject under discussion is not of great importance or if we are chatting simply to pass the time, we must be less demanding. Yet there are people who are inflexible even in matters like this; for instance there are people who refuse to speak except on subjects of great importance; they cannot adapt to the interests of others in the group and are unable or unwilling to identify with them.

We have mentioned the importance of an ability to listen and to identify, at least partly with the interests of the other members of a group, but we must also observe them. In a normal conversation, we should notice when we are talking too much, when the others have lost interest in what we are saying, when the interests of the others are different from ours etc. This is essential if we are to learn anything from them or even if we are to be sociable.

We have also suggested that flexibility helps us to learn in new situations. In fact, this is one of the problems we find with teenage children, who believe they have to try out everything, whether to learn or simply have a good time. Therefore, it is worth repeating that we must not sacrifice our basic principles for the sake of a new experience, even though it is perfectly legitimate to make every effort to benefit from such new situations, provided they are licit in themselves.

Some people are very efficient so long as they are working in a familiar area but if they are asked to undertake something different, something unknown, they feel frightened or become so uneasy that they waste the opportunity. This is a trait of character that can be harmful to flexibility: we refer to the tendency to remain tied to the familiar, though not necessarily to what is fundamental. We find examples of this attitude in the father who gets into a bad mood because someone has taken his favourite seat or who gets angry when the normal time for dinner has to be changed. Here, the virtue of orderliness needs to be balanced by flexibility so as not to become an obsession and transformed into an end in itself. There is also a certain inflexibility in a child who cannot study unless the television is switched on or who objects to any change in the household routine, even though it cannot be avoided.

In brief, the two opposite extremes to flexibility are rigidity in trivial matters – which is very different from firmness in matters of principle – and what we might call fragility, which means that we let ourselves be carried away by any influence, without reflection on the meaning of what we are doing, in other words, spontaneity in the mistaken sense of the word, understood as something which does not need the support of the intelligence and the will.

Teaching flexibility

We might now ask how our children may be taught this virtue. There is no need to repeat how essential it is to teach children to have a deep understanding of the permanent principles and virtues in their life or the importance of helping them to relate their everyday activities to these principles; let us only say that without this, flexibility is impossible. Instead, let us concentrate on other aspects of the practice of this virtue.

In educating younger children, we may concentrate on two points – new people and new situations. Children should learn to behave in a natural way with other people and therefore they should have friends who can visit them at home and who invite them in return, so that they may see that there are different rules and habits in every family. There is no point in protecting children so that no effort is required on their part in these matters. If they find it difficult to go out into the world on their own, we should help and encourage them lovingly and show them that we have confidence in their ability to handle the situation. Furthermore, such visits to other families, whether they be relatives or not, will help the children to learn the difference between adapting to other people's way of life and giving in on fundamental principles. For instance, a nine-year-old child is left with his uncle and aunt while his parents go on holiday; the child's cousins are allowed to watch anything they like on television; on their return, the child tells his parents that he has seen several programmes which they had forbidden him to watch. His parents can only say, 'What a pity! You have missed a great chance to give good example to your cousins.' What we are suggesting is that children above the age of reason should know many people and many families, so that they can learn to distinguish between ways of life to which they should adapt and basic rules which should never be abandoned. Another point is that, if children experience new situations, they can learn to adapt readily to new requirements: for instance, to travel on their own, to go shopping, to go to the bank to pay in some money, to stop playing when a younger brother needs them.

As children grow up, they will have to learn to be flexible in getting on well with others, making allowances for each individual's idiosyncrasies. In this sense, flexibility is closely related to the virtue of respect for others: it should be explained to them that a certain type of behaviour is appropriate when they are with certain people but not with others, and how they can benefit from their contacts with other people if they are able to adapt and find an area of mutual agreement.

The intensity with which this virtue is practised will depend on the number of different situations in which one can behave properly and one's ability to adapt to others, by exercising one's powers of listening, observing and expressing oneself. In this regard, it is clearly important to teach our children to express themselves verbally, not only in their own language, but in foreign languages too, so that they can be flexible in other countries and with people of other nationalities.

Lastly, it is important to teach our children not to be over attached to superficial matters or points of mere opinion. This will require that they develop a critical attitude. Especially in adolescence, they must learn to moderate their opinions and realise that perhaps they are not right in everything they say. They must be willing to admit that they can learn from others – even from adults! – but, in order to be flexible, they should compare what others tell them with their own criteria and not deliberately submit to harmful influence. They need their parents' guidance to distinguish matters of opinion from matters of certainty; the example of their parents should show great flexibility in the former and unwavering firmness in the latter. In discussing these matters with their children, parents should show great respect for their views, giving clear and precise information without smothering them with the weight of their own knowledge and experience.

Flexibility does not mean giving in easily; on the contrary, it means learning to say yes and learning to say no at the right time. Apart from that, it means being open to the process of improvement for which opportunities arise in the countless situations of every day.

SELF-ASSESSMENT

Briefing Note: see pages 29-30, above.

Am I flexible myself?

1. *I have personal standards which help me decide how to act as circumstances arise.* (Flexibility does not mean trying everything, nor letting oneself be borne along by every outside influence.)
2. *I do have opinions on matters which are debatable; but I don't try to impose them on others.* (Being flexible means using phrases like 'in my opinion...', 'I feel that...', 'maybe...'.)
3. *In questions related to objective truth, I can be firm, but I adapt to the people I'm talking to or to the situation I find myself in.* (One shouldn't try to talk to everyone in the same way. A 'gift of tongues' is needed in order to say things in different ways or just to know that it is time to keep quiet.)
4. *I usually make an effort to distinguish between those things which are debatable and those others which are not.* (One of the actions which is most confusing for young people is when these aspects are mixed up. Talking dogmatically about debatable questions is especially damaging, for it tends to break down the communicative process with the youngster.)
5. *When studying, I try to recognise what information is certain and, therefore, can and should be accepted.* (It is a question of assessing the reliability of

the sources, of the authors. Or, if one doesn't know, seeking the opinion of someone who does, and who is trustworthy.)

6. *In debatable questions I use my critical faculties as best I can, in order to accept what is acceptable and to reject what is not.* (Flexibility will lead a person, in certain occasions, to stop reading a book because of the damage it may do him.)

7. *I try to adapt myself to others, and to their needs, if I see that, in that way, I may improve the relationship or help them.* (The flexible person knows how to distinguish between different kinds of people, and they know what sort of vocabulary they should use, what degree of abstraction they can develop and so on.)

8. *I try to help other people – my friends, companions etc. – as far as I can, without sacrificing my own values but without being too rigid, either.* (We should seek the good of others, and that is why it is wise not to rush things, to be prudent.)

9. *I try to know myself, to check if I am talking too much or too little, or when it is useful to give information or when it is better to keep quiet.* (This kind of 'situational sensitivity' is necessary in order to be flexible. Sometimes a helping hand will be needed from the spouse or from a friend to discover how others see us.)

10. *In general I try not to be rigid and not to be weak. And if I make a mistake I know how to make amends.* (To rectify is simply knowing how to cope with having made a mistake. Some educators never want to say they are sorry, never admit that they've made a mistake, believing that, if they did so, they would lose their authority. That is not true. Their authority will increase as long as they don't make mistakes too often!)

Teaching others to be flexible

11. *I teach the smaller children the basic rules that they must obey.* (Small children have few criteria and those they have, they don't know how to apply to everyday situations. Therefore it is better to insist on specific aspects of behaviour in order to keep them on the right track.)

12. *I try to create or take advantage of occasions when the children will have to relate to people they don't know.* (Children should visit their friends' homes, stay for a time with relatives or go on an exchange programme, but only if they know the rules they must not break.)

13. *I try to get the smaller children to have different kinds of experiences, getting them to try out hobbies, go to different places etc.* (As children grow, one can see how some do not want to 3leave their known friends, or places;

and this is because their educators have not helped them get used to adapting to new ones.)

14. *I give the children different kinds of jobs and things to do so that they learn to make their way around.* (We are referring to things like going to the bank to cash a cheque, going shopping alone, or travelling alone, for example. The things we get them to do will be different according to their age and level of maturity.)

15. *I teach the children to listen to and observe others, in order to be able to adapt what they say or do to their real situation.* (One thing which will help them in this way is encouraging them to think of pertinent questions to ask in order to get the others to open up: 'What are your hobbies?' or 'What do you do at the weekends?', for example. And then suggest other things they can observe – the interest the other person has in some subject, for example.)

16. *I help the youngsters to speak without being dogmatic, or making others feel they are being dogmatic, because of their tone of voice.* (This 'dogmatic' way of speaking is very common in teenagers and it greatly limits their chances of getting on well with others.)

17. *I explain to the youngsters how easy it is to give up one's own criteria in a desire to be the same as their peers or, at any rate, not wanting to be different.* (Sometimes the influence of the group can be enormous. If educators realise this, they can try to link the child up to other children whose parents share the same sort of values.)

18. *I help the youngsters discover how television, films or magazines are influencing them and their personal values. In the end, these influences can make them feel that 'anything goes'.* (Relativism is one of the greatest enemies of flexibility as it excludes any kind of solid criteria.)

19. *I help the children overcome their possible fear of the unknown so that they can begin to take advantage of the marvelous things the world has to offer.* (The cause of this indifference or apathy may lie in a sense of insecurity, in laziness or in fear.)

20. *I teach the children to be prudent and to make amends when need be.* (Today one frequently hears youngsters saying they are sorry. Saying 'I'm sorry' can be an authentic expression of a person wanting to make amends but often they don't mean it at all. The expression is just a convenient excuse for not having thought out the possible consequences of their actions. Unfortunately some youngsters do whatever they like and then trivially say, 'I'm sorry', afterwards.)

12 Loyalty

Loyal people accept the ties implicit in their relationship with others – friends, relatives, superiors, their country, its institutions, etc. and defend and reinforce the system of values which these respect.

When we think about the best way to teach the human virtues, we frequently notice that they are all closely interrelated. Loyalty is directly connected with perseverance, responsibility, respect for others, prudence and some other virtues. Nevertheless, it is possible to discuss one and the same reality from different points of view and thus stress certain aspects which were previously considered partially. With this in mind, let us look at the virtue of loyalty.

We have said that a loyal person accepts the bonds implicit in relationships with others. This acceptance involves taking a decision, but a very different type of decision from the one involved in perseverance. Perseverance allows us to do whatever is necessary to attain the objectives we have set ourselves; in other words, there is a situation planned for the future which encourages us to make every effort to overcome any difficulty in our way. On the other hand, when we accept a bond in our relationships with others, we are not looking forward to a future situation, but accepting the present reality. The bond does not change with time, except to grow stronger, deeper and more mature. Therefore, as time passes, it is important to behave consistently in accordance with the nature of that bond, taking care of it, defending it and reinforcing it. Here, indeed, it may be necessary to practise the virtue of perseverance in order to foster the relationship, but loyalty itself is the virtue which helps us to behave according to our word or, in certain cases, simply to become aware with the help of reason or faith of a particular relationship so that, without any need to pledge a word, we are conscious that it is binding and that we have a moral obligation to accept it freely.

As an example, let us take the case of loyalty to a particular friend. Leaving aside for the moment the nature of the commitment involved here, let us imagine a situation in which that friend begins to behave in a way that endangers the friendship. Loyalty will ensure that the other person should do all in his power to help his friend by virtue of the system of values involved in the relationship, despite the unfriendly way in which he is being treated. In other words, he will try to help his friend to bring his behaviour into line with the bond existing between them, so that the relationship will not disintegrate. At the same time, he will almost certainly need perseverance to undertake and carry out whatever is necessary to bring his friend back into line with the values represented by their relationship.

From what we have said, it will appear that this virtue requires a recognition that a bond or relationship exists and that there are certain values involved in that bond.

The relationship of loyalty

Human beings tend to form relationships with others, because they need one another for various reasons. Young children establish these links without realising it, but, when they get older and more conscious of what they are doing, they sometimes wish to destroy them, in the belief that they constrain them and limit their freedom. We wish now to discuss these problems and say a little about the educational factors involved.

When we say that young children are involved in certain links though without being aware of them as such, we refer to the relationship with other members of the family, with their classmates, with their friends and playmates. Normally they are unaware of the values involved in these relationships; consequently, they do not practice loyalty in regard to them, at least on many occasions. Yet, on other occasions, they are too loyal with regard to a relationship which may be of very minor importance. This presents us with a problem, for not only have we to recognise relationships but also we must place them in order of priority. If it ever happens that loyalty to one's family appears to be incompatible with loyalty to God, for instance, we must be willing to accept that loyalty to God is more important than any other. In fact, these loyalties can never be incompatible. It is quite possible that, in a particular situation, it might seem, on a human level, that we have done something against the interests of our family, but if we have a supernatural outlook on life, we will realise that when we do what is best for God's sake, we are also doing what is best for our family, even though this might not appear to be so at a particular moment.

However, on another level, it is important to have a clear hierarchy. For instance, a married man should realise that his first duty of loyalty is to his family and that friends come afterwards, but both these loyalties are compatible. That is to say, it is possible to accept the bonds implicit in both relationships. However, when it comes to interpreting this bond, when it is a matter of doing something to defend and reinforce it, it will be necessary to establish an order of priorities in order to behave appropriately.

So far, we have mentioned various points relating to the question of loyalty, and these could be summed up by saying that there are four aspects to teaching this virtue:

- How to teach them to recognise the bonds implicit in their relationships with others.

- How to make their various relationships compatible with one another.
- How to have a correct understanding of what loyalty means in each particular case.
- How to realise that their freedom is not constrained by such relationships.

Let us now look at each one of these problems.

Recognising relationships

We have said that it is important to be faithful to our word, as a formal or explicit declaration of intention. There may well be an ongoing activity or attitude upholding the values of a relationship with others, even though nothing has been said on the subject. However, it is likely that this situation will not oblige one to look after the relationship, unless, at least in his mind, it becomes clear and explicit that he has undertaken a permanent duty towards the others. In this regard, we see that loyalty depends on a mental process: it comes from an act of the intelligence and must not be confused with the habitual tendency to react emotionally or favourably in certain circumstances. For instance, very often people who take part in a public demonstration are not expressing loyalty to their country or to the group being supported by the demonstration; they are only expressing a desire to respond emotionally to something which offends or concerns them. Loyalty, in this case, would cause someone, who had intellectually recognised and accepted a bond to do everything he could in favour of the other party to the relationship: he would work conscientiously, he would improve those areas in which he really had some influence etc. We repeat, therefore, that loyalty, deriving from a personal commitment, is a very different thing from those other signs that derive from an emotional approach.

We find this same problem in children. How can we expect them to be loyal before they reach the age of reason? The answer is simple: very young children neither are, nor can be, loyal in the strict sense of the word. Nevertheless, they can begin to learn about the virtue because they do enter into relationships, and later on they will be able to recognise these and act accordingly. What young children can do is learn, at least, to feel the importance of a relationship and to defend or help the people involved. Perhaps we should explain that this is different from what we shall expect from them later on, namely, that they acknowledge the relationship itself and protect and reinforce the system of values which it involves. We repeat, however, that relationships should exist before they are recognised as such. In due course, they may become explicit and form a basis for one's actions.

To be specific, the practice of all virtues in the service of others is an essential basis for loyalty later on. A child who is helpful to his parents, brothers and sisters is beginning to discover the family as an entity. At the same time, he is helped by the other members of the family and he realises that in this unit he has found something that cannot be found elsewhere. Nevertheless, what he is aware of is other persons or individuals, and not of the value of the relationship as such. That is why 'loyalty' can sometimes go too far, at least in certain cases, because the child thinks only of his friend, for instance, and not of the importance of friendship. Let us take an example: a grown up accuses a child of having broken a window; he denies it, although in fact he is the culprit, and another child backs him up out of 'loyalty'. This kind of personal loyalty is not what we are advocating here. If he were truly loyal, although at first he would have certainly protected his friend from the adult's anger, he would then go on to suggest some way to get his friend to do the right thing. In other words, one of the values of friendship is that it involves mutual help to get all parties to behave properly and to improve, and this is possible precisely because of the close relationship that exists between friends. If there are no values, as we have been calling these positive factors, around which the relationship can exist, loyalty is meaningless or can actually lead people to support something which, in fact, is wrong or harmful.

Let us take another example: a youngster's loyalty to his team-mates. If the most important aspect of the team for him is the possibility of winning, then, whenever the team loses, he will criticise the others unfairly and might even want to leave the team altogether; or he might indiscriminately criticise the members of the opposing team or blame the referee, once again showing an interest only in winning. On the other hand, genuine loyalty to the team would ensure that the child play to the best of his ability, even when losing; even if they kept on losing, he would continue playing, practising and doing his best to help the others as players and as human beings. In other words, what we have called the 'system of values' involved in the notion of a team would include sportsmanship, playing ability, good humour, helping the others and so on.

Once again, we are emphasising that one of the values of a relationship is the element of improvement for oneself and others; this improvement involves defending and reinforcing other values connected with the relationship, such as justice, respect for others, personal initiative etc.

This brings us to another very important matter. Loyalty is meaningless unless these values, as we have called them, are permanent and, in fact, one sign of mistaken loyalty, when the values involved are not permanent, is defence of personalities or institutions irrespective of the values they represent: in other words, an indiscriminate support for those personalities or institutions out of selfishness or to satisfy one's desire to belong to something. Consequently, we may stress that, in teaching loyalty, it is essential:

- to ensure that children practise all other virtues in the service of others, and
- to help them to distinguish between the personalities or institutions with which they have a relationship and the values involved.

Some examples may clarify the latter point still further. Loyalty to one's parents does not mean approving of their behaviour even when it is wrong, but rather defending them, protecting their good name against groundless slander and helping them to improve. It also means being sincere and generous with them. Loyalty to one's country does not mean concealing the defects to be found in it or responding emotionally whenever its name is mentioned, but rather defending and reinforcing the permanent values we find there. Only in God is there perfect harmony between his words and his deeds, between what he is and what he does. It is easy to see that the only truth, the only permanent values, are found in God's revelation, because the 'values' created by man are precarious and can vary according to man's own interpretation of his needs.

Before going on to the second of the problems we have mentioned, perhaps we should ask what are the most normal relationships which children experience. Undoubtedly, the most immediate one is that of the family, after which comes the group of friends and then a few closer friends. Besides these, if a school has a spirit of its own, where certain principles are deliberately cultivated, then the child could come to recognise his relationship with these principles.

Compatible relationships

On the subject of ensuring that relationships are compatible with one another, we should first of all ask ourselves how the children envisage them. A child might consider that the virtue of respect is practised among his friends, but not within his family and, consequently, he might defend his friends and criticise the family. As he sees it, there is a certain incompatibility between the two relationships, and his tendency is to abandon one in favour of the other. This brings us back to the problem we mentioned earlier, namely, that loyalty should not depend on finding our own views reflected in others, because in that case it would last only as long as these views are held by both sides. Loyalty involves seeking and recognising the values which are permanent in any human situation whatsoever and, at the same time, identifying the specific and particular elements in the various relationships in which we find ourselves involved, almost without realising it. In this same sense, for instance, the value of justice can be experienced more intensely within the family and in dealing with our friends, while companionship can be practised more easily at the school level than at the level of one's country.

This shows that loyalty is meaningless unless certain permanent values are accepted. It also shows that there can be no incompatibility between relationships unless we forget these values and replace them with a personal interpretation of the relationship. Our first duty is to be loyal to ourselves and this involves seeking and fully understanding the values in question; once that is done, we have to take a decision and acknowledge a number of bonds, allowing us to act in accordance with these values, for we know that some of them present better opportunities than others to defend or reinforce a particular value. If we act in accordance with these values, there will be no incompatibility, although we may have to act in a different way in each particular case in order to defend and develop them. This requires that all the virtues be highly developed and we can conclude, therefore, that loyalty is a virtue for the mature person.

Learning to be loyal

Our last remark does not imply that this virtue cannot be practised to some extent by people who are not yet mature. A young child learns to be loyal by doing his best to help others, though he cannot yet really understand the nature of the value he is developing. In the early stages, these values are based on a very elementary, though essential, distinction, namely the distinction between good and bad. For the young child, who is making every effort to do what his parents and teachers tell him is good and to avoid what they tell him is bad, it also means trying to get his friends, brothers and sisters, and even his parents, to do the same. If parents encourage their children to tell them when they think they are breaking the rules, they will soon begin to concentrate on being loyal to these rules, which are values, after all, rather than on their parents as individuals. Similarly, if they learn to obey the rules relating to their personal cleanliness and the conservation of the environment, they will begin to see the value behind these things: integrity, justice, respect etc.

On another level, the children should be introduced to the notion of improvement and they should be told that they have a duty to improve themselves and to help others to do likewise. For instance, when they have to take decisions, this is a criterion to be kept in mind. Disloyalty in the form of not helping others to improve in a particular situation may be due to weakness or to not realising that their capacity for improvement may itself show whether or not they are doing the right thing and whether they are being loyal or not. Sometimes, even for adults, it is hard to know whether one is being loyal; for children, it is all the more difficult because their principles are not yet clearly worked out. It is therefore important to take advantage of those situations where the element of improvement is clear and obvious.

Sometimes a situation may arise between brothers and sisters where a question of loyalty may have to be settled. For example, one child may accuse the others of having done something wrong; his loyalty should make him help them to improve, whereas it is the very opposite of loyalty to accuse them, in front of their parents, insincerely or for revenge or out of thoughtlessness. What he should do is try to put things right and, if he fails, discuss the matter with his parents privately so that they may use their authority to help. In other words, the important thing is that children should be helped to identify the real motives behind their actions and, consequently, change their minds or go ahead depending on their intentions.

It should be clear then, that the virtue of respect for others is closely related to loyalty. Respect, as we have said, involves acting or refraining from acting so as not to prejudice, and indeed so as to benefit, oneself and others; while loyalty encourages us to act or refrain from acting according to a certain relationship. A child who is aware of the relationship between himself and his school will do nothing to harm it, such as criticising it or painting on the walls, and he will do everything he can to foster the values and principles which it represents.

However, just when children seem to have understood what is meant by loyalty and have established a number of relationships, another problem arises. They think that being loyal in a relationship may limit their freedom.

Relationships and personal freedom

This problem seems to arise from confusing freedom with 'liberation' – which equates freedom with independence. Thus, as C. Llano Cifuentes says, 'human freedom and the human being become absolutes: the free man is seen as one who depends on nothing and no one, he is the 'Absolute Man', unattached, uninvolved. This leads to a kind of idolatry of freedom taking freedom to such an extreme that it becomes a utopia.'

For teenagers, this is a problem relating to ideas, and parents need to be ready to clarify the child's incomplete and confused notions. They need to explain that our freedom is only partly a matter of independence. We gain our independence from something only insofar as we become dependent on, or bound to, something of a higher order. Freedom consists in ability to choose between bonds. We are free, not only because we can choose between bonds which seek us out, but also and in particular because we are capable of choosing the bonds which allow us to develop personally, that is to say, those which are closely related to truth and goodness. In this case freedom increases: it is an ability to become oneself and transcend oneself.'

If a child avoids any type of relationship or commitment, he will find himself unable to practise any permanent principle properly. His standards will all be merely provisional and he will end up by adapting to any situation, to the majority opinion and to mere fashion. On the other hand, if he works out the pemanent values involved in his relationships, he will find that he has a solid basis on which to base his whole life.

Parents should discuss these matters with their teenage children and explain what is meant by these values in themselves, as well as how they should be practised in connection with their various relationships. Initially, it may be best to deal with the relationships between the children and their family, their friends and their school. Indeed, the notion of friendship seems to be losing ground; there is no time to be loyal to our friends, and we simply get on with whatever we are doing without paying any attention to the values involved in the relationship.

Nevertheless, parents can still exercise an influence on these relationships in a positive way. When it comes to loyalty to one's country, on the other hand, we see that many of the permanent values involved at this level are easily reduced to emotional demonstrations or merely to support for national sport. Parents should therefore emphasise personal loyalty to those institutions with which the individual is most closely associated. Loyalty to one's country or to one's city will be meaningful only if the people of that country or that city are loyal to themselves, to their basic principles and to truth. Loyalty to these fundamental values is essential in a world which is destroying itself by frantically concentrating on things which are merely transitory.

SELF-ASSESSMENT

Briefing Note: see pages 29–30, above.

Am I a loyal person?

1. *I recognise the commitments which arise from natural law, from being a child of God.* (Loyalty requires thought. It isn't an easy virtue; it is not a matter of emotions or feelings. First of all we need to recognise and therefore be committed to being human beings, social beings with a need to improve all through life and help others do the same.)

2. *I recognise the commitments I have acquired as a result of formal or implicit promises or covenants.* (We owe loyalty to our spouses; it is called fidelity. Loyalty is also owed to our friends although we have made no formal promises to them.)

3. *I am conscious of the values which underpin the commitments I have acquired.* (For example, in marriage these values will be the constant concern for the welfare of one's spouse and the procreation and education of children. In a football team the best values to support it can be friendship, things well done, companionship but not 'winning at all cost' or financial gain.)

4. *I keep to commitments I have acquired, because I think about the relationship between what I do everyday and the values I have committed myself to upholding.* (Loyalty requires thought. Frenetic, incessant activity can lead us off the track.)

5. *When I give my word, I do so seriously, aware of the consequences it entails.* (The human being has no more profound or solemn way of committing himself than saying 'yes'. Sometimes one may give one's word without thinking about the possible consequences of having done so, and whether one is able to do what one has promised, or worse, without any intention of keeping one's word.)

6. *I try to do something to defend the rights of people in need, trying to live solidarity, being loyal to my brothers and sisters who are children of God.* (Some people reduce loyalty to a very small circle – just the family and a few friends – for example. The virtue of loyalty leads us to broader commitments.)

7. *I am conscious of the commitments I have acquired.* (There are all kinds of commitments that there is no need to take on. But once one has taken them on, one should be loyal. For example, one can belong to an old boys' association (an alumni association) or not. If one does become a member, one should try to pull one's weight.)

8. *I recognise a hierarchy in the commitments I have acquired.* (Out of 'loyalty' towards their work colleagues, some people are prepared to sacrifice their family. The family comes first.)

9. *I am conscious that it is easier to be loyal when my feelings support the commitment. But I make an effort to carry out my commitments even when it is not easy.* (If a friend behaves in a bad way, loyalty should lead me to tell them so, even though it costs me an effort and I don't like doing it at all.)

10. *I understand that there should never be, nor can ever be, conflict between my commitments as a child of God, and any other kind of commitment.* (We serve God, by serving our families, our friends and needy people.)

Teaching others to be loyal

11. *I help the smaller children realise the importance of relationships with others – in the family or in the classroom.* (As a previous step towards loyalty, it is important that the small children recognise that they are an important part of the group.)

12. *I teach the smaller children to obey the rules, to train themselves to be loyal in different commitments.* (They need to learn how to behave in a team, with their brothers and sisters, with their grandparents etc.)

13. *I teach the small children to distinguish, in simple terms, between what is good or correct and what is bad or incorrect.* (In this way we are training them to act in the right way later, when they have the intelligence and the will to do so.)

14. *I manage to get the children to recognise their responsibility towards other family members and to understand what being loyal in that situation means.* (To pursue the virtue of loyalty one needs to recognise the commitments one has – in this case personal responsibility in these relationships – to understand what values underpin each commitment.)

15. *I manage to get the children to recognise their responsibility towards their friends, and to understand what being loyal in this situation means.* (Frequently teenagers think that being loyal to a friend means defending them at all costs even if they have done something wrong. Being loyal means always seeking the best for the other person.)

16. *As the children get older, I manage to get them to see their responsibility towards other members of the class, teams they belong, members of clubs etc., and to learn to be loyal in these situations.* (One will notice this loyalty in such things as: not talking badly about the school in front of others, not painting or dirtying the school premises, celebrating other students' triumphs, supporting the sports teams when they play, going to activities organised by other students – theatre, concerts, exhibitions.)

17. *I talk to the youngsters to help them see the different kinds of commitments they can make in their lives.* (Sometimes they don't realise that they should commit themselves in specific relationships.)

18. *I help them understand that committing themselves does not go against their personal freedom.* (Authentic freedom means choosing between different kinds of commitment. The virtue of loyalty requires help to think things through. It is one of the virtues which will require most explanation and reasoning.)

19. *I explain what kind of commitment they are making in each case.* (What being a member of a team means, or being a good friend or a member of a club.)

20. *I help them learn to find a good balance between their commitments to different people and organisations.* (Sometimes a youngster will virtually forget about their family in favour of their team or their youth club. Children need to have a hierarchy in their values and to learn how not to neglect any of their duties.)

13 Industriousness

Industrious people are diligent at things essential to supernatural and natural maturity, and help others to be industrious too, in everyday work and other duties.

The cardinal virtue of fortitude is made up of two parts: resisting and undertaking. The virtue of industriousness helps one in a specific way, to do the second part, the undertaking part. A capacity to undertake something, to carry out a series of activities, staying with it, presupposes that a person has adequate motivation to overcome any obstacle which may arise. The main motive industriousness or hard work relies on is love. The ability to act out of love depends, in turn, on a person being suitably equipped to love; he has to know how to love and he has to be prepared to love. Therefore, hard work and diligence combine to form a single virtue 'Diligent' comes from the verb, *diligo*, which means to love, to appreciate, to choose something after careful consideration and attention. The diligent man does not rush into things. He does his work thoughtfully and lovingly'.

At first sight it may seem odd to link this virtue with love, for normally it is identified with making a big effort, with being serious and tough. True: there is this dimension of disciplined effort; but hard work leads a person to consider the fulfilment of his daily duties as a fertile field for achieving personal maturity, both natural and supernatural: i.e. for fulfilling his duty to be an even better son of God, and an instrument for helping others to do the same.

Work and other duties

It is important to realise that hard work is not a virtue which is developed only in the area of one's daily work, one's job. The word 'work' can be understood as describing a collection of activities which are hard, disciplined, productive, and directed to some goal. It is true that in daily work a person normally finds more discipline than in other spheres, in the sense that when we work we are subject to a series of controls in the line of timetable, the sort of activities we engage in, the procedures for carrying it out, etc. In the home there are also activities which demand an effort (doing repair jobs, for example) but they do not have to be done within such a strict framework. In other words, we can do them when we feel like it. Anyway, the point is that outside the area of everyday work there is a whole series of duties which we have to do which call for the virtue of hard work.

We can take work as meaning a series of hard, disciplined, productive activities directed to some goal. Work, therefore, is subject to external determination or conditioning; but so called free time is also conditioned. We cannot attain total freedom from every form of conditioning nor is it desirable to attempt this: life is just not like that. We spend a great deal of our time in a social context and whenever we live with other people this conditioning occurs. The various forms of conditioning turn into rules, rules which normally are quite consistent with the goal that is being pursued by the group. For example, the internal rules of a school seek to regulate relations between teachers and pupils so they get on well. The virtue of order helps each person to appreciate and to keep to these norms. Of course, these actions can be performed with technical excellence without even realising their purpose; a person can also perform work in any old way without worrying about it.

I have stressed that industriousness is important as a virtue not only in the context of work but also in the fulfilment of other duties done in so-called 'free time'. Doing these things can derive from really deep motivation, or they can simply be the result of doing what has to be done with technical proficiency. Industriousness implies doing things carefully, out of love, so as to take good care of what God has given us, to try to be an even more worthy son of his, and to help others do the same.[32]

Up to this point we have been moving on a more or less theoretical plane. Now we will look at how this particular virtue may be taught, bearing in mind some specific difficulties, many of them very familiar to parents.

Doing things diligently

To do things diligently, first of all we have to do them. Is it love that allows us to do the thing, is it love that motivates fulfilment? Or once we have done the thing well, is it then that we can work with love? Let's take children and their studies. These are hard, disciplined, activities directed to some goal. In other words study is work. But, is it reasonable to ask children to try to work out of love? Should a child's studies show signs of his having put love into them? I think it depends partly on what we mean by love. We can consider it as a tendency towards good and towards its possession (J. Hervada). Love is to be found not only in the personal motive with which we work, in why we are working (a young person who tries to do a job as well as possible so as to please his parents or help some companion), but also in the extent to which the work itself is in keeping with norms which in some way reflect permanent values (an appreciation of a poem prepared with advice given by one's teacher, for example); in this example we get a combination of the value of obedience to the teacher with the intrinsic value of such things as order, beauty, etc., which a good appreciation implies.

For work in itself to be worthy it must be done in accord with certain objective norms. In other words, work badly done is not justified by reference to the effort we have put into doing it. The effort is meritorious, but work well done depends on a proper connection between effort and the quality of the end product.

There is not much chance of the virtue of hard work being developed if a person engages in activities unsuited to his abilities. For example, if we asked a child of eleven to write twenty pages of a critique of some work by a philosopher. Similarly, it would give a wrong impression of this virtue if we misled a child by telling him that he had done a job well simply because he had worked hard at it – when in fact it was badly done, objectively speaking.

A piece of work well done must fit certain objective standards. Conformity to these standards is already a sign of love. This work well done will help develop the virtue of hard work when it is connected to a worthy purpose which in turn stimulates the person to make the effort needed to do the job. To put it in a nutshell: 'Work is born of love; it is a manifestation of love and is directed towards love.[33]

Problems involved in getting things done

As we have said, being industrious implies:

- knowing the standards that apply to work well done in each particular case;
- being sufficiently motivated to make the effort required; and
- having adequately developed a series of ancilliary abilities needed for doing the particular job properly.

In referring to these aspects, not only will we be thinking about children's studies but also about other duties they have in the home or in connection with their friends and with society at large.

How are children going to do things well if they don't know what 'well' means? Sometimes we educators ask young people to do things without giving them clear indications of what we expect of them. 'What we expect of them' brings up another question. When we give these indications, up to what point are they in fact the instructions the child really needs in order to comply with essential standards or to what degree are they in fact matters of opinion? Take, for example, children's duties in regard to order and personal cleanliness: is it a matter of telling them what to do, or should we try to reason out for them the importance of these things and leave it up to them to work out exactly what to do? Our common sense will suggest that with small children we need to spell out some rules because the child needs to learn from his parents whether he is doing things in the right way or not. But once the child is able to reason things out a bit and establish his own standards, the parent's role consists more in getting him to think than in spelling out exactly what he should do.

Young people need *clearer* information *the less they know* about what they have to do. And they need more information the more *technically complex* an activity is. For a teenager to rig up his own radio he needs quite a bit of information. If he does not get it he will probably fail. So, we can distinguish two factors – *clarity* and *scope* of information. Clear information but not a lot of it applies to those actions which naturally admit of greater freedom of personal interpretation: how to help others, how to be more responsible, how to be a better friend, because once he sees clearly what the object of the exercise is and has a few general instructions, he has enough to allow him get on with the job?' On the other hand we cannot just tell him to 'make a radio' and expect him to do so automatically.

For children to be hard-working we need to help them get clear in their minds what the goal of the activity is and tell them something about how to go about it, sometimes more and sometimes less.

Even then difficulties can arise. For example, the teenager who doesn't keep to the basic rules of presentation, tidiness, etc. in doing an exercise, because he says that the teacher is not going to look at it. In other words, even though he knows how to do it, he does not want to do it.

The problem of motivation

In the example just given, the virtue of hard work will lead the young person to do the exercise well because he realises that doing a job well is an act of love.

In any activity we can identify a number of qualities – in ourselves and in the activity itself. Motivation to work hard comes from the discovery of these qualities and abilities by one's self and the explicit recognition of them by one's teachers. Going back to our example: in some way the young person was not going to do a good job because his teacher by *not* looking at the end product was showing that he gave *little* value to this piece of work. He didn't value it: he didn't appreciate it. Moreover, it is possible that if his parents had insisted that he make a good job of it, still they would not have got him to change his approach, because for the child there is a direct relationship between the person who lays down the rules and the duty of evaluating the work done. That is the first step towards personal recognition of those values which each person adopts for his own life. As long as children do not appreciate these values, their motivation necessarily has to come from outside.

We can now ask a question referring to the parents' approach: Should parents go for being demanding and motivating the child from outside – or should they be concerned to help him discover personal motives of his own for working?

There can be no one answer to this question. Both approaches are necessary, but the ability to work hard depends especially on a person's awareness of what he is doing. Being a hard worker means *wanting* to make an effort and I want to when I want to because I want to. What stimulates a child is knowing how to do a job (we'll look at this later) and having ability to do this autonomously. Outside pressure is one way of developing his fortitude but the virtue of hard work includes a personal desire to be of service to others.

Initially, it can be good for parents to notice those things their child does with special affection. We have all observed a little girl carefully cleaning and combing her dolls. Or a boy whose bicycle gets more attention than all the work given him by teachers and parents combined. What a lot of care he gives it! And how pleased the children are that everything is in order, just as it ought to be. We can smile thinking about children but the same is true of grown ups: a lady getting all dressed up for going out into town; a man carefully checking his equipment before going off shooting or fishing.

But how can we put the same affection into less agreeable activities, into those duties (such as work) which are hard and disciplined? In these other activities we mentioned we can see the beginning of the habit of hard work: but this virtue is also needed in the more or less routine affairs of everyday life.

Work is a type of activity carried out, in a personal way, by human beings ... It is a human activity – involving a certain amount of originality, initiative and creativity – and its end-product, whether material or not, has to do with changing something. To the extent that originality, initiative or creativity is missing, or something is not changed at all, it cannot be regarded as human work: it is something purely mechanical. Originality, it is worth remarking, lies not only in the way one performs the actions: it also has to do with their purpose and how one goes about organizing a series of actions which at first sight don't seem to leave much room for originality (for example, little chores like putting out the lights, clearing away the table, tidying a press, etc.).

The main motivation for carrying out work is that it is human: that it allows a person to express himself in his own way in a particular context; it lets him develop certain qualities and abilities; and it leads him to natural and supernatural maturity.

The satisfaction a little girl gets from her dolls or a boy from his bicycle comes mainly from feeling that he is in control of the situation by having done something personally which really means something to him. Work lets one combine external action with certain values which you already hold – order, cleanliness, getting things to work properly.

Doing one's ordinary duties will give one this feeling in so far as one can put some of oneself in them: it's not a matter of merely repeating actions on someone else's instructions.

There are two ways to ensure that actions become something one feels about personally: (1) by doing them successfully in a different way, a way suited to one's personal qualities and abilities; (2) doing things which don't involve much originality in themselves but making out of them something that is different, due to the meaning we give them.

Depending on the kind of activity, one can give more emphasis to one or other of these approaches. And one has to try to achieve some sort of balance. I remind the reader that we are discussing onerous, disciplined activities aimed at some particular purpose.

Motives and ages

What specially motivates a small child is the connection the action has with his own world, his own interests. For example, novelty-experiment, he finds very attractive: doing something he hasn't done before and then doing it again because he likes it. A small child likes opening the door, answering the telephone, laying the table. But then, after he has done it a number of times, his interest wanes and he stops doing it. He also likes solving simple problems provided he knows the way to go about it. He likes gathering up things, collecting things etc. The problem is that as the years and even the months go by, his interests change and he puts his effort into other things. To get him to keep putting effort into particular activities the educator needs to play an active part, and to motivate him. For example his personal presence, encouraging the child, being demanding with him, giving out to him, smiling – whatever suits the child's character and the particular circumstances.

Almost every thing is original and new for the small child; but later, when it stops being new, one has to try to get him to persevere in making an effort: this requires the active involvement of the educator – at the beginning by using what the child still likes, showing that one is pleased by his efforts, and later by making demands in a reasonable way so as to get him to acquire the habits he needs for things which take more of an effort.

The main problems in connection with this virtue of hard work usually arise when the child is about ten years old. As far as study is concerned, progress is being measured more specifically at this age, and not so much time can be allowed for 'free expression'. At home good behaviour has to be spelt out more explicitly to ensure that family life goes smoothly. It seems that there are fewer opportunities for stimulating originality in work and at the same time the children are not yet able to reason out what their actions mean; they can't yet give them their full value. I feel that at this age one has to use all possible means available, requiring them to develop the virtue of fortitude, especially as far as physical effort is concerned.

Of course, educators still have to be demanding in an explicit way, even though this takes more effort than before. But there are other ways of being demanding which might be worth trying. For example, team work at school gives scope for the child's companions to be demanding; the pupil rises to the occasion out of a sense of duty. In the family, the different jobs can be given out in such a way that one child has to do something for another: if he fails to do it, it will be his brother or sister who will require him to do it. It is also good to keep looking out for the sort of interests each child prefers, his likes and hobbies – and then to get him to put affection in the small things these involve. But it is also good to try to ensure that the more routine actions have some personal meaning for the child, so that he feels motivated to keep on making an effort.

This matter of 'meaning' and of 'recognising the value' of actions can be the direct result of understanding the actions or it can be connected with something else. For example, the child can do things in order to please his parents or he can realise it is important to do them because his father has made an effort to come home early to be with him when he is doing his homework. In the second case he comes to realise the value his father puts on study, and so he takes it more seriously himself. In the first case, he makes an effort because he realises the importance of study and for that reason wants to do it well.

One should begin to make him question the first kind of motive, getting him to see that it really is important for him to do his work, even if he doesn't like it, as a way of contributing to other people and to please God: in other words developing his concept of duty and generosity.

Also, while remembering that this is a time to keep on stressing quite a lot of 'routine' aspects, it would be good as far as possible to complement them with exercises which involve more originality and creativity. In this connection, it could be good to consider how in fact his life at home and at school is focussing the child on the *solving* of problems. Would it not be a more interesting activity and one calling for more originality to *identify* problems?

Once adolescence is reached, we may meet another type of problem in the line of motivating children to be hard-working. In their studies, they have to learn to do lots of things which have no direct connection with their interests, with their world. For example, learning how to comment on some text or to prove a geometry theorem. Moreover, teachers have to insist a lot on the technical aspects of work due to the amount of new subjects being put into the curriculum. They have to pass on to the pupils more and more information and the pupils may become passive; they cannot see the way to doing their work in an original and creative way.

This can show us the value of career guidance as an on-going subject. One thing that helps is contact between parents, teachers and children/pupils so that they appreciate that their studies have some real point. Motivation can also come from: the real interest the pupil acquires in the subject; and knowing and accepting the objectives pursued by teachers, and by their parents in conjunction with them – but in the end it is quite probable that students will have to engage in many onerous, disciplined activities with little or no motivation. It is good for them to realise that that's the way life is, and that these routine, almost meaningless, activities acquire a new meaning depending on how we go about them: if they offer to God the effort to do things well or do them in order to serve other people or out of a Kantian sense of duty. For there is a close connection between hard work and generosity. And as I have said elsewhere, it is not good to *require* young people to be generous: rather, you have to guide them so that they do things on their own initiative.

In other words, at the adolescent stage it's a matter of continuing to suggest to young people why they ought to act in a certain way but *without obliging them* to act from the same motivation as oneself. Returning to the case of the adolescent who didn't want to do his work in the way laid down, his father could say to him: 'Don't you realise that even the way you present your homework has a value in itself – independently of whether the teacher is going to look at it or not?' But if the boy doesn't respond, does one have to then require him to do the homework? There may be reasons for saying 'yes' but if one does lay down the law one has to remember that one is not helping him develop the quality of being industrious. One will just have to be patient and try to approach it from another angle. (Patience does not mean that parents should never become angry or express their annoyance: A child may even need this sanction, this help. But it does mean that they should not lose their interior calm.

The child's sheer ability to do what he is asked to

A child needs a certain level of technical skill if he is to do the tasks required for achieving personal maturity and for helping others to go in the same direction. How can a student study a book if he doesn't know how to read? How can a daughter prepare a meal for her brothers and sisters if she doesn't know how to cook?

Technical skill is a necessary condition for developing the virtue of being hardworking. And the more skillful a person becomes, the easier is it for him to do his tasks and the greater satisfaction he will get from them – for once you have a good grasp of the technique of doing things, you can begin to introduce a certain personal style into them. So, one way of producing a situation where a child has no desire to study is to give him homework which is far too difficult; but you get the same effect if you give him too easy jobs, because he needs to make no effort to do them: and so gets no real satisfaction from them.

Childrens' problems with their everyday work, i.e. study, are never a simple matter of just 'not studying'. Rather, it is either that they haven't got enough motivation to make an effort – or haven't yet developed their ability to do what the job requires. As far as the second aspect is concerned, parents should see their childrens' teachers to find out how they can be of help. What sort of difficulty might the youngster have? Perhaps he needs to develop his:

- capacity to read and understand what he is reading; powers of observation;
- ability to synthesise;
- ability to relate facts to each other;
- ability to speak in public;
- ability to distinguish between facts and opinions.

Once his shortcoming is identified, it will be much easier to help the child do his jobs with genuine interest and affection.

Two vices

Finally, I should like to comment on two vices which go against industriousness – laziness and frenetic, non-stop activity.

Laziness is defined not so much by the mere fact of doing nothing as by that attitude which leads one to become depressed because one can't summon up enough energy to do some spiritual good. Therefore, industriousness also is a spiritual attitude which leads one diligently to do one's own duties.

Laziness is contagious: so parents should watch those aspects of their own lives where they are most inclined to be lazy. This might be in the area of their duties to their family: if one doesn't get home until late because it suits one to stay at the office; once home, not helping one's wife; etc. Or one could be lazy about one's duties to God: not praising him, not praying etc. Or in relation to work: absenteeism, or not working hard.

In this connection an interesting point arises. A man (a woman) in principle seems to be industrious, because he throws himself energetically into his work. But he is not in fact industrious; he is lazy. Work is where he hides from having to do his other duties diligently. A man needs to be active and he also needs to contemplate, and the two things are perfectly compatible. He needs time for really making an effort and time to do things which call for less effort.

Effort is one of the causes of tiredness which, in turn, calls for rest and recovery. Therefore vacations, free periods, rests, ought not to be considered a luxury; nor are they incompatible with hard work; in fact they are a necessary part of hard work. Not only *because* the need for rest is produced by tiredness, but also because rest equips one to work.

Industriousness is a virtue of a lover, of someone who knows he can serve God and man in every detail to do with the fulfilment of his duties. He does not shine out through being hard working. Yet, if he does have this virtue, other people will notice that what sustains him is love, and maybe they will want to drink from the same fountains.

SELF-ASSESSMENT

Briefing Note: see pages 29–30, above.

Am I industrious?

1. *I usually try to do what I should, to take the steps necessary to do a job well.* (Being industrious does not just mean filling one's time with activity, but doing things well. It is easy to substitute quality for quantity.)
2. *When I do things, I put some good intention behind the effort it takes to do them well. I do things for someone, as an act of service.* (It is a question of acting 'for' love and 'with' love. The Christian offers what they do to God. They do things for love of God.)
3. *I recognise the various areas where I have duties to carry out.* (Industriousness applies to work but also to what I should do for the family, for friends and for fellow citizens.)
4. *I understand that any activity which can really be called 'work' must be done in a disciplined way. It involves effort and must have some purpose to it.* (This means that industriousness does not exist when we do things that are a result of whims, that don't take any effort and that don't help oneself or others improve.)
5. *I strive to carry out my duties; I don't invent excuses if things work out badly.* (Industriousness involves responsibility; when a mistake is made, it should be made up for.)
6. *I try to make sure that all my actions are truly human.* (In this sense, everyday routine actions are especially relevant. We should try to put initiative and love in to them, either by giving them our own 'personal style' or by putting some good intention behind them.)
7. *I look for ways to improve my skills etc., in order to be able to carry out my duties better everyday.* (Also, we should develop new capacities, to be able to act competently in wider fields.)
8. *I have a hierarchy of values which allows me to give priority to the things which are most important.* (The married man should attend his duties as a spouse first. Then come his duties to the rest of the family, then to his friends and to all those who have a call on him.)
9. *I think about what I do everyday, to make sure I am giving enough attention to each field of action.* (Some people tend to be industriousness in just one field. It is not easy to find the adequate balance.)

10. *I do all I can to avoid feeling down (and showing it) when I see how much effort it is going to take to do my duty.* (If one doesn't manage to do this, probably one has fallen into the vice of laziness.)

Teaching others to be industrious

11. *I give a good example as regards doing my duty in different fields of action.* (It is not a question of giving perfect example, but rather of striving to improve in those areas which one wants the children to develop.)

12. *I get the smaller children used to carrying out their duties according to a set of rules or regulations.* (When we give orders to the small children, it useful to think clearly about what are the criteria for a job well done in each case. For example, what does 'tidy up the cupboard' or 'study lesson 3' mean?)

13. *I give more and clearer information to the children, depending on the degree of technical complexity involved in what I am asking of them.* (One cannot carry out an action well if one does not know what the criteria for the action well done are. Often we do not give this information to the children or we give it in a confusing way.)

14. *Before asking a child to do something, I try to make sure that they are up to carrying out the action.* (If the child doesn't know how to do the job, first of all we shall have to teach them how. If the child fails to do the job well, often because of their lack of competence, they will probably lack motivation and will not make an effort in other actions in the future.)

15. *I try to get the children to be industrious in those things which they like doing, first.* (At first, the child needs to learn to do well the things they like and which they are good at. Later we can insist on those things which they don't like so much.)

16. *As soon as the children show that they want to know more about 'why' they have to carry out specific actions, I give them clear explanations.* (The smaller children usually obey simply because the educator has ordered them to. Later on we need to explain why. If we don't, the children will probably do what they ought when we are present, but will not do so when they are by themselves.)

17. *I try to motivate the smaller children by 'being there', and because what I ask them to do is related to their age group's natural interests.* (A certain degree of industriousness can be achieved through back-up from the educator; smiling at the child, or putting on a serious face or simply being present when the child is carrying out the action.)

18. *When the children are older, I try to motivate them through team work, helping them learn to carry out their personal duties and trying to interest them in the job to be done.* (Motivation is a real problem in many cases, but the most important motivation of all is the satisfaction which comes from knowing that one has done the job well.)

19. *I coordinate with teachers/parents to ensure that each child gets sufficient attention.* (Parent-teacher relations are always important but particularly as regards the virtue of industriousness.)

20. *I try to create an atmosphere in which the youngsters can become enthusiastic about life and therefore put a real effort into all they do.* (We should not forget that adolescents have a great capacity for becoming enthusiastic about things. But if we do not channel this 'effervescence' positively, they may end up, instead, being destructive.)

14 Patience

Patient people keep calm, in situations where they experience some difficulty.

The cardinal virtue of fortitude is made up of two parts – undertaking and resisting. Putting up resistance calls for a series of virtues which are interconnected – patience, endurance; perseverance and constancy. Here we are going to examine the first two of these. Strictly speaking, patience comes into play only when one puts up with some difficulty in order to repel a greater evil, whereas endurance helps one bear with difficulties when some good is long in coming. However, I have combined the two virtues in my description at the beginning of this chapter, because in everyday language we use the word patience to cover both of them.

At first sight it seems that patience is a virtue more important for parents than for children. We can remember lots of situations where children led us to lose our patience. However, it would be a mistake to identify patience with the situation where parents just bear with their children's behaviour: patience, like every virtue, has two opposing vices; one is impatience but the other is insensitivity or hardness of heart.

Yes, we parents need to develop the virtue of patience (I will go into this) but our children also need to learn to be patient – for a whole series of reasons. If a person doesn't realise the limits of his present abilities, there is the risk that he will want to go too far, too fast. An adult, if he is prudent enough, can assess the situation and work out how to get what he is aiming at. But children, due to their age and intellectual development, may not be as prudent as that – so there is a danger that they will set themselves targets but never have the patience to achieve them. For example, the child of ten who decides to save up his pocket money so he can buy a bike when he is fifteen.

Patience implies that it is worth while waiting, and that it is possible to wait. It also involves serenely putting up with the difficulties which keep arising.

The influence of the environment

It would be useful to think a little bit more about this business of reasonable targets. I don't aim to give any precise rules but simply to point out some features of modern society and modern youth.

Nowadays, a lot of people fill their time with frantic activities, looking for instant results. They usually see the consequences of what they do but they don't take a long term point of view; they don't worry very much about what will happen in ten years' time. They worry about tomorrow or next week. One result of this is that they look for payback, economy: they try to get the same results, only faster or with less effort. Or better or more results, in the same time etc. What they cannot obtain instantly ends up (without their realising it) having little importance and little effect on what each of them does.

What are these things which take time to come? The most natural things. For example, all the intellectual or human virtues (wisdom, justice, etc.); a man's natural maturity. This is a big problem, because one can never say 'I am now a generous person'. A person can always improve, and it is in this effort to improve that each person's prime value lies.

One of the basic things a person looks for in the world around him is the solution of problems *today, now*. People want a totally just society *now*, a free society *now*. So they keep on changing structures – failing to see that the only way to achieve a just society is to have a society where everyone is just. And that takes time. We very rarely arrange things to ensure that our great-grandchildren have a better life. We want immediate results. I am not trying to say that we should not look for instant results. I am merely stressing the danger of looking only to what you can do in the short term – or of making the mistake of thinking that things can be done overnight when, by their very nature, they take time. It is impressive, for example, to look at our ancestors who started on the building of a cathedral which they would never see finished or who laid out a garden thinking of how it would look when trees had been growing fifty or a hundred years.

Another feature of modern society worth keeping in mind is the tendency to see no value in putting up with difficulties. Along with the flight from pain comes hedonism, the pursuit of pleasure. Anything which means controlling your instincts or basic passions is considered to be 'anti-natural'! Self-control entails effort and therefore it is not acceptable. Yet living in harmony with other human beings involves self-control on everyone's part out of respect for other people's autonomy. The only way to make 'uncontrolled living' compatible with 'living with others' is in a situation where the individual loses his identity and forms part of one amorphous mass.

Yet, it is a fact that pleasure, whether licit or not, can be attractive, and a young person is going to need help from his educators to distinguish good and bad pleasure. Also, he needs to be helped recognise that happiness implies not only pleasure but also pain. A lot of patience is required to keep searching and striving to find more and more happiness. Surface pleasure is presented to us as a highly attractive 'product'. Maybe we ought to see how to present happiness, pleasure and pain in an attractive way: that could give us part of the answer to the question of how to motivate a child to develop the virtue of patience.

We must also take account of the state of development of our children. The smaller ones have very limited power of *concentration* and often give up a game or a task before they finish it – out of sheer impatience. It is also quite reasonable that when they want something they find it very difficult to *reason out* why they can't have it immediately. And they have not much *will power* to help them carry out their resolutions. In other words it is quite reasonable for a small child especially not to be automatically patient. We should not require our children to be patient in the way I have described (they have no duty to be patient); instead we should understand them, and gradually give them what they need, little by little, to develop patience. It really is bad if they reach adolescence or even their thirties or forties, without having learned to reason things out or to concentrate, or to develop will power.

However, from puberty onwards, it is good to remember that many young people's explicit bursts of impatience – getting angry, arguing, fighting etc. – have a lot to do with the biological change they are experiencing, and therefore should not be treated very severely. Or, at least, if they are treated severely they should also be shown that they are understood. During adolescence, too, young people need to be helped resist the barrage they get from the consumer society. They do have to experience new situations, and interpret situations personally. But they do not need to buy the latest new products. We should also point out that teenagers are often unfair and quite unnuanced: they tend to be very understanding with some people and completely impatient with others. They will put up with all sorts of difficulties in matters they consider important, whereas on other subjects they have a very low threshold.

So we can see that patience is very important – but not so easy to acquire.

Stage one

Is there any kind of activity you can practice in the family which will teach the virtue of patience? Isaak Walton in 1600 describes one such activity: 'It was an employment for his idle time, which was then not idly spent a rest to his mind, a cheerer of his spirits, a divester of sadness, a calmer of inquiet thoughts, a moderator of passions, a procurer of contentedness; and that it begat habits of peace and patience in those that professed and practised it.'

What is he referring to? Fishing. Of course, I am not suggesting that all parents should take their children fishing. However, we can usefully think about fishing in order to notice the kinds of situations which elicit patience and find parallels in our ordinary life.

Fishing is, first of all, an activity which calls for a certain amount of time. And it implies waiting (letting time go by) without doing anything in particular. It means putting up with such things as bad weather, not being able to move, keeping still, and the risk that you won't get a bite. Additionally, your mind isn't allowed to think about other matters – at least to any great degree.

Thus, activities suitable for stimulating patience probably require putting up with some inconveniences in order to obtain what we want, or to avoid even greater inconvenience. Specifically:

- there must be a time gap between what we are doing and what we are aiming at;
- we have to try to control certain passions;
- we have to make an effort to tolerate some physical discomfort or avoid unnecessary movement;
- through the activity we have to seek the value of the self-control it involves.

Motives for being patient

Patience calls for special motivation which comes only from an even temper. In the description at the beginning of the chapter I said that it helps a person bear present difficulties with serenity. Serenity prepares the ground for a meaningful exercise of patience. 'We must try to keep our peace, even if only so as to act intelligently, since the man who remains calm is able to think, to study the pros and cons, to examine judiciously the outcome of the actions he is about to undertake. Only then does he act, calmly and decisively.'[36]

Therefore, if we fall into the temptation of activism it will be difficult to act serenely, and the very activity we are engaged in will make us impatient. 'Serenity of mind is not indifference or insensitivity, it is not isolationism or resistance to change. Serenity means giving pride of place to reason; being vigorous in our conversation; looking at the facts carefully and objectively; it means distinguishing between essential factors and accessory ones, between what is important and what is accessory. Serenity allows one avoid precipitous or nervous or shock reactions, and it smooths the way for prudent, responsible actions; it helps you reach the most equitable solutions.'[37]

Serenity, calmness, is a necessary condition for developing patience, although being patient does not imply that we ought always dominate our passions. Anger can be harmful but it can also be quite in order, and it can be a useful aid to educating children. It must always be controlled, and it is controlled when the angry person is aware that he is angry and tries to continue to stay annoyed, because he has a right purpose, rather than trying to calm down.

We have said that control of the passions via the mind – an even temper – is a pre-condition for becoming a patient person. But what sort of motivation can we have for developing patience? Later we shall take this question of motivation at different ages; now I just want to look at some general points.

Putting up with inconveniences only makes sense in relation to some benefit one expects to result from this effort later on. Otherwise we would be talking about masochism. Therefore motivation comes from thinking that, through making the effort of patience, you will derive some benefit for yourself, for other people or for the honour of God. In fact, these three aspects coincide, although possibly, depending on the situations, each person may be more conscious of who is to be benefitted. Therefore, we can say that the main motive (not necessarily the one we are most conscious of) is conformity with the will of God, who knows better than we do what is good for us. Which is why he allows us have problems, pains, difficulties.

This single final goal, we have said, is translated into partial motives, depending on each person's situation. Thus, a father can be patient with his son in order to rear him better. You can be patient with someone you know by listening to him and trying to understand him, because you realise how anxious he is and you want to make it easier for him. A child can put up with the nuisance of explaining to another child the rules of the game, because he wants them both to have a good time.

As you can see, a purpose is called for if the virtue is to develop. It is important to realise that patience is a virtue which calls for sensitivity. If we don't feel any pain, any joy, if we don't experience everyday triumph and failure, then patience doesn't arise. Insensitivity as we said, is a vice contrary to patience because it leads a person not to concern himself, not to be impressed by the prospect of any good or of any inconvenience.

Patience at different ages: small children

One might think that one way to avoid being impatient is to develop that indifference and hard-heartedness which seems to enable a person to cope with difficulties. But, can you call someone 'patient' who does not feel what he has to bear with? I have already said I don't think you can. We are not trying to neutralise our children's feelings: they form part of their personality. What we must try to do is let them have strong feelings – but train them to control those feelings through their own willpower. Parents should help their children to develop their feelings and, at the same time, get them to be patient; in this way their desire to reach good goals will be a vital factor in their lives – not just an intellectual idea.

The setting for developing this virtue will depend mainly on the warmth and security which surrounds them. If the parents are rather capricious in the demands they make on the children if they react emotionally and unpredictably to what their children do, making a mountain out of a molehill, then the children will feel insecure. The interior peace which the smaller children need is the result of the understanding and affection their parents show them and the demands they make on them. Any and every contact parents have with their children tells them whether they are being rejected or accepted as people. It is vital to all of us to be accepted by the people we admire. That is the only way a small child can learn that it is good to accept certain inconveniences and difficulties. For his parents have told him that it is good to act in this way.

Parents can teach their children to accept the annoyances, inconveniences and difficulties that crop up, and they can encourage them to wait calmly for good things to happen. I stress that it is good for children to have strong feelings, but they have to learn to control them.

In this connection, we might say that there are two kinds of children: those who react intensely to difficulties and will tolerate no waiting, and those who are by character easy-going. The first get angry with their brothers and sisters and can't control themselves; they won't go through a visit to the dentist without shouting and getting 'hysterical', they change activities without finishing anything because it is going to take time and continuous effort to finish it; children who will not wait until the end of the week to get paid, children who are always interrupting and butting in at the wrong minute.

To train a child who has these characteristics you have to make demands on him in a trusting, calm way, trying not to solve problems by giving special rewards and punishments, and letting him see you are pleased when he has made an effort to control himself. You also need to work out what is particularly important to the child, for normally he won't use the same standards as his parents to arrive at the answer. For example, for a six-year-old it may be very important to tell his parents some problem he has: and he may not see why he should wait until they have finished the conversation they are having. In this case, it is surely best to let him speak, realising the importance the matter has for him. But the same would not apply to a ten-year-old: he should know better and wait.

It is also good to teach children that pain and inconvenience are not something to be avoided at all costs. It is not a matter of protecting them from suffering but rather of being beside them to help them see that they can cope with a difficulty by making an effort. Parents will also notice that their children are impatient in some situations and not in others – or that they put up with something hurtful when caused by one person and not when caused by another. It is normal, for example, for a child to accept more readily – though still with a certain amount of displeasure – something done him by his very little brother, but he will get more angry with someone more his own age. This is only natural. In fact, it gives a good opportunity to show the child that he has this tendency and to use him as co-educator of his smaller brothers and sisters, by saying to him for example: 'we have to put up with the younger ones: that way they will learn to do things better.' It is more difficult for children to recognise they can make the same sort of effort at self-control when dealing with children of their own age or older. They will come to realise this later on, when they are able to work things out for themselves.

Children who are indifferent to difficulties are a different problem. They seem to be patient, because they don't react. However, the reason for this is that they are not interested in other people or in their own abilities. In these cases you have to try to get them interested in any activity they can do well; you even have to get them to exaggerate their pleasure in what has been accomplished, wakening them up to a side of life which they have not yet discovered.

For these children, and also for the first group, human contact with the members of their family and also with other people is very educational: in people they discover attitudes and ways of feeling and acting which clash with their own. So they have to make an effort to knit in with others. An example of this is the only child who, since he gets too much attention from his parents (who rather expect him to act in a grown-up sort of way), loses a certain naturalness and cheerfulness. Once you put him into a situation with other children of his own age he changes radically.

Through these contacts children discover their feelings. Generally they come to discover this aspect of their personality in the most natural way – through contact with others – but also through contact with nature. Emotion, feeling, can arise from noticing a combination of colours or of shapes; or from hearing noises like the wind in the trees or the sound of insects; or from eating wild fruit or tasting sea air or smelling hay or letting a stream run through one's fingers. A person who has a contemplative turn of mind can find in nature lots of ways of being 'filled' with interior peace. The stimulus of television, cinema and other forms of technology often disturbs this peace, distracting one's attention from what gives one a feeling of being part of God's creation. And, of course, it is possible to find this peace by entering God's presence, and speaking to him, leaving some moments of the day for directly uniting ourselves to him, through the sacraments and through prayer.

Older children

The best time to stress the virtue of patience is from the age of ten onwards. Prior to this it is a question of creating the right atmosphere, based on a sense of security which comes from children realising that the demands made on them are reasonable and well meant.

Once children are this age we can give them criteria to use, and we can reason with them. It is specially important to maintain the right atmosphere for that interior peace we were speaking about, but now children can understand better why they ought to make the sort of effort we have been suggesting to them or requiring of them. They have to learn readily to accept difficulties and inconveniences and look forward optimistically to obtaining the things they like.

What sort of activities can help them to be patient? If we go back over the suggestions made earlier on we will find lots of possibilities. Some of these activities will be imposed in some way and will be that much more difficult to accept – a long illness, the loss of some prized possession, continuous jeering by some of their companions, realisation of their defects and short comings, or having to make a special effort in study and then failing some exam. What you have to do is complement these situations (where the affection and good arguments offered by parents help the child to overcome his gloominess or his impatience) with agreeable activities which also call for patience.

For example, fishing or acquiring any ability by dint of being patient: playing the guitar or some other instrument, learning a language, learning to typewrite, etc. Other activities could be collecting, aero-modelling, or carrying out some plan for improvement worked out by the child himself. But the kind of patience which most interests us is that which has to do with serving other people.

Being patient with children

Saint Thomas says that patience is that virtue by which present evils (mainly those inflicted by others) are borne in such a way that no supernatural sadness results from them.[38]

Patience is the key to being a good educator – simply because normally an educator cannot see the results of his work in the short term. Or, at least, what he does see in the short term is not the most important result. Also, many difficulties arise in the process of educating and in the way the pupil acts, and the educator has to put up with a great deal in order to reach the desired goal (if indeed he ever does reach it).

For many parents the highest degree of patience they aim at is that of resigning themselves to what happens without complaint or impatience. Of course, they should try to control their desire for immediate results, to have their children behave and develop along preconceived ideas of how a good child should behave. But if we realise that it is a matter of achieving not so much what we want as of using the means available to enable our children to do what God wants, it will be easier to be patient, accepting inconveniences not in a resigned sort of way but peacefully and calmly. This attitude means overcoming that depression or gloominess which seems always to come with mere resignation.[39] To the extent that we realise the value of the difficulty and disappointment our children cause us, we can be really happy in accepting them – to the point, even, where pain and pleasure coincide. 'I have reached the point of not being able to suffer, for all suffering is sweet to me' (St Teresa of Lisieux).

So much for parents' attitude of patience with their children. But in day to day life, should children be able to notice that their parents are being patient with them? Insofar as patience involves acceptance and understanding, yes. Children need to see that their parents are ready to listen to them and be concerned about them. They need to know that their parents want them to be happy. This acceptance presupposes that parents do not make their children think they are an unwanted burden, but rather the genuine, essential object of their love. Nor should we limit ourselves to this; we should teach our children to have the same attitude towards us, their parents, and towards the rest of the family and towards their friends.

However, this does not mean that we should passively be resigned to accept whatever they do or say. Parents have a duty and a right to tell their children if their conduct is good or bad. Therefore, anger, joy and other passions, intelligently controlled, are quite in order: anger expressing itself as justifiable indignation, or joy shown because the child has acted generously towards others, for example.

Each child needs to be treated differently by his parents: more or less affection, more or less time devoted to him, more or fewer demands made on him, etc. But all need an equal amount of understanding. It is the virtue of prudence that 'moves us to be understanding with others, for we are convinced that souls, like good wine, improve with time.[40]

SELF-ASSESSMENT

Briefing Note: see pages 29–30, above.

Am I a patient person?

1. *I make an effort to overcome my present worries and wait calmly for the arrival of better times.* (Life presents us with an endless series of trials and tribulations. For example, a child who takes ages to pass a particular exam, another who is untidy in their bedroom, another who never seems to worry about others. But we educators have to learn to wait for the child to pass the exam, for the time when they eventually do keep their bedrooms tidy or stop being so selfish.)

2. *I know how to put up with, and accept, the consequences of a decision I have made, in the child's best interests.* (It isn't easy to put up with the long face or hostile behaviour of a youngster which is the result of having refused

them something they wanted, because we thought that there could be serious physical or moral danger in it.)

3. *I do all I can not to be indifferent or passive towards negative things in life.* (Sometimes people confuse indifference and patience. The indifferent person does not react. They don't know what is good or bad, or, at any rate, they aren't interested in doing anything about it.)

4. *I distinguish between those things which it is really worth waiting for and those where the effort is not warranted.* (Patience has its limits, as all virtues do. We should not forget that the virtues refer to the golden mean. In some situations it is best to try to change the circumstances or avoid the situation rather than wait for things to change.)

5. *I distinguish between those things which I can reasonably wait for and those where it would not be reasonable to do so.* (Life is not an exercise in developing patience. Patience is not naivety nor is it stubbornness in relation to fictitious situations.)

6. *I usually face up to things serenely, avoiding being too active, in order to see what is important and what is not.* (If one is constantly active, one cannot be patient. That kind of person wants to see results tomorrow and, if that can't be, then they want them the following day.)

7. *I realise that if I am going to wait for the good things to come and put up with the difficulties which arise from accepting a lesser evil in order to avoid a greater, then I shall have to suffer. I accept this suffering serenely.* (Suffering is part of life. It is a question of learning to suffer with a smile on one's face, realising that waiting is worthwhile, or that it is worthwhile putting up with a lesser evil in order to avoid a greater one.)

8. *I know that excessive activity or excessive noise are two ways often used to avoid having to wait or put up with something.* (Patience requires having clear values or goals in one's life. If we don't have them, why wait? But one quite often finds people who avoid the effort of waiting, by increasing their activity or producing noise.)

9. *I do whatever I can to understand others better. And I do this to be able to help them in the best possible way.* (We usually have problems in being patient with people whose personality upsets us, or with the children at a particular moment in their development – for example, when they enter adolescence and it is particularly difficult to understand them.)

10. *I realise that it is important to understand and accept others although we don't notice any improvement in them.* (One of the problems about

patience is that people take a long time changing in important areas. For example, in acquiring a number of human virtues.)

Teaching others to be patient

11. *I normally give a good example of serenity and interior peace.* (Educational and anti-educational contagion is high. If we ourselves are seen to be patient, that will probably influence the children a great deal.)

12. *I insist on the small children learning how to overcome a whim and how to wait for the arrival of something good.* (The main problem with the small children, as regards patience, is that they have little will-power and are likely to be led along by their basic tendencies. They will not understand why they should be patient, but it is useful for them to get used to having to wait for something they want, and having to put up with their whims not being satisfied straightaway.)

13. *I help the children recognise the needs of the people who are closest to them so that they see why they need to be patient.* (It is easier for the small children to understand their grandparents' needs, or a smaller brother or sister's needs, or those of a close friend than those of others in general.)

14. *I am as supportive as I can be to the preadolescents when the situation requires them to be patient and yet their will-power is probably not developed sufficiently to let them live the virtue well.* (Examples of this kind of situation are an illness; when they don't pass an exam; when they lose or break some prized possession.)

15. *I try to introduce the smaller children to interesting activities that require some degree of patience.* (For example, learning to play a musical instrument, using a computer, making collections, modelling.)

16. *I get the teenagers used to being quiet without noise and with little activity.* (Excursions to the sea, the hills or to the countryside can be useful in this regard.)

17. *I help the youngsters to recognise, in each situation, and according to their age and degree of understanding, why patience is needed.* (When we give them information, we should try to be as clear and concise as possible. They will need time to think through the situation.)

18. *I try to introduce the teenagers to activities which require patience in some degree, but that are also attractive.* (These are activities which require a certain sustained effort, which require having to put up with something and in which it is necessary to learn to dominate some passion.)

19. *I encourage the youngsters to have strong passions but controlled by their wills. I try to get them to abhor indifference.* (There are such a large number of negative situations in society today that it is easy to switch off in order to avoid pain.)

20. *I help the youngsters understand more and better the motives for being patient.* (Overall, the most important motives will be to encourage personal improvement and to help others in the same way. And so accept God's will.)

15 Justice

People who are just strive constantly to give others what is their due, so that they can exercise their rights and responsibilities (the right to life, to own property, to political freedom, etc.), as parents, as children, as citizens, as workers, as rulers, etc. – and they also try to see that others do likewise.

Justice presents certain difficulties and certain advantages when it comes to commentary. On the one hand, it is one of the few virtues which might be called fashionable; but for this very reason and also by its very nature, it is one of the most complex of virtues.

This virtue regulates our relationships with God and with others; it ensures that we respect each others' rights and that we fulfil our duties; it calls for simplicity, sincerity and gratitude. In fact, if every member of society had a well-developed virtue of justice, general well-being would be almost at a maximum. Justice also brings peace, although, as Saint Thomas explains, peace is indirectly the result of justice – in that justice removes the obstacles to peace. Peace is the direct result of charity, for that is the virtue which produces union of hearts.[41]

Another problem involved in discussing justice is that it is connected to a whole series of other virtues, each of which is very relevant to educators: obedience, piety (which covers childrens' duties to their parents and to their country), sincerity, friendship, religion, etc. My plan in this chapter is to deal only with justice, and leave the other virtues for later.

A few points about the notion of justice

In order not to confuse justice with other virtues, it is useful to bear in mind three aspects which are present in every just act: 'otherness', strict right, equality.

Otherness: Justice is done only in respect to other persons. A child could break another child's toy, and that would be a fault in justice if he failed to remedy the situation by buying another toy or fixing the broken one, for example. But if the child breaks his own toy, no injustice has occurred. Perhaps a fault against poverty is involved.

Strict right: This means that justice has to do not with a gift but with something which one owes. For this very reason, justice is a function of an individual's capacity to recognise that he owes a debt. And we can see that, if it has to do with paying exactly what is owed, being just can be very 'tough' on people. Therefore, in considering the virtue of justice we must not forget always to keep charity close by.

Equality: This refers to perfect parity between what is owed and what is given. For an act to be just there should be neither more nor less.

It is also good to realise that an act of justice involves three structures:

- relationships between individuals
- relationships between society and its individual members
- relationships of individuals with society.

These three structures are usually called commutative justice, distributive justice, and legal justice, respectively.

We should bear in mind that being a just person, being just, is not a matter of acting in a just way in isolated events: It is the habit of constantly acting in accordance with the rules of justice. It is also good to remember that this virtue has to do with one's will, not with one's mind. Justice does not govern intellectual acts (as prudence does); it aims at making one's actions right.

Children's relationship with others

To consider which aspects of justice should be tackled, we have to keep in mind certain characteristics of children, their age, mental development and the character of their relationships with others.

When you look at children at different ages, the stage when unjust acts are most obvious is that of the youngest children. This is easy to explain, because they make no attempt to hide these actions – simply because they don't regard them as wrong. A small child can want something belonging to someone else and just because he wants it he feels entitled to take it. But once a child has reached the use of reason and has a clearer idea of what is reasonable in this connection, when he does something unjust he prefers to hide it or else tries to justify himself in some way.

Following Paiget's studies of the development of children's concept of justice, it seems that the most important norm for a child of seven or eight is what his parents tell him. From that age onwards, he steadily discovers the need to treat everyone equally, and only from the age of eleven does he begin to realise that the really just thing is not to treat people equally but rather equitably, in accordance with each person's responsibility and his circumstances. All this might suggest that the parents' role should be different depending on the child's concept of justice.

As we have said before, you cannot have justice unless the individual recognises what is owing. Nor can you have a just action unless, once the need to give a person his due is recognised, the individual acts in a way suited to the particular situation: this means that he has to apply his intelligence and will properly.

Justice up to the age of nine

A small child can find it difficult to consciously act in a just way, but he can learn, with the help of his parents and the older children, what is 'not right', what is unjust. This he learns initially in relation to children of his own sort of age and with his companions and friends. This is the time to insist on the rules of the game. The parents should start the process; later will come the rules imposed by the group. In fact, every parent must have noticed how small children frequently appeal to their parents to solve justice problems which arise in games. But, from the age of nine or ten, more or less, children argue about rules among themselves and only go to the parents when something happens which they cannot themselves control. Sometimes, indeed, they prefer to stop the game rather than accept recourse to parents.

All this could lead us to think that up to eight or nine the best approach to teaching justice is to emphasise certain rules of the game and at the same time point out what is unjust. You don't do this by having a deep understanding of children's motives but rather by helping them to acquire habits by being affectionate, understanding and demanding. Specifically, parents could think along the lines of these objectives:

- learning to establish an agreement with a brother or sister or friend and then keeping this promise
- accepting the rules of a game, once these have been made clear
- telling the truth, to the extent that they grasp it
- respecting other people's property: not stealing, not breaking things etc.
- respecting certain needs and rights of others: the rooms of the other members of the family, keeping quiet during study time, respecting privacy (knocking on the door before entering, not interrupting a conversation).

All these things prepare for the time when they begin to realise that rights and duties do exist. And in a way this is the problem they will experience throughout the rest of their lives. That person is most just who appreciates which are the rights and which are the duties he himself has and others have, in accord with their situation as members of the same family, as parents, as citizens, as people in the same society, etc.

This can give us a framework to discuss the development of this virtue in the case of children who have more use of reason and more will of their own.

From nine to thirteen

Earlier I referred to that point in a child's life when he claims he should be treated like everyone else. He does not realise that each person should be treated in accordance with his particular position; he fails therefore to distinguish between egalitarianism and justice. We will see the results of this attitude when we look at how parents exercise justice. A child's grasp of what is just comes, at least in part, from having learned to keep the rules of the game in the various activities he shares with his brothers, sisters and friends. Only little by little can he realise that these rules, and moral principles in general, are – to put it pragmatically – measures to allow equals to get on together. Justice then takes on a new meaning for the child. It allows and promotes harmony in one's relations with others. It leads to order and a certain well-being. He also realises what injustice is through his feeling of 'rebellion' when unjust situations arise; he realises that the accepted order has been destroyed.

However, the problems keep occurring: the children want to be just but they don't know what being just implies. You might think therefore that justice is a virtue which can only be practised when a person is older. But that's not the case. An understanding of what is just will direct a just act in the right way. In order to be just, a person needs to have acquired the habit of acting in a just way, even though the criteria he uses may be wrong. This indeed is the very reason why the virtue of obedience is so important.

Through obedience to their parents, children act justly and learn to be just towards their brothers, sisters and friends. If they don't get this training the whole process will be much more difficult.

From what we have said, it would appear that parents' attention to their children during this second stage should be centred on four aspects:

- Keeping on insisting that they do just things and explaining to them what is unjust.
- Helping them to understand and practise better the grounds for being just.
- Making clear to them the difference between the circumstances of different people.
- Teaching them to control themselves and make up for their mistakes in this area.

You will notice that points (1) and (4) have to do with the will; point (3) with the intellect; and (2) with will and intellect.

Let us just look at the points connected with the will. What kinds of acts of justice could young people of 10 to 13 or 14 carry out? Obviously we can repeat the list of suggestions made for younger children, but we can add on others. For example:

- helping them to think about the best thing to do, if someone has been unjust to them. (A classical writer says: 'Three things there are which are especially difficult: keeping a secret, bearing the outrage of injustice, and making good use of the time available for leisure'.[42] In these cases the most just thing to do may be to report the injustice you have suffered to a person who is competent to get the problem sorted out; to try to get the person who has acted unjustly to make up for it; to take steps to get your own back; or, even to forgive him – because he needs to be forgiven. One way or another, you have to try to avoid any act of revenge, that is, replying by means of another unjust act, because in the last analysis, by acting unjustly it is yourself you damage most.
- speaking of others with respect, looking on the positive side of things. Showing the lack of justice involved in the action of secretly defaming a person to a friend of his, an action which is an especially serious act of injustice, because no one can live without friendship'[43]
- returning something lent in the same condition as you got it
- making them see the opportunities others have to do some good act, so that they can help them to act in a responsible way
- obeying the express orders of their parents and other people in authority
- being very careful not to commit small acts of injustice which may seem unimportant but which can create an environment in which it is difficult to do positively good acts (taking a bus ride without paying for the ticket, getting into the cinema when one is under age, telling 'fibs' in order to avoid making some effort, etc).

As far as apologising is concerned – this is a way of making amends for being unjust – obviously the virtue of prudence should come into play here, to ensure that this does not happen too frequently. And when it does happen you have to try to teach children to ask for forgiveness and to make reparation. Some children will find it easier to ask for forgiveness than to make reparation; with others the opposite is the case. Parents' example is basic, but they should also try to show the child the reasons for making this important effort.

The reasons for being just

It would appear that from a very early age a child is aware of something we might call justice, even though he doesn't understand it completely. Piaget explains how children from seven to nine years of age believe in what he calls 'immanent justice': that is to say, the justice which arises from the very act one commits. Piaget, in fact, told a story to a large number of boys and girls of different ages. The story tells how a boy stole an apple and, on his way home, he fell into a stream because a little bridge broke under him. The great majority of the children under nine saw this as a direct result of his having stolen the apple. But his percentage kept going down the older the group was. This sense of justice suggests that in some way the small child recognises that it is good there is a certain order in things and the main reason we can offer children for being just is by way of recognising what this proper order is in each situation and why it is right.

But, as we said before, explanations are not enough. They also need the affectionate help of their parents; sometimes parents have to be demanding; sometimes more affection needs to be shown them. When a child recognises that the just act makes sense, it is possible to get him to do it just out of fear of his parents but later he will do it because he knows it is his duty or because he genuinely wants to do it, realising that it is for others' good.

Taking account of each person's circumstances

We mentioned earlier when a child reaches the age of about eleven he may begin to recognise that justice means necessarily treating each person a different way. But until he is thirteen or fourteen it is quite possible that he will not make much progress at this, but it is good to begin to take steps so that children can, as they begin to understand things better, perform genuinely just acts, as far as possible.

At the ages we are considering, it is a matter, above all, of helping children to realise that we are all different and this implies that they have to learn to be more sensitive. A person does not simply do things: he also has a soul of his own, his own emotions, his own thoughts. So it does not make sense to act towards every person in the same way: that would work only if people were machines.

Therefore, you have to try to help children to distinguish between:

- brothers and sisters of different ages,
- brothers and sisters with different needs (to be helped in some way, to be asked for something specific, etc.)
- various people depending on the way they are feeling. A just act can be done at the right time or at the wrong time etc.

Older children

Up to now we have been concentrating on justice in the context of the family and therefore we have looked at activities as a function of the people who live in that group. We can take it that the child's will is now strong enough to allow him to act justly in other contexts, now that he can appreciate these better.

We must also remember that adolescents, by their very nature, tend to be very idealistic; they look for grand solutions to 'important' problems, and they are more concerned with justice as an ideal than as a series of actions towards one's neighbour.

The adolescent has to be shown what his duty is in his role as a brother, a companion, a citizen, so that he can establish a direct link between his legitimate concern and his everyday activity. It is no longer a matter of getting the child to behave in one way or in another but rather of helping him to understand what is just in every situation.

Following on Piaget's surveys, a number of psychologists have looked at the concept of justice and morality among children and young people. In a recent study Rest suggests six stages in the development of the child's ability to make moral judgements. The last two stages are reached only when he is around the age of twenty, so we won't go into those here. The first stage is one in which the child learns as a result of being obedient to adults. This changes, in the second stage, into a realisation that it makes sense to establish agreements with others; that there can exist a duty and a moral debt on both sides. But this is at the level of mere exchange. Then he goes on to recognise that in order to live in harmony with others one has to act justly towards them: this leads to having a basic plan for co-operating with others. In the fourth stage the individual recognises law and his duty to society at large. No ages are ascribed to these stages, but the fourth one coincides with adolescence.

These studies support the view that in adolescence it is good to teach children what law is – not just civil law but also natural law. Children need to have criteria which will help them take up a position in regard to the countless problems of justice which arise in everyday life.

Parents' justice

Perhaps one of the things a parent is most in doubt about is whether he or she has acted justly towards the children. The Romans used to represent justice as a blindfolded woman trying to balance scales. It is true that we parents should try to be as objective as possible in our dealings with our children. However, it can be extremely difficult at times, for parents and for children, to act justly. Which is why everything they do should be done with affection. The parents' role is one which can be put under the heading of 'distributive justice'. And 'acting rightly' means that we have to try to overcome any kind of special sympathy or antipathy we have towards particular children. Each child is different and needs to be treated differently, but this has to be harmonized with general rules which apply across the whole family.

These rules for the family as a whole must be made in line with basic standards connected with:

- the right to be respected by others
- the right to help others reach human and supernatural fulfilment
- the right to play one's part in keeping with one's ability
- the right to live in harmony with others, according to a certain order

Obviously, these rights are balanced by corresponding duties. But the way each right and duty is interpreted can be different, depending on each member's character and circumstances. It is a question, therefore; of orientating each child's activity with a great deal of flexibility.

When children don't do what they ought, we come up against the question of punishment. It is silly to say that one is for or against rewards and punishments, because in fact we are imposing sanctions on other people all the time, smiling at them, listening to them (positive sanctions) or reading a newspaper and not listening, or looking at one's watch when one of the children is telling us something which to him is important (negative sanctions). What we should be trying to do is ensure that the sanctions we impose fit the situation, that they help the child to improve. Children, whether young or old, expect their parents to be just to them, and this applies also when it comes to rewards and punishments.

A small child usually volunteers that a severe punishment should be given if someone has broken some rule. And this idea only changes to the extent that the direct control and demands coming from the parents begin to be seen in terms of mutual co-operation among all the members of the family. At this point the child discovers that the best punishment is reparation in some form (if he has broken a window you do not punish him by not letting him watch television for a week but by insisting that he should pay for a new window, for example, or put the window in). This is a case of the 'punishment' fitting the 'crime' exactly.

Finally, parents also have to learn to rectify. It is not easy to be just, especially when we don't have all the relevant data or when we are not fully in control of our reactions.

Final remarks

We are trying to see that our children acquire the virtue of justice not only so that they will act well at home and with their friends but also as responsible citizens. In this connection we should bear in mind that 'automatic criticism, blind censure, without weighing pros and cons, is an act of injustice, an attack on distributive justice, which is the only virtue that allows states to operate.

What we are trying to develop is the desire to be just, an appreciation of what is the just thing to do in each situation, realising that sacred scripture speaks more than 800 times about justice and 'the just man', which means the 'good person', the 'saint'.

SELF-ASSESSMENT

Briefing Note: see pages 29-30, above.

Am I a just person?

1. *I am conscious of the rights of the people around me.* (Justice is based on the people's rights and duties. Each needs to receive what is their due: spouse, child, student, teacher, parent, local authority, etc.)

2. *I try to understand each situation objectively in order to act justly in each case.* (Justice does not mean always acting the same way in the same circumstances; each person is different.)

3. *Although I know what I am entitled to, I am prepared, in charity, to let it all pass, for the sake of others.* (Family life, in particular, would be very, very tough if parents always acted according to the tenets of justice. Affection and love are also needed.)

4. *I recognise my spouse's rights.* (Apart from the conjugal obligation, each spouse has the right to be given help to improve all through life.)

5. *I recognise the rights of other members of the family.* (For example, the right to privacy, the right to participate, the right to receive help to improve.)

6. *I recognise and respect other people's rights at work, in the city where I live or in my country.* (Other virtues come in here, such as honesty, loyalty or patriotism.)

7. *I recognise the commitment I have acquired towards my friends. I realise that we have made an agreement and I have to keep my side of it.* (I have a duty to my friends. I have acquired the commitment to help them improve all through life and to learn from them.)

8. *I am sufficiently aware of what rights I should respect, especially those related to natural law.* (In this field there are absolute, basic principles like the right to life, the right to a job and to a home, and the right to acquire and own goods.)

9. *I keep my promises, and uphold commitments I have acquired.* (Although there are such things as solemn commitments or formal agreements with papers and witnesses, we should not underestimate the value of giving one's word.)

10. *I understand that opposing, criticising, or censuring others on the basis of little or no information is a lack of justice in itself.* (People have the right to know the truth and also the right to their good name.)

Teaching others to be just

11. *I teach the small children to come to an agreement with a brother or a friend and then keep it.* (Before beginning to understand what natural law is, or what other people's rights are, the child can learn to carry out actions related to justice through making agreements.)
12. *I teach the smaller children to keep the established rules.* (Although rules are established on the basis that everyone should be treated in the same way – that is egalitarianism – small children should learn to keep the rules because living together with others requires it.)
13. *I teach the children to respect other people's property – not stealing, or breaking things or making a mess.* (When the children are small, they do not have an abstract notion of justice. Therefore they will behave in a just way only if educators insist that they do.)
14. *I help the children recognise the needs and rights of others.* (Respecting times when other people want silence; not interrupting; knocking on the door before entering.)
15. *I reason more with the children between the ages of 9 and 13 so that they begin to understand what is just, and what is not, in different circumstances.* (Children of this age are very centred on the rules of the game as the way of living justice. All the same, they can begin to understand some situations involving true justice.)
16. *I give them information to help them understand some motives for being just with others.* (For example, information about the sort of behaviour expected of students if they are to show respect for their teacher, or about how to show respect for their parents.)
17. *I reason with the youngsters to help them see that justice means making amends.* (It is not just a question of saying 'I'm sorry' but of realising the damage one has done the other person.)
18. *I get the youngsters to commit themselves to some teamwork and then insist on each doing his/her job.* (Teamwork is an excellent way to show the need to carry out one's duties, in relation to agreements or commitments.)
19. *I get the youngsters to create the rules for living together in the family or at school.* (If the youngsters have had the opportunity to participate in setting up the rules, they will understand them better and will be better motivated to keep them.)
20. *I teach the youngsters aspects of civil law which affect them, so that they can act in a responsible way. I also teach them what natural law is.* (They need this information. If we don't give it to them, it is unlikely they will find it elsewhere.)

16 Obedience

Obedient people accept as their own instructions which come from authority, provided they do not go against justice, and they act promptly to comply with them, striving faithfully to interpret the will of the person in authority.

It is interesting to speculate on why the virtue of justice is so fashionable whereas obedience (a potential part of justice) is out of fashion. Obedience awakes in some people the uncomfortable feeling that their own will is going to be controlled by someone else. They think that obeying the very opposite of freedom, initiative and creativity. And it is precisely because they entertain doubts about the justification for obedience that some parents let their children do whatever they like.

But obedience, understood as a virtue, is not the blind submission of a slave. In fact, if someone were to obey on the outside but be rebellious on the inside there would be no virtue there. The virtue in obeying exists when one does something because one recognises the authority of the person who issues the commands.

It may well be, therefore, that the main reason why this virtue is so poorly regarded – at least by older children – is that they question the very need for 'authorities' of any kind. It would be simple to conclude that this is a clear example of uncontrolled pride, but I think that we need to study some of the features of the society in which we live in order to understand better the true meaning of obedience.

The permissive society

In a society where all the basic material needs of people are catered for – food, shelter, clothing – most people at least have a certain sense of security which allows them to question whether they will subscribe to the existing structures governing relationships with others. It all depends on the standard of living: if it goes up one tolerates the government, if it goes down one is against it. If things are not to one's satisfaction, one seeks to change either the government or the structure of society. He very rarely realises that the solution lies with himself (provided public authority is acting in accord with justice): if he acts more responsibly, working harder or working better, he will obtain just what he wants and all this refers to a sphere in which he recognises the value of what he is looking for – a better standard of living.

But if the person does not realise that other things exist which are also worthwhile (I mean non-material values), he does not even pose the question and, logically, public authorities in these spheres cease to have any relevance and obedience ceases to make any sense. For example, if a person ceases to take any interest in truth and does not believe that the Church is the depository of truth, what sense does it make to obey the indications of the Pope? If one is not seeking more order, more justice, more goodness, why obey the philosophers? In the past, philosophers played a very important role in solving the problems of societies, but now their role is in a state of crisis. If a person does not regard as important, if he does not understand, what love and service are, what reason can he have to obey his parents, who are people delegated by God to educate their children in love?

When permanent values – which are all partial reflections of the Supreme Good – cease to be of interest to people, then public authorities, whose function it is to help people to discover these values and apply them, find that they have to convince others of the values involved. And that is not easy to do.

The permissive society is a society in which the only value is material well-being – pleasure centred on the present. Neither the past nor the future has any relevance. And therefore the best thing a person can do is blindly follow his instincts.

Obedience, then, only has meaning in relation to the values one accepts in one's own life. There are lots of examples. Young people who refuse to obey their parents as to the kind of clothes they wear – but they obey the fashion of their own little set, because for them the most important value is 'to be like everyone else'. Young people who operate in a completely untidy way in everyday things but then, in the area of sport, obey their trainer. Others reject civil authority but they accept the orders of leaders of street demonstrations. What is the problem? Is it that young people don't obey, or is it that they obey 'authorities' who represent counter-values or very poor values?

The moral is quite clear. We parents should seek the development of our children in the virtue of obedience in relation to the values which we consider important in life. If these values are poor ones, then probably the demands parents make will not produce this virtue in their children, because they will do these things for motives other than respect for their parents. Children who do not learn to recognise the value of obedience when they are young, will find it more difficult to discover it later on and to acquire the habit of obedience.

I should clarify one more point: obedience is not a virtue designed for small children, it is not meant to make life easier for parents. It is a virtue – like all virtues – for one's whole life.

Motives for being obedient

We can distinguish deep motives which parents ought to recognise so that they can go on to explain them to their children, and partial motives which small children and young people need for acquiring the habit of obeying as they make their way to a full appreciation of what obedience is.

As a Christian virtue, obeying lawful authority is like obeying God. And there is no higher motive than that for doing what one is told. This motive provides the certainty that, by obeying, we ensure we do not make mistakes. The person who gives the order can make a mistake; but the person who obeys cannot, provided he does not do something which goes against justice.

Obedience is also the source of true freedom. Attachment to one's own will makes one a slave. We know that the will, by its very nature, tends towards the good, but very often the intellect does not recognise where good really lies. Very often we have to have recourse to competent authorities to check whether what we want and what is really good are one and the same thing. Obedience, in these situations, helps give us strength and perseverance in reaching out for the goals we set ourselves in life. The motives available for obeying are then, quite profound – you do not come across them every day, especially not in young children. However, if we parents fail to keep them very much in mind, there is a danger that we expect our children to be obedient for very poor motives.

What sort of motivation could we suggest to small children for being obedient and what is the best way to instill this motivation? A small child can obey because he intuitively recognises his parents' authority. They give him security, affection, and a sense of well-being, and all this leads him to do what his parents want, even though he feels also inclined to disobey in order to test his own strength and his scope and ability to act independently. Unconsciously he recognises that he has a will of his own – and this causes the 'no' stage. After the age of three or four, a child starts developing his own will – much to the annoyance of his parents. If previously Daddy was 'all-wise', now Daddy is not quite so 'all-wise', and the child begins to want his parents to convince him before he obeys. He understands the need for the rules of the game and, once he knows what these rules are, it is easier to get him to do what he is told, because he realises that a certain amount of organisation is necessary to make life run smoothly. From the age of five his motivation to obey starts to change. At first he can obey with the sort of motivation which allows his obedience to be a virtue: he obeys because of his parents' authority. Even though this authority is never lost, parents need to use other complementary methods in order to get him to obey because of their authority but now understanding the process better.

From five onwards parents need to make explicit demands on their children and give reasons for those demands, so that the child obeys because he sees it is reasonable to do so. He can also obey out of affection for his parents, knowing that his obedience is a way of showing that affection. When we come to dealing with problems particular to this age level we will go into this in more detail.

From the age of thirteen or thereabouts, it is good for obedience to be the result of a thoughtful attitude. And the motivation for obeying should be consistent with the values which the young person is beginning to apply more consciously in his life.

One small clarification at this point: we have been speaking about the obedience-authority relationships between parents and children. This relationship, strictly speaking, is not governed by the virtue of obedience but by the virtue of *piety* which requires that we should give due honour and service to our parents. It does not matter if here we combine these two virtues. However, knowing this distinction can help us recognise the importance of helping children to learn to obey authorities outside the home (which is the specific area of obedience). It follows therefore that well-used authority of parents should be responded to by children's obedience-out-of-love, and on the other hand that the authority conferred on other people be complemented by obedience deriving from justice.

In both cases it is a question of aiming at an obedience which is a function of someone else's authority – not only because he possesses that authority (it has been conferred on him) but also because he exercises it.

Obedience up to the age of thirteen

Up to the age of thirteen, approximately, lack of obedience does not give rise to serious problems: it is more a nuisance and source of exasperation to the parents. Often disobedience results in physical danger rather than moral danger. (For example, a child who disobeys an instruction not to play in a particular place because it is dangerous, and then disobeys and breaks an arm.)

Yet this is the best time for teaching children to obey for high motives, the aim being to have them acquire the habit of obedience before they reach adolescence. So, it is not a matter of just getting children to obey: they have to obey well. We shall look at this more closely, examining some typical faults.

It is easy for parents to rest content with a more or less blind obedience on the grounds that this produces the desired results – peace and order. But we fail to realise that 'there is danger of mere involuntary collaboration whenever demands are made without appealing to the individual's conscience'. It is not enough for the child to do what we order him to do; and certainly it does not produce the virtue of obedience.

Let us look at some of the more common faults in the way children obey, and then suggest some criteria which parents might use.

Problems like these:

- where children obey out of routine, just doing the physical thing, but not trying to do it well or paying attention to the real aims of the person giving the instruction;
- where children focus on the minimum necessary to justify obedience, instead of obeying generously, even to the point of doing more than they are asked;
- where they obey, yet criticise the person who gives the order;
- where they dodge in order not to have to obey or are deceptive, offering false excuses, sometimes by appealing to some other authority ('Mummy said I didn't need to do it');
- where they try to convince the person in charge to let them do something else instead, or try to convince him that they really don't need to do what they have been told to do;
- where they do it, thinking that they will get credit for it, credit which they will then try to trade on;
- where they say that they are going to do it and then they don't;
- where they look for the backing of other children to form an 'opposition' group.

How should parents approach problems like these?

What parents should do

Obedience is made easier if parents are consistent in the way they elicit it. If they act now one way, now another, depending on their mood, so that one day they demand one thing and the next day something different, it is quite likely that their children will not develop the virtue of obedience. Otto Dur's view is that 'any lack of unanimity in educational approach, any lack of unity in what one is aiming at and how one goes about it, kills the seeds of obedience'.[47] It is true that unity is important but we must also remember that we are only human and we cannot expect always to act in a completely uniform, consistent way. In any event, the important thing is to make a real effort oneself to live those values which one regards as important and to make sure that the children recognise these values very clearly.

This means, in practice, that you have to elicit obedience in fewer things than one might expect. If we want our children to obey so that they grow in quality and avoid what is evil, we should not waste time in looking for superfluous obedience or obedience in areas where really the child runs no great risk: that is, we should not look for obedience in regard to things which annoy us, because we don't like the way the children do them but which are really a matter of opinion.

But on fundamental matters, we need to let the child know exactly what we want him to do; we should make sure that he has grasped it all, and then we should tell him to do the thing, spelling out when and perhaps *how* he should do it.

But we have said that we have no interest in blind obedience, minimal obedience. In this connection it is good to count on the help of one's partner and of the older children, or relatives, to get the idea across to the child that he should try to do more than the minimum required of him, whether the command be expressly or tacitly given.

This brings us to the three classic degrees of obedience:

- simple external compliance
- internal submission of the will
- full submission of one's own judgement.

Training in obedience also calls for powers of observation and for sensitivity on the part of parents, because many factors can contribute to a child's having a rebellious, disobedient attitude.

In the case of small children, if you give them clear information at the right time and then make demands in an affectionate way and follow them up, in a general, orderly atmosphere the results are usually positive. But from this age up to thirteen or fourteen you often get a recurrence of the 'no' stage typical of the three- or four-year-old.

There are all sorts of reasons for this. For example, excessive insistence by parents on things of secondary importance; nervousness on parents' part; misuse of threats and empty promises; and also a scries of factors on the child's side. It is worth while thinking about the connection there might be between, for example, a lack of purity and disobedience, and an injustice and obedience (the child who has copied in an exam). If children feel that all is not well in their conscience they are ill at ease and they may show this by disobeying.

All of us parents have to keep an eye on the little ways in which our children act, mainly to know how things are going. We have to show that we are aware of the sort of difficulties in obedience which we have mentioned above, and we have to then give them support and show our confidence in them.

Once children realise that they have to grasp and fulfil what their parents want, even though they may not have made explicit demands, the right time has come to show them an affection and gratitude. We have a right to be obeyed, yes, but children will be keener to obey if they know that we appreciate the effort they are making.

Obedience in the case of older children

Up to now we have been concentrating on obedience to parents, because in that relationship (together with relationships with teachers) there is a better chance of getting them to develop the good operative habit of obedience. But we should not forget the obedience children owe to other authorities. At the earlier ages they usually obey these other authorities because their parents and teachers have told them that is what they should do. They will learn to obey the team captain, the babysitter, a traffic policeman. And they learn to obey God through a well-trained conscience.

When adolescence is reached, they may begin to question the need to keep on obeying these authorities, and, sometimes, they may begin to obey other people, whether consciously or not.

In our initial definition of obedience we said that it consisted in accepting as one's own decisions those which come from whoever holds and exercises authority provided they do not go against justice. This means recognising the real authority of particular people, being able to distinguish between what is just and what is unjust, and being able to make one's own decisions made by others. The ability to make one's own other peoples' decisions is dependent on previous development of the habit, on recognition of the other person as someone with authority and on recognition of the command or indication as something just and reasonable.

It is good to stress these factors during adolescence. The first problem has to do with the ability to distinguish between:

- people who have authority and who exercise it
- people who have authority and who do not exercise it
- people who have received no authority but who are very capable of exercising influence.

Parents have received authority from God to educate their children, and it should be exercised. Parental authority should be 'a positive influence which supports and increases each child's autonomy and responsibility; this authority is a service to children as they go through the educational process, a service which implies power to make decisions and sanctions; it is a form of help which consists in directing the way children play their part in family life and in orientating their growing autonomy, making them responsible people; it is an essential component of their love for their children which expresses itself in different ways depending on the situation, in the parents-children relationship'. To the extent that we fail to exercise authority in a reasonable way it is likely that the children will think that there is no need to obey either us or any other authority.

We can help our children to recognise those persons who have authority conferred on them: authority in the Church, authority in civil life, in social life and in cultural life. A person is given real authority in order to guard and strengthen good values in others. In so far as the values which he tries to transmit are impoverished or equivocal, or if there is an inconsistency between what he says and what he does, his positive influence on young people will be that much less. (For example, authorities who preach peace but practise unjustified war.)

This brings us to the greatest difficulty: that children accept the authority of other people not for the validity of the values they foster but because of their capacity to influence others. This ability to influence others may be described in this way: 'without having received any authority, a person can manage to enthuse and move others to action, by means of his presence, his words, his organizational ability, and can keep them obeying him until he obtains what he wants'.[49] It could be someone who plays on the instincts of others, on their passions; who convinces them with half-truths or falsehood well presented. It could be someone, in other words, who manipulates others.

What resources do we educators have to cope with all these difficulties? I think it is a matter of getting children to obey on one basic thing: that they think before they act. The development of the virtue of prudence and a series of abilities (especially the ability to exercise critical judgement) is what best equips young people to distinguish between what is true and what is false, between good and evil, between authority which ought to be obeyed and a manipulator who seeks ends other than their personal improvement.

Obedience is a potential part of the virtue of justice. It is important that people see it from that angle. One has to reason with children so they see that they ought to obey because their parents and other authorities have the right to be obeyed. Then they will be able to obey out of love and out of a deep sense of duty.

SELF-ASSESSMENT

Briefing Note: see pages 29–30, above.

Am I obedient?

1. *I realise that authorities are necessary in life and that therefore it is also necessary to obey all through life too.* (This will become clear if we realise that we should obey in all those things in which we ourselves are not authorities.)

2. *I accept the decisions that authorities over me make, as long as they don't go against justice.* (Obedience is relational. If I recognise that there is a person who has a special mission to defend and protect some value which I cherish, the best thing I can do is obey – at work, in an association, in the parish.)

3. *I try to interpret the real will of the person who has given me orders.* (Real obedience is not just a question of carrying out the letter of the law but rather of interpreting what has been ordered so as to carry it out the best possible way.)

4. *When I receive an order, I try to carry it out straightaway without looking for excuses to put it off.* (It is easy to find excuses to put off things that are probably going to require a special effort or that are not very enjoyable. We should try to detect those moments when we have the tendency to deceive ourselves.)

5. *I try to do what authorities order, accepting the order fully as part of myself.* (To obey outwardly, but resist inwardly, is a very strange sort of obedience.)

6. *I try to obey all those people who have authority over me.* (It is easy to end up obeying only those people whom we get on particularly well.)

7. *I understand that people who hold authority in things to do with skills etc., lose that authority if they become incompetent.* (It would be ridiculous to obey a driving teacher who drove badly or obey a climbing instructor who didn't take safety precautions.)

8. *I try to think through the immaterial values that I want to live, and I look for an authority, as regards those values, who can help me along.* (We always need to have some competent person to help us lead our lives of faith. And the same holds for cultural or social development.)

9. *I recognise that almost the only value in the permissive society is material well-being, And that for this reason, other values tend to be ridiculed.* (This is probably why the virtue of obedience receives so little attention at the present time.)

10. *I understand that obeying lawful authority is almost the same thing as obeying God as long as it does not mean going against truth or justice.* (Obeying authorities is largely a function of knowing where true authority lies.)

Teaching others to be obedient

11. *I manage to get the small children to obey because I give orders in the right way.* (When the children are small, we should order one thing at a time. As they grow, we shall have to give them more reasons for the order.)

12. *I teach the children to recognise the different authorities they should obey.* (There are various kinds of authorities. For example, parents, teachers, policemen, traffic wardens, an elder brother when the parents are away.)

13. *I try to give the clearest sort of information to the small children so they know exactly what they've got to do.* (Among the many causes for disobedience, one of the most frequent is that the children really don't know what we want. It is a question of giving clear, concise information, and ordering one thing at a time.)

14. *When the children reach the age of ten, I try to explain to them some of the reasons there are for obeying in different situations.* (We need to avoid eliciting a blind, routine obedience that gives no thought to the authority's real intentions.)

15. *I reason with the teenagers to help them learn not to look for excuses or put the blame on others when they have not obeyed.* (We should realise that a lot of the things we ask the adolescents to do are not particularly agreeable and that it may take quite an effort for them to obey. Tidying the bedroom may seem important to the parent, but the child may consider it irrelevant.)

16. *I explain to the youngsters that saying that one is going to do something and then not doing it goes against the virtue of justice.* (This action is especially negative, as it involves two mistakes. First, not obeying; second, changing the situation so that it is probably too late to find another solution.)

17. *I explain to the youngsters what personal responsibility means - and that if they aren't going to do what they should, they should tell the person responsible.* (More than anything, we don't want the youngsters to start forming 'pressure groups' in order to defend themselves against authority.)

18. *I help the youngsters recognise the people they are in fact obeying.* (Although some youngsters think that obedience goes against their freedom, they will find that they are always obeying someone. For example, the coach, the group, the leader of some protest.)

19. *I try to insist on what is most important for each age group without getting involved in too many details.* (To begin with, one should probably look for obedience in those things where physical or moral danger may arise.)

20. *If I have to use punishment at some stage, I try to make sure that there will be positive educational results.* (For example, physical punishment is usually interpreted by the child as vengeance, as are punishments such as 'two weeks without going out' or 'three days with no television', or 'I'll stop your allowance'. Most of the time, it is better to explain, or insist firmly. We should avoid physical or psychological violence.)

17 Prudence

In work and in dealings with other people, prudent people assess situations in the light of right standards: they weigh the favourable and unfavourable consequences for themselves and others prior to taking a decision, and then they act or refrain from acting, in keeping with the decisions they have made.

When looking at other virtues we saw that it is essential to understand what they mean in order then to act in a rational way when training children to acquire these virtues. At first, the way to teach a virtue may not seem very clear, but after taking a good long look at it one finds all kinds of ways to encourage its development. It can also happen that some parents who seek their children's good and know what they are about fail to recognise the danger involved in stressing one virtue to the neglect of another. Or they may not take special account of the characteristics, qualities and potential of each individual child. The virtue of prudence comes to their aid; it equips them to consider the matter carefully before deciding what to do in each situation, in keeping with right standards. We parents need the virtue of prudence 'in order to be just, in order to live charity, and to give good service to God and to all our fellowmen. Not without good reason prudence has been called *genitrix virtutum*, the mother of virtues,[50] and also *auriga virtutum*,[51] the guide of every good habit'.[52]

Obviously this virtue has nothing to do with not committing oneself in case something goes wrong, yet there are people who propose no kind of ultimate purpose to themselves as they go about living and who spend their time 'protecting themselves' from being responsible for their own lives. Negligence is a vice which goes against the virtue of prudence – just as imprudence is. We will look later at the difficulties involved in developing this virtue, but first I want to stress how important this virtue is for parents themselves.

Prudence and parents themselves

One of the great difficulties parents meet is the fact that family life is something continuously active. This activity does not make for thought and reflection: parents have a strong tendency to react to all the new situations which constantly arise, rather than face them calmly and so be able to make the right decisions. It is quite possible for parents over quite a long period not to take any decisions which could be called 'important'. And yet, they do take a whole series of little decisions, which should really all fit in with standards which they have assimilated over a long period. It can happen that some of these decisions do not in fact fit in with the values they want to incorporate into their family life – simply because they were not well-thought-out decisions. It is also possible for parents to operate towards their children in a 'technically' very effective way but with petty, impoverished, even selfish, motives.

The virtue of prudence 'is both intellectual and orientated towards action: it grasps the essence of a situation and then 'guides' one's will and action'.[53]

So, parents who develop this virtue are better able to see clearly what they are aiming at and then discover the best ways to achieve this aim.

One of the problems related to this virtue is what we might call 'false prudence' which 'is at the service of selfishness and is expert in using the best means to achieve warped ends. In such circumstances, cleverness and perspicacity only serve to worsen one's dispositions... Parents should think seriously about the goals they regard as important for themselves and for their children, in order for them to be able to act in a way consistent with those goals. An educator can regard this role in part, as helping the child to freely assimilate a series of values in such a way that these have a real, definite meaning for him. If he has not got these values clear in his mind, prudence, in the sense of virtue, is meaningless.

Other problems have to do with the ability needed to gather together the necessary basic information, with assessing the relative importance of the different bits of information; with distinguishing between fact and opinion; etc.

Imprudence – which includes precipitance, thoughtlessness and inconstancy – is very much connected with failure to control one's passions. Imprudence can lead parents to pre-judge their children or pigeon-hole, not realising that a person is dynamic and changes a little every day. We all have some sort of mania – big or little – and this can influence our objectivity. There are parents who insist blindly on their children following the same career as themselves. Others, through excessive anger or envy, make unjust demands on their children; others, who are very clear on what they want, think that their good ends justify whatever means they use to attain them.

So, there are many areas in which a person can improve at being prudent. But in order to do so, he needs right motives. There is really only one motive for being prudent – the desire to make a decision consistent with the action we take to achieve our purpose. This virtue can be looked at in terms of getting on well with people or being efficient in one's work but if a person is a Christian his basic motive should be to do God's will.

Developing the virtue of prudence

I hope it is clear, then, that the virtue of prudence calls for a certain degree of intellectual development. It is a matter of discerning, of having standards, of judging and deciding. Does this mean that there is no point in trying to get a small child to acquire this virtue? In one sense, yes. A small child finds it very difficult to act prudently. But in so far as he begins to take personal decisions in a limited area of autonomy he does need this virtue. Normally, the most prudent thing a small child can do is to obey his teachers. Once he has learned the criteria necessary for being able to make decisions in a particular situation he can begin to develop this virtue provided he is given the right help. The learning process develops from obedience in almost everything, to the point where he makes his own decision based on the advice he has freely sought. He should be told clearly what things he can decide freely for himself and what things he should look for advice on. Specifically, a child needs advice from others on those matters where he lacks the necessary information and cannot obtain it, either because he is not old enough or because the situation in itself is complex. He also needs advice to deal with any new situation which arises, where he lacks experience.

From this point on, the process of developing this virtue concentrates on the young person's gradual acceptance of responsibility for acting prudently in taking decisions in more and more types of situations. To do this he needs to size up a situation accurately, to know the standards which should guide his judgement and to take the right decision.

Sizing up the situation

In considering the various aspects of this virtue we are going to concentrate on children between fifteen and twenty years old, because this is the age when their reasoning powers are developing, although we will make some reference to younger children.

Although prudence operates in concrete situations, this habit does need to be based on certain dispositions which encourage its development. To size up a situation, in the first place one needs to want to do so and one must recognise that one is not in possession of the whole truth. A proud, self-sufficient person can think that he is so well able to assess a situation that there is no need for him to question his initial assessment or to try to check such information as he has. The attitude which we should try to develop is one where, without underestimating the value of one's own judgement, a person recognises his limitations and tries to look objectively at the data available to him.

Teenagers usually see things in a very black and white sort of way. This produces a tendency to judge a situation without trying to see if they have enough information to go on. For example, they can accuse a companion of acting unjustly without making sure that the act occurred at all. Or they can judge a person simply on the basis of partial or incomplete information in a newspaper. Others can decide on a course of action without stopping to think if they have the capacity to see it through and without taking account of the possible consequences of this action.

All this leads us to stress the need for us to develop a series of abilities in our children:

- the ability to distinguish between facts and opinions,
- the ability to distinguish between what is important and what is secondary,
- the ability to seek out information,
- the ability to select sources of information,
- the ability to recognise their own prejudices,
- the ability to analyse critically the information they receive and to check out anything which looks doubtful,
- the ability to relate cause and effect,
- the ability to recognise what sort of information is necessary in each case,

Any kind of ability connected with information at some stage calls for making a choice. And this in turn implies that one must have some sort of standard on which to base this choice.

We have said that it is necessary to flee from that choice of information which is based on possibly unconscious prejudice. It is quite possible to go to a source of information because one is well disposed to it – and not to another source because one is turned off it or because it means making a greater effort. We should seek the most objective, complete, and suitable information available.

A child can go about choosing suitable information as soon as he has attained the basic ability to do so: by this I mean the ability to *observe*, but also the ability to read and assimilate what he has read, and the ability to listen. By observing, reading and listening he can come to grips with reality, but as we have said it is also a matter of knowing what to observe, what to read and whom to listen to and how.

In regard to sizing up a situation, it makes sense, with younger children, to put a lot of emphasis on their powers of observation, helping them to discover new aspects of life, getting them to concentrate, and making them more sensitive. In this way they can be gotten to watch a bird, for example, and notice its colour, size, song etc. They can also be led to classify different animals and plants and so forth: this amounts to making judgements in accordance with certain standards. The 'important information' for recognising a bird might be its shape, colour, song, etc., and the 'secondary information' whether it is on a seat or a tree, etc. If brother and sister have seen the same bird, you can show them that each has seen it in a different way. This way they learn that there is a difference between facts and opinions, and that each person can see the same facts in a different way. If they note the facts they have observed, they can perhaps look up the bird later in a reference book. That way they will learn by using different sources, that one source is better than another. Perhaps their mother is not the best person for identifying an animal. Up to this point we have been following the list of abilities given earlier and we could continue with the same example right down to the last point in the list, the 'ability to remember'. The net result of this process is that the child is able to judge correctly in accordance with suitable standards.

By getting children to focus their attention on interesting things like this, parents can develop their powers of observation – playing simple games like 'I spy' or asking their children, after a TV programme, what happened in the programme.

Ability to read can be put to use in connection with the virtue of prudence as a basis for distinguishing between facts and opinions (reading the newspaper, for example), so that they distinguish what is important from what is secondary, so that they learn the need to use different sources of information, etc. But reading is perhaps especially useful for learning the standards they should use when it comes to making a judgement. In order to do this, children need the help of their parents and teachers.

When it comes to listening, a child needs to learn to discern the reliability of the person who has given him the information – a friend, his parents, etc. He should try to listen carefully and retain what is important.

We have tried to indicate how a small child's capacity to arrive at the truth of a situation can be stimulated – focussing his attention on interesting things so that, by observing, reading and listening, a process can be begun which leads to his making a judgement.

The process is the same in the case of older children, but the things they focus on will become more and more complex. They will perhaps want to adopt an attitude to whether it is a good idea or not to have atomic power stations; who should run schools; whether to read a particular book or go to a particular film. To reach prudent decisions they need to follow the steps outlined. Translated into questions parents might ask their teenage children, these steps would be:

- What do you know about this subject?
- Where did you get your information?
- Are your sources reliable? Are they adequate?
- Have you already formed an opinion about this matter independently of the information you have? In other words, are you prejudiced in any way?
- Are there any gaps in the information you have gathered?

- How can you supplement this information?
- Have you sifted this information, to distinguish facts from opinions, secondary material from important material?

And then comes a key question:

- What standards have you chosen for assessing the situation? Are these the right standards?[55]

Knowing how to judge

Ability to judge is made up of two elements: establishing suitable standards and evaluating the situation in the light of these standards. And up to this point we are speaking about an ability known as 'critical judgement' which can be described as follows: 'once suitable standards are established for assessing a given situation, critical judgement recognises the various elements in the situation and evaluates them correctly in the light of these standards'.

Technical ability to evaluate a fact in the light of a standard or criterion is absolutely essential. We can teach children this ability by using everyday situations. Take, for example, advertisements on television. I stress that this is a technical capacity and therefore, at this point, we are not concerned about whether the standards we are using to train children are the right standards (we will presume that moral standards do not apply in this case). As far as TV advertisements are concerned, parents could look for possible standards to define whether an advertisement is 'good'. They might suggest, for example, that it should have lively background music, that the name of the product should be repeated a number of times and that the advertisement should emphasise what makes this product different from other similar products. We do not mean that these are the right standards for defining what makes a good advertisement. This is an exercise. Having established these standards, different advertisements can be analysed and given marks in relation to the established standards. In this way, children can be taught to analyse, to establish standards and to evaluate a situation in keeping with these established standards. It is also possible to examine more deeply how advertisements affect us, and what the criteria for a good advertisement are from the advertisers' point of view. In the same sort of way, you can think of standards suitable for judging a book, a film, a newspaper article or any occurrence which the child should adopt an attitude to.

But this sort of thing need not be restricted to older children. Small children can be asked to work out what makes Christmas presents good and exchange impressions about this: they can establish, for example, that they should not be easily breakable; that they should not be too expensive; that they should be able to be put to different uses; that their brothers and sisters should be able to use them. Then they can use these standards to assess particular presents one by one.

In this case it is obvious that we are also trying to establish *correct* criteria. We will look at this question later. But first, it is important to help children to realise when they are making valid assessments and when in fact they are being critical for no good reason. We constantly use words which need to be clarified if they are to be properly understood. We say, for example, 'this is important' or 'that is a very good experience'. But what do the words 'important' and 'good' mean? The effort involved in describing the meaning of words of this kind helps the development of this aspect of a child's critical capacity. In other words, a person needs to go through life with a clear awareness of the various criteria he applies when evaluating situations.

Prudence as a virtue takes on its full meaning when a person recognises the real purpose of his life. Pieper says: 'Only that person can be prudent who in advance *loves* and *desires* the good; besides, only he who is already prudent can act to achieve the good. But since love of the good grows thanks to action, the more fruitful one's action the more the roots of prudence grow in solidity and depth'.

Loving the good presupposes recognising the permanent values which go to make it up. Only in this way can a young person manage to judge correctly. For example, if a child did not accept the importance of justice, he could decide to do something selfishly, making perfect use of his critical capacity but being imprudent and also unjust towards others. He could examine all the various strategies for getting some superficial pleasure and choose very accurately from among them using his likes as the only criterion, instead of choosing from among a wide range of activities which he could engage in to the benefit of other people using their needs as his criterion.

This means that we parents must steadily give standards to our children, so that they know which standard to use in each situation. To give some examples, from early childhood up to older ages:

- standards for behaviour in the home: the relationship between work, free time, helping others, etc.
- standards for evaluating what other people do: the injustice of a companion; who is right in some argument; etc.
- standards for judging whether it is good to read some book or see some film;
- standards for evaluating social and personal problems;
- standards for seeing if one is acting justly, generously, sincerely, respecting others, etc., and prudently.

To sum up: it is a matter of helping the children to judge according to *the established rules of the game, according to the basic norms which apply to everyone and according to higher principles.*

Making decisions

Prudence implies deciding to take steps to do good. It is not enough to judge situations: one has to make decisions in line with those judgements.

At the moment of decision, a person has to take into account the information and the judgement we have described, realising that the decision itself can be taken at the right time or the wrong time. Secondly, he has to foresee the consequences of the decision he takes, because action does not always clearly follow on from a judgement. For example, a situation in which there is lack of loyalty between a man and a woman can be judged, in accordance with correct and true standards, as something intrinsically bad. But it does not necessarily follow that the victim of the disloyalty should be told about it. The possible consequences of the various alternatives must be weighed. And this is the basis of the act of deciding: consideration of the different alternative ways of achieving some end, in accordance with a correct assessment of the situation.

It might be thought that a person is prudent who never makes a mistake, because he never makes a decision. This is wrong. A prudent person is one who knows how to correct his mistakes. 'He shows his prudence in preferring to miss the mark twenty times rather than give in to an easygoing 'do nothing' attitude. He won't rush into things foolishly or behave with absurd rashness. He will run the risk of his decisions. Fear of failure will not make him give up in his effort to do good.'[57]

The decisions which children have to learn to make have to do with their work, their relationships with the family, their social relationships. These are decisions they should take after judging people or events, when faced with conflict situations, when adapting to change, after reflecting on the values which they consider important in their own life, in the planning of their future career, etc.[58] And parents can help their children here: first, by helping them to understand the things they are told to do, then getting the children to act and to do them on their own initiative; then, by helping them to think about the various options open to them, and finally by asking them questions to check whether they are in fact thinking carefully before making decisions. There is no cut and dried solution. The risk of leaving children to make their own decisions should always be a calculated one.

Lastly, it is worth realising that, depending on the nature of the particular problem, the most difficult step, or the one which takes most time or effort, could be either gathering the information or formulating a judgement or trying to make the best decision. In some cases, the prudent person will act immediately because he already has all the necessary information or because if he does not act he will cause harm to others or to himself. In others he has to spend quite a bit of time before making his decision.

Being prudent calls for guidance; it means seeking advice – and it also means that parents have to learn to give advice without necessarily imposing it. You can notice that a child is developing in this virtue if he asks for advice, if he looks for sufficient sources of information, if he weighs up this information and discusses it with his parents and with other people, if he is becoming a person with standards, if he acts – or refrains from acting – after examining the possible effects a course of action may have on himself and on others.

SELF-ASSESSMENT

Briefing Note: see pages 29-30, above.

Am I a prudent person?

1. *I have a good memory in the sense that I remember things as they really happened, as they really were, and I use experience to understand new situations.* (Prudence is based on memory to a large degree; if I don't remember anything of what has previously happened, of what I have studied or what I have observed, for example, how can I have an adequate basis for judging a new situation? What a shame teachers don't pay more attention to the development of the memory at school!)

2. *I normally manage to overcome the desire not to suffer, in order to come to grips with difficult situations.* (Another reason for not wanting to know what is going on is pure laziness.)

3. *I study regularly in order to be familiar with things that affect me as a parent or as a teacher.* (We can come by a lot of information through study, but we also need to develop a 'situational sensitivity' which we could call intuition.)

4. *I develop my capacity for observation, to be more familiar with what is going on in the family or in the school.* (We also need to find the time and opportunity to listen to others.)

5. *I can distinguish between what is important and what is secondary in the family or at school.* (In fact 'important'refers to anything which can influence family or school values positively or negatively in a significant way.)

6. *When the subject is important, I check the reliability of my information sources before accepting information, and I try to supplement this with information from other sources in order to get as objective a view as possible.* (It isn't easy to get an objective view of things, especially when they happen unexpectedly.)

7. *I try to identify my own prejudices, and overcome them.* (Prejudices cause us to have biased and incomplete information. For example, we may only

listen to those people whom we get along with, or we may have a preconceived opinion about some child's capacity to say anything interesting.)

8. *I think about what criteria I should use to assess each situation.* (It is easy to make decisions or just react on the basis of inadequate or incomplete criteria. For example, send a child to study in abroad just because it is useful to know that language to get a good job. But a good educator would have taken other criteria into account; for example: the child's good, their level of maturity to cope with that kind of situation, the kind of place they are going to live.)

9. *I normally make a decision thinking about what is best for the child although it may have a down-side.* (We could make a bad decision if we gave too much weight to the child's convenience. But often the reason we don't want the children to suffer is because, if they do, we suffer ourselves.)

10. *I usually manage to take in a situation at a glance.* (Some people are so analytical that they get lost in the details of the situation. They don't grasp what is most important, and they end up making bad decisions.)

Teaching others to be prudent

11. *I take an interest in the children's reading comprehension.* (To know how to read is essential for prudence. And reading comprehension should be developed by parents and by all teachers, whatever their subject.)

12. *I help the children develop their capacity for observation.* (Observation is especially relevant for learning about interpersonal relationships. There are simple games that can be used in order to develop this capacity.)

13. *I create situations in which the children have to learn to listen.* (One gets a lot of information by listening to other people. It is especially important for the smaller children to listen to their parents and teachers.)

14. *From adolescence onwards I help the youngsters to distinguish between what is important and what is secondary, between what are facts and what are opinions.* (Prudence is, more than anything, an intellectual virtue. It requires critical capacity to make this kind of distinction.)

15. *I help the youngsters discover the prejudices they have, so that they can have a more objective view of life.* (This is particularly difficult in adolescents, as they tend to be people of extremes, people who don't know how to say 'maybe' or 'in part yes and in part no'.)

16. *I help the children distinguish between reliable sources of information and others that are unsound or only partially to be trusted.* (This is virtually the same as telling them who are recognised authorities in each matter.)

17. *I insist on the children looking for as complete information as possible before taking a stand or before making a decision in important matters.* (Opinions are commonly held on the basis of very poor information, on slogans or on what they have heard on television.)

18. *I insist on the youngsters memorising important information.* (Youngsters need to, and should, memorise certain kinds of information. If they don't do so, they will never be prudent in their lives as they will be unduly influenced by their feelings when making decisions.)

19. *When the youngsters need to take a stand or make a decision, I help them distinguish what criteria they should be using. I then help them apply the criteria to the situation.* (All too frequently the youngsters react to situations. They don't bother about looking for information or thinking through the criteria they should be using.)

20. *I insist on the youngsters carrying out their decisions when they have duly considered the possible consequences of the action for themselves and for others.* (The intellectual process should result in action. Prudence is not a question of rejecting action; it is a matter of doing the right thing.)

18 Audacity

Audacious people set out on and complete courses of action which may appear imprudent, convinced that – after calm assessment of the facts and taking account of possible risks – they can achieve a genuine good.

Before considering audacity as a virtue we will first comment on it as a passion, for the development of this virtue depends largely on the strength of the passion behind it. Audacity is a passion of the irascible appetite which sets vigorously about dominating some evil or achieving some good. Passion in itself is blind, and therefore it can lead to rather imprudent results. That is precisely why we are more interested in the virtue than in the passion of daring. A passion is only an instinctive movement, born of an instant realisation that something can be achieved, but it can evaporate as quickly as it arises.

For audacious action to occur, prudence must be present, a necessary factor, but also the passion has to be strong. Undoubtedly, a person can find some type of motivation which leads him to be daring in pursuit of a good. But if he already has a certain inbuilt energy, it will be much easier for him to achieve more. As Saint Thomas says: 'Audacity increases with good health, energy and youthfulness'.

But audacity can also lead a person into situations which hinder his improvement. Horace says: 'Mankind, which takes on anything, ventures even into what is totally forbidden.'[59] The virtue of audacity, which is part of the virtue of magnanimity, helps a person to pursue the good and to set about great undertakings, convinced that he can really achieve something worthwhile. And for it to be a virtue, prudence is called for. 'Anyone who takes all kinds of risks without a thought or a care is not brave: by acting like that he shows quite clearly that being game for anything, not stopping to think, is more important to him than his personal safety if he puts it so easily in jeopardy.'[60]

We would have to ask therefore: why run risks? And: How can you justify an action which seems to be imprudent? Precisely for this reason, no one is better equipped with motives and reasons for practising this virtue than a Christian. The Christian bases his audacity on supernatural hope: he is convinced he has received the promise of goods which far exceed any human expectation, goods he should seek no matter what the risk.

After thinking along these lines, we are perhaps better equipped to examine the problems involved in teaching this virtue. At first, it is a matter of creating the right conditions in children so that they are capable of having a strong passion. But it is also a matter of helping them to see a goal or goals which are really worthwhile, and then to make a consistent decision, which is well thought out and is rooted in convictions and not just in intuitions and whims. These are the questions we will go on to examine.

Conditions for audacity

Normally a human being is able to do much more and much better than he himself thinks. He continually limits himself, sometimes unconsciously, out of false prudence, laziness, lack of self-confidence, or because he has not developed himself – his body, his mind, his abilities – so as to be able to rise to the opportunities which present themselves. Therefore, audacity presupposes that the child has learned to recognise his potentialities and has actually experienced them. That is the only way he will be able to have reasonable self-confidence.

Among the conditions necessary for being audacious or daring one is particularly important: control over one's body. For two reasons. If he lets himself be led by his instincts into a search for superficial pleasures, he will never be able to recognise clearly any genuine good. Secondly, the body needs to be looked after if one's other attributes are to be developed properly. Health, feeling in good form, makes for good resolutions – for both making them and carrying them out. Obviously, this does not mean that a sick person cannot be daring; what it does mean is that a person who can have good health and be physically fit should do whatever it is necessary to be so because if not he is despising something which plays a very important part in achieving a genuine good.

Physical education is something that many parents do not know much about. Most parents' efforts in this direction have to do with giving children medicine or at least vitamins when they see they need them. But children need the opportunity to get exercise in sport and other activities which demand physical and mental effort, forcing their body to do a bit more than it would do instinctively. The body is kept fit through taking the necessary exercise and it develops through making a reasonable effort and getting enough food. In this connection we should not forget the importance of a balanced diet, not only for physical health but also to give scope for the child's moral development.

There are two vices which go against the virtue of audacity: rashness and cowardice. Let us look at cowardice. A person who lacks confidence in his own abilities and qualities can become cowardly through not daring to do anything worthwhile. We have seen how this lack of confidence can have a real basis or derive from the child's imagination. In other words, it may be an objective fact that the child simply does not have some ability or quality; or that quality may be latent and he may not know he has it. It is up to the parents to help their children to discover all their potentialities. We have already referred to physical capacities, but other abilities must also be looked out for.

I do not propose here to cover all the areas in which a child can be developed. I simply want to make the point to help parents think about all the countless ways their children can strive to do better. It is good to help them to develop one or other specific ability so that they realise just how possible it is for them to improve if they make an effort and stick at it. And it is good to help them learn to some extent at least about both what they are capable of and what their limitations are.

In any event, it seems essential that children make constant efforts to develop a range of human virtues, because without those virtues they will be unable to be daring. A person acts audaciously when he is tackling some other virtue, be it justice, generosity, patience. That is to say, daring increases to the extent that one is learning to express love.

Finally, as regards the conditions necessary for being daring, it is good to remember that a person will feel more able to be daring if other people support him. A child can be daring on his own or he can contribute to a daring action of his parents, or brothers and sisters, or of the whole family. Confidence – which is the result of the unconditional love which should obtain in a family, of the enduring nature of the family relationships and of the opportunity to be accepted for what one uniquely is – produces the conditions that allow for each member to develop in his own style. The unity of the family both fosters and is the result of the effort of all its members to strive for noble ideals. Society nowadays has perhaps greater need than ever before of enterprising, daring families.

Discovering noble goals

For a small child the most important thing is to have the opportunity to experience actions, situations, things, which involve some value. This gives him the experience he needs (helped by his parents) to recognise – in other situations – actions and events which are devoid of those values. He will notice a small act of generosity, he will realise the difference between a tidy room and an untidy one, he will come to learn what factors make any action useful: even though he does not realise their underlying value.

One will then go on to help the child to accept or at least tolerate these experiences – not run away from them because he feels lazy or because he does not like the results. Many valuable experiences are disagreeable until one discovers their real meaning. At first, the child manages not to turn his back on them because he gets help from his parents and other people who are over him – his brothers and sisters, relatives, teachers.

If previously the child went through these experiences without grasping the difference between one value and another, the next step will be for him to put a name on each value and thereby learn to distinguish one from another. Parents can ask children to describe what each experience means for them. And then they can ask them to continue to perform good actions.

A logical consequence of this training is that the child begins to do certain things voluntarily or on his own initiative, connecting them with the values mentioned, although he will also do things using poor values or bad values which he has experienced. The important thing at this point is that he should get genuine satisfaction from having done the right thing. And here we should stress the importance of positive sanctions on the part of educators.

As a result of these steps, the child can come to act in a way consistent with the values which he is now really beginning to discover. He can try to create a good climate of study with the others in his class, or can try to listen to and accept others.

At this stage he needs to apply his intelligence a bit more to the values which have to some degree become part of him. And his parents should consciously talk to him about this – suggesting to him different points of view so as to get him to think. This way he will acquire a basis for whatever opinions he has. Obviously the process we have been describing, without pinning it down to any precise age, can really only take shape during adolescence, not earlier. This is the time when the child is able to express clearly, with conviction, the values he holds, and to act in a decisive way to promote his beliefs.

From this moment on, he will try to connect up all these values and act always in a consistent way, trying to establish a genuine hierarchy of values[61]

Obviously, if parents succeed in getting their children to assimilate a series of values and develop a unified value system, the children will also at the same time be acquiring experience of how to relate their own actions to these values; they will learn what is the prudent thing to do or not to do in each situation that arises. They will act confidently and their audacity will make sense, because they will realise that certain actions are worth the effort because of the good they are trying to achieve. They will acquire a better sense of their real capacities and qualities and they will therefore try to achieve more than others.

If a person carries out some valuable action, convinced that he will succeed, aware of the means available to him to do it, he is not being imprudent. But if he does not know the value of the action and does not have these resources to do it, he is being imprudent on two scores.

The problem of prudence

The virtue of audacity involves the search for a genuine good, as we have said. Audacity is based on prudence and justice, but it allows the person to see clearly the resources at his disposal to embark on great and noble undertakings. In practice, if he already recognises the value of the undertaking, how can he set about calculating the risk? (Here we are looking at audacity as a human virtue; later we will see it in a Christian context.)

There is no point in being daring in search of something which does not lead to fulfilment in life. It does not pay, it is not worth the risk. On the other hand, 'the greater the undertaking a person desires and hopes to carry out, the nobler his goal and the clearer its connection with his ultimate goal, the greater must his daring be'.[62] Therefore, the first rule is to check the value of the action in relation to man's overall purpose.

After that it is a matter of seeing all the dangers and advantages of the action in question, the helps one can count on and therefore all the resources available to overcome the difficulties. A person usually has more resources than it seems, provided he has been striving to develop himself in line with certain good standards, for he already has a whole series of human virtues and knows where he can find friends to help him in his efforts. And in particular he can draw on his past experience.

A young person who has values or standards and wants to be daring will have tried to do all sorts of things. Some of them will have worked out all right, others not. He needs to be encouraged in his efforts, even if they don't seem to us to be very prudent – provided no serious risk is involved. This way he can learn from his own mistakes and, what is more important, he can come to know his real potential. And in this he will surprise even his parents.

Trying to influence a group of friends to behave better, might seem imprudent, and so might pointing out to a teacher that he has acted unjustly, for example. However, it is everyone's duty to help others to improve – even on the purely human level.

The Christian virtue

A Christian bases his daring on supernatural hope. He knows that everything is for the best, even if he does not understand everything that happens. He knows he can count on Christ's grace through the sacraments and prayer. He knows he can count on the help of Christ's mother who is also our Mother. A Christian should be ready to expose himself to all kinds of risks. because he can count on God's continuous help. 'God and daring! Daring is not imprudence. Daring is not recklessness.'[63]

Naturally this way of acting, 'for someone who does not practise faith and hope, would be meaningless and would go beyond the limits of human prudence and would seem to be madness, but a Christian approaches it with the clarity and certainty which the practice of these theological virtues gives him'."

SELF-ASSESSMENT

Briefing Note: see pages 29-30, above.

Am I audacious myself?

1. *I try to have strong passions, but ones dominated by my will.* (In certain kinds of education there is a tendency to want to eradicate passions and develop cerebral capacities instead – to avoid reacting to what is good or what is bad. To be audacious, one needs to react to good and evil with passion.)

2. *I focus on those things which are a real service to others and to God in order to perform actions of authentic worth.* (Audacious acts can focus on the goal to be achieved or on the means to use to get there.)

3. *I make an effort, which some would think out of the ordinary, in order to control some influence or action which is objectively bad.* (Audacity means not only looking for what is good but also defending oneself heroically from what is bad. Sometimes we do not resist evil influences, out of laziness or fear.)

4. *I try to keep my body in good condition because I know that it will make it easier to carry out audacious actions.* (According to St Thomas Aquinas, audacity increases according to one's degree of physical vigour, health and youth. It is useful to remember that we can keep ourselves 'young' by making sure that we have future projects. Future projects are a sign of true youthfulness.)

5. *I get as much information as I can about possible future projects, and I think seriously about them in order not to expose myself to unnecessary risk.* (One should not accept unnecessary risks. Some projects may put one's own life in danger, and others may need other people's help to get them going.)

6. *I try to know my own capacities and limitations as well as possible.* (If one has qualities well suited to a project, there will be less risk of failure.)

7. *When I think about possible projects, I take into account the real importance of each, and the degree to which it fits in with my general objectives.* (If the project is going to be of great benefit to others, there is more reason to be audacious.)

8. *I recognise that the most important projects are those that help people fulfill their end, that is, to glorify God.* (In fact, audacity makes little sense to

those who do not believe in God. Almost all projects which can be considered audacious for the Christian, and possible (because they believe in the help they will receive from God), would be considered unreasonable by a nonbeliever.)

9. *I receive God's help through prayer and frequenting the Sacraments, with the idea of starting projects of real value.* (Audacity in the Christian life is essential. Without audacity, the saints would never have done the deeds they did.)

10. *I understand that I have an untransferable mission to glorify God and love him as best I can.* (Audacious actions will frequently show this duty in a palpable way. For example, one person may take part in a radio or television programme although they know that the others in the programme will try to ridicule faith; another may try to organise a trip to the Holy Land; yet another may try to enter politics in order to influence society positively.)

Teaching others to be audacious

11. *I help the children discover their qualities and capacities and, when they are older, to learn about how their virtues are developing.* (Audacity calls for the development of other virtues in order to make it really possible to carry out projects.)

12. *I help the children discover their talents through having had to act in 'new' activities and situations. I also encourage them to focus on some specific action so that they get to know what they can do when they apply themselves.* (Usually the children tend to overestimate or underestimate themselves. They need to try things out and also concentrate on certain things.)

13. *I help the adolescents discover what basic tendencies they are not controlling well.* (Lack of temperance makes it difficult to discern what is good, and that discernment is essential to audacity.)

14. *I look after the physical development of the children, making sure they have exercise, sport and a good diet.* (Each of us is a complete unit. When the body is ill, it influences the soul, and when the spirit is sick, it influences the body.)

15. *We try to create an atmosphere that favours the development of audacity in the home or at school. We try to pursue noble goals.* (We know what the effects of good and bad example are in all aspects of education. But, as regards audacity, a teacher might be tempted to settle for mediocrity and lack of enterprise, preferring to 'play safe'.)

16. *I try to help the children participate in activities which are related to high ideals.* (Perhaps a youth club, some parish activity or a non-governmental organisation.)

17. *I counsel the youngsters to encourage them to have initiative and then pursue their plans.* (Having initiative is a habit. If the educator always takes over, never letting the children take the helm, they will not learn to have initiative and they will not be audacious.)

18. *I give theoretical information to the youngsters and I also make sure they know what is going on in the world so that they can develop personal convictions.* (A person who is not convinced that any real needs exist will never be audacious. Helping the youngsters take part in ambitious plans of others is not enough. They need to learn to be ambitious themselves.)

19. *I reason with the youngsters to help them see that taking risks is a good thing, depending on the amount of good they think can be achieved through specific actions.* (We need to talk to the youngsters frequently, helping them to think things out. We should not forget that audacity must not go against prudence but it does require having high ideals.)

20. *I help the youngsters realise the importance of what they are thinking of doing, and also of knowing what resources are available to do it.* (If one doesn't see the point of doing something, or when the necessary resources are not available, then one will be doubly imprudent if one decides to act).

19 Humility

Humble people recognise their own inadequacy, qualities and abilities, and press them into service, doing good without attracting attention or expecting the applause of others.

The virtue of humility helps a person to control his disordered desire for his own excellence, and therefore it helps to create an atmosphere which makes it possible for people to get on together. However, our description of this virtue speaks about recognising one's strong points and shortcomings and this has nothing to do with rejecting one's self: pride is not the only enemy of humility; there is also the vice that has to do with abdicating one's honour and good name. Therefore, it is clear that, to be humble, one needs to be realistic, recognising one's self for what one is. That is the only way to use all our qualities etc., to do good.

We can all find things in our make-up that we don't like – potential we fail to realise, qualities which are not developing. The truth of the matter is that if we begin to take a good look at ourselves we come to realise we are not worth a great deal. The logical thing to do is to accept the situation and try to take oneself in hand – though some people take refuge in pride, emphasising what they have, what gives them the edge over others, in order to justify their whole existence.

The virtue of humility takes on its fuller meaning when a person looks at himself in relation to God, because in that way his inadequacies are compensated for by God's greatness. 'Humility means looking at ourselves as we really are, honestly and without excuses. And when we realise that we are worth hardly anything, we can then open ourselves to God's greatness: it is there our greatness lies.'[65]

According to Saint Thomas the true measure of a man is not taken by looking at him alongside others but rather in his relationship to the Creator. 'The same happens with pride, which is not primarily thinking one is better than others, but rather an attitude to God. Man's position as a creature – which is inherent in his make-up – is the first statement of his humility, and it is this that in practice pride desires and destroys.'[66]

It seems obvious from what we have said that humility is a virtue basic to the development of faith. Saint Teresa of Avila said: 'Humility means walking in the truth: pride means walking in falsehood.'[3] Humility is a virtue which parents can develop in their children for a number of different reasons. They can try to get them 'to walk in the truth'[67] in the name of efficiency or they can be trying to get their children to recognise their possibilities as true sons of God. Humility is useful for both natural and supernatural life. 'The right disposition for faith is recognition of everything that has to do with natural honesty, with love for the truth, with openness to everything noble, just and beautiful to be found in human life. To say it in just one word: 'in the natural order, what disposes man to faith is humility.'[68]

Many spiritual writers have dealt with the subject of humility. Some of them identify stages in its development; we might take, for example, Saint Bernard's classic description: 'one type of humility is sufficient humility; another is abundant humility; another, superabundant humility. Sufficient humility consists in submitting to him who is one's superior and not imposing oneself on him who is one's equal; abundant humility consists in submitting oneself to him who is one's equal and not imposing oneself on him who is lower than oneself; superabundant humility consists in submitting oneself to him who is lower than oneself.'[69]

If we take these three types of humility, connecting them with family life and with education in general, we will be able to draw a number of conclusions about how to teach this virtue.

Sufficient humility

At this stage in humility, a person submits himself to God, recognising God's superiority, and to competent authorities in the different areas of his life. He also tries faithfully to do his duty and when he does it he avoids the pitfall of being vainglorious about doing things 'so well'.

From the viewpoint of teaching this virtue, it may well be that this degree of humility is quite suitable to young children. It is fairly obvious that a child's natural humility (he clearly knows less and will usually do things technically worse than older people) could turn into a fear of God and fear of life in general – and fear is no good basis for the growth of love. With a small child it is not necessary to draw attention to his inferiority; it is natural for him to be underdeveloped. The thing to do is to point out to him affectionately what he does well and what he does badly, so as to get him to see exactly where he stands and to accept that. Up to the age of seven or eight, a child usually realises his need to obey those in authority over him, although he will test the ground to see how far he can go. A small child's humility is something quite spontaneous; in view of this, what we parents must avoid is the tendency to develop our children's pride rather than foster their genuine humility. Let us look at a few family situations. When a small child, through not looking where he is going, bumps into a table, there are some mothers who say 'bad table', instead of 'silly boy'. It may seem harmless: but if this sort of thing happens quite often, the child could even think that it was not his fault at all. A small child needs to learn that he does make mistakes and that sometimes he does not keep to the rules of the game. In situations like this he should obey the established rule: for example, he should say he's sorry. This is an expression of humility, because he has to say explicitly that he has not done something very well. Humility, for a small child, means, therefore, learning to obey and to make amends by accepting that he is subject to authority or that the game does have rules.

As far as parents are concerned, this should mean that they tell him what the rules are and who is the right person in authority in each situation; they should help him recognise facts for what they are – not praising him when he does not do things well and not going overboard when he does what he ought to do, in case that would make him opinionated. On the child's side it means trying to be simple, sincere and truthful.

Abundant humility

The basis for this second stage of humility is recognition that God is present in every single person and, therefore, that we should not consider ourselves superior to anyone. Everyone always has some hidden qualities. And, besides, everything we are is a gift of God. Our job is to make an effort to give back to God something of what he has given us. If we think like this we will not try to impose ourselves on people who are 'below' us, because we simply do not see people in that light.

As the years go by, a person gets more and more scope to lose his humility and become proud. There are hundreds of quite common and subtle ways one can be proud and look down on others: 'the pride of preferring our own excellence to that of our neighbour; vanity in our conversations, thoughts and gestures; an almost sickly touchiness that takes offence at words and actions that are in no way meant to be insulting.'[70]

We shall now look at some of the more common difficulties experienced in trying to reach this stage of humility.

Self-sufficiency

Self-sufficiency is usually the result of quite unreasonably thinking that one's own abilities are a reliable guide to the way one should act. It is a desire to be free from any kind of help, so that one does not need to recognise one's inadequacy. In a way, it implies turning one's own mind into a god. Self-sufficiency obviously results in a person being unable to talk about anything but himself. The only thing he is really interested in is himself. And even when he does listen to other people it is only a device to allow him to then go on to talk about how great he is. Even when it does not express itself in talking, self-sufficiency can be noticed in other things one does: it is particularly obvious in the person who does not seek help or advice, who does not think he needs any form of guidance. The net effect is that he reads indiscriminately, goes for any kind of experience, and is proud of how much knowledge he has acquired – useless knowledge, for the most part. As Cowper put it: 'Knowledge is proud that he has learned so much; Wisdom is humble that he has learned no more.'[71]

At all events, this is a real problem among teenagers. They want more independence. Sometimes you can point out to a young person his failure to take reasonable account of different views people express on some particular subject. But this sort of exercise is not very useful unless the child has a good idea of the standards which should govern the whole purpose of his life. If he has good standards and values, you can show him how a particular action does or does not fit in with them. But if he has no such standards, there is no way he can assess the value of the action. Therefore, once again we must stress that the most important job of parents is to share values with their children, values which give them guidelines for behaviour. Undoubtedly, if the child has learned and assimilated the fact that God is Truth, he can become humble. If he does not accept this fact, all that humility can do for him is give him a better chance of achieving his own personal goals in life.

We parents have to help our children a great deal in their efforts to develop self-control. Showing them unconditional affection so that they learn not to be so boastful about their achievements; to accept other people's ingratitude; to forget themselves, to give themselves generously to the service of others for love of God.

In relationships with others

Although really there is no clear distinction between matters which affect a person's internal life and those which have to do with his relationships with others, we have stressed how humility should express itself in one's personal, private life and in one's relationships with others. The question is: how can we help our children to be humble in their relationships with others, especially with their companions?

The stage of humility which we are discussing has to do with not thinking oneself superior to others. This means that we should recognise the, perhaps hidden, qualities, which every person has. This implies that everyone has qualities which can be appreciated. However, it can happen that a child puts no value on these particular qualities. For example, perhaps someone does not appreciate music: in which case he gives no importance to the fact that one of his companions is a very good musician. Whereas, because he is good at sports, he does appreciate the sports abilities of other friends; in which case his attitude to his musical companion is one of disdain, because he does not admit the value involved in being musical. Thus, acceptance of other people depends on one's grasp of the values they enshrine. Obviously therefore we should try to get children to admire other's natural and supernatural endowments. Pride leads one to want to be greater, or to be better at something, than other people are. A doctor who in some social gathering talks about nothing but medicine shows, perhaps unintentionally that he is not interested in other subjects. He writes them off because he is wrapped up in his own experience.

It is a matter of teaching children to take an interest in other people because other people are interesting. Taking an interest means asking them about their interests, and in a nice way getting them to see that you also have a right to be listened to. A person can keep quiet or make no effort to speak because he thinks others are not at his level. Or he may not accept opinions or suggestions on the subject under discussion, because he is the expert.

Basically the person who is humble in his relationships with others is he who knows that he can learn from them. He focuses on their qualities and forgets about their defects.

But let us pin this down a little more and make a list of those situations where there can be a tendency towards pride and, therefore, an opportunity to learn to be more humble:

- owning or wanting to own things; money, toys, equipment, tools, clothes, valuables, etc. Especially something one's companions do not have.
- Having or wanting to have qualities and abilities: being able to read, do sums, be good at some sport, speak, etc: something others do not have or have to a lesser degree.
- Having in fact done or wanting to do things which the others have not done.
- Being or wanting to be first there, the 'best' or the 'most'.

In order to be humble, in these situations, there are a number of connected virtues which can help a lot. Specifically, modesty, gentleness and studiousness, moderation, flexibility, etc. All these stem from doing things in accordance with good standards. And parents have the job of helping their children to incorporate into their make-up these rules which help them act correctly. With smaller children it is a question of not encouraging their pride by making a big fuss about their achievements, making exaggerated comparisons with what other children have done and pushing them to seek success rather than try to find the way to serve others without looking for applause. Modesty will control their tendency to attract attention through what they wear or by exaggerated kinds of self expression (gestures, posturing etc.). If parents overdress their children and encourage them to affectation, they are put at a distance from humility. Gentleness makes for obedience and steers them away from uncontrolled anger (where they exult in their own strength). Studiousness will control their appetite to know too much out of curiosity. Really, parents have to ask themselves whether they prefer their children to be seeking noisy public success or whether they think that what they should rather be doing is working in a quiet but effective way, to the extent that their potential allows.

On the other hand, humility must be compatible with work well done (work which is successful or leads to success) and an ability to relate well to other people – this means that people accept you and it can also lead to a lack of humility. Here the only thing that can guide us is an upright intention. Avoiding being loud or odd, as far as possible. Using the ordinary resources available to one without going to extremes, and learning to correct one's intention when one starts going off course. And a final word about those who normally do not fail at things because they are intelligent, good students, good companions, good at sports etc. It is very important for everyone to be an achiever and to know he is an achiever. But it is also important for a person to learn to lose, to recognise that he does not do everything right, that he is not indispensable, that the reason he has endowments is that God wanted him to have them. With young people of this sort one has to find ways by which they do experience small failures – and, of course, one has to make more demands on them. A person can only reach the highest level of humility when he realises his objective personal inadequacy.

Superabundant humility

'Humility reaches its maximum perfection in those who see themselves as worse than others. All the saints have regarded themselves as great sinners. And this attitude of theirs does have an objective basis in the context of God's grace, for without that grace, on the one hand, no one would continuously be able to act in a fully upright way, and, on the other hand, everyone would be liable to commit the very worst sins.'[72] In Sacred Scripture we find a constant example of humility in the way Jesus acts; and in the light of his teaching the saints explain what humility means for us sinners: Saint Paul says: 'I shall be happy to make any weaknesses my special boast so that the power of Christ may stay over me, and that is why I am quite content with my weaknesses, and with insults, hardships, persecutions, and the agonies I go through for Christ's sake. For it is when I am weak that I am strong.'[73]

A person can be truly humble only if he is so out of love of God. Otherwise, it would not make sense. Submitting to the will of God, continuously thanking him for his goodness, being trustingly dependent on him: all this makes us more aware of our limitations but it also gives us experience of the grandeur of being sons and daughters of God.

In this life a Christian needs faith and he needs humility. Humility is man's necessary input for developing a supernatural life based on faith.[74]

SELF-ASSESSMENT

Briefing Note: see pages 29-30, above.

Am I a humble person?

1. *I recognise my greatness as a child of God but also my wretchedness as compared to him.* (Humility means being realistic, not abdicating from one's rightful dignity but not exaggerating one's own importance, either.)
2. *I know my own shortcomings and I strive to improve as regards some of them.* (The proof that we are really conscious of those shortcomings lies in the fact that we are striving to improve.)
3. *I don't usually compare myself to other people. Instead, I try to know myself and the degree in which I have managed to improve after making an effort.* (Each person is different, and there is no point in considering oneself superior or inferior to others. One should try to use one's talents as best as one can.)
4. *I try to submit to those in authority over me and, at the same time, I try not to impose myself on those who might be considered my inferiors.* (We are looking for an attitude which allows us to take advantage of the talents of those who work with us or who live with us. We count on them because we know we are not superior to them.)
5. *I try to help those who depend on me to achieve the success that is their due, and I prefer to see that happen than to have my own successes recognised.* (Because they are envious, some people underestimate others. They try to make problems for them, or they simply are not prepared to accept their successes.)
6. *I try not to overwhelm others with my own real or imaginary excellence.* (This kind of vanity shows in the way one talks, in one's gestures, in an extreme and unhealthy capacity to take offence for no reason at all.)
7. *I accept that authentic authorities really do exist and that I should take them into account instead of conceitedly overestimating my own intelligence.* (This is probably one of the most common ways of lacking in humility in the modern day. Self-important people are usually intolerant towards others.)
8. *I realise I can learn a lot from other people and that is why I listen carefully to them.* (Self-sufficiency leads to underestimating others. Not only is it a lack of justice; it is also an expression of pride.)
9. *I recognise the different areas in which I may lack humility and I try to avoid them.* (The principal areas are: having or wanting to have more material

goods than others; having or wanting to have qualities or capacities that others do not have either; doing things or having done things that others have not done, or pretending to be No. 1.)

10. *I realise that the best way to avoid doing things out of pride or envy is to think about why I am acting. And I realise this will sometimes mean having to apologise.* (To be realistic is to know how to admit one's faults: no one does everything perfectly.)

Teaching others to be humble

11. *I make sure that the objectives I set up for my children are not just academic success, success in sport or social success.* (We should be trying to help children learn to serve others to the best of their ability. Undue insistence on success will lead to vanity.)

12. *I give clear information to the children so that they know when they are doing things well and when not; I do so affectionately and I encourage them to improve.* (Although the smaller children are never going to live the virtue of humility fully, they can learn about their capacities: they can learn to be realistic.)

13. *I get the children used to obeying and to recognising who are the authorities they should obey.* (If the parents imply that their children are their equals – for example, by inviting them to give their opinion on matters where they have no competence, or keeping to the same bedtimes as adults – the children will probably come to overestimate themselves. The same thing will happen if the teacher treats them with too much confidence or asks their opinion about things of which they are ignorant.)

14. *I am careful to make sure that the adolescents do not think that they possess more capacities or qualities than is the case.* (The opposite would produce conceited and rather nasty children. Sometimes this happens as regards their studies: 'What a bright child!'; or their looks: 'What a beautiful girl'; or as regards moral values: 'How good she is!')

15. *I teach the youngsters to think about they have done and to say they are sorry and make amends if necessary.* (Much of education could be summed up as 'making children think'. We can do that, by giving them clear and concise information and asking questions to make them think.)

16. *I help the adolescents recognise what it means to be a child of God.* (It is not easy to understand the importance of humility if one does not accept the existence of God the Father. At any rate, the virtue would be reduced to 'being realistic'.)

17. *I help the youngsters to have criteria for knowing how to relate to others.* (This is another kind of information which youngsters need. Some criteria which we can share with them will be, for example: Don't talk too much about your own prowess, learn to accept ingratitude from others, forget about your feelings when you think that you have been treated unjustly.)

18. *I try to give good example in my personal way of practising humility.* (A parent or a teacher who is always insisting on their own ability will scarcely be a good example for encouraging children to be humble.)

19. *I help the youngsters discover different aspects of a person which can be appreciated in order to recognise their merits.* (Sometimes a youngster may not appreciate another, or they may even despise them, because they do not recognise the value of some talent they have. For example, the other's musical talent.)

20. *I help the youngsters cope with their failures when they tend to have low self-esteem at some stages in their lives.* (Some people fail too often in life and we need to help them discover their positive points. Others always come out winning; it is useful to put children of that sort into situations where they are going to fail. Without failing once in a while, it isn't easy to be humble either.)

20 Simplicity

Simple people ensure that their normal way of acting – their speech, the way they dress, the way they behave – is consistent with what their real intentions are; they allow other people to know them accurately: they are what they seem.

The virtue of simplicity is a sign of a person's genuineness; and something is genuine when it is humanly sound. In other words, simplicity calls for a person to have a clear mind and an upright will.

From a more practical point of view, we can get a good idea of simplicity by contrasting it with some of the vices which go against it. A person can, on the inside, lose sight of man's true goal and become complicated and devious in his thoughts and desires. It is also possible for a person who knows very well what the purpose of his life is – to express himself in a two-faced way for various reasons. He can express himself in an obscure, complicated or misleading way, in the way he acts, speaks, dresses, by being pedantic, sarcastic or hypocritical. These are some of the vices which express the opposite of this virtue, but there is also a vice which is due to excessive simplicity: naivety. The right thing is to be straightforward and transparent in our attitude towards others and towards God.

We are dealing here with a virtue which has an important influence on the development of a person's intimacy. But it has to do not only with intimacy: in a special way it has to do with complete rapport between how one acts and how one feels in one's heart. Simplicity is the opposite of duplicity, which amounts to thinking one thing and doing another, making one's external action contradict one's real attitude. Obviously, therefore, this virtue is closely connected to humility and sincerity.

Letting oneself be known

The virtue of simplicity allows someone to be known for what he is in his heart. But, is there not a danger of a lack of modesty and reticence, if simplicity allows oneself to be 'discovered' in this way? Simplicity implies that the person has reflected on what he wants to express. Prudence will advise him as to whether it is right or not to express things which are intimately his. Simplicity will help him to act consistently with his intimate intentions. I am referring to truly personal intentions and not to attitudes imposed by rules or conventions foreign to one's convictions.

This virtue, therefore, has particularly to do with one's relations with God and with other members of one's family and with friends – intimate relationships, relationships of intimacy. Not that simplicity is not needed in relationships with other people – but the quality of the relationships we have just mentioned depends on simplicity. In other words, I can have a relationship with a business connection, for financial purposes, with a certain duplicity, and still get good results – good for me, and perhaps for the other person. However, if one does not act with simplicity towards a friend, friendship automatically disappears, because the relationship operates only in terms of formal rules which make for only an apparent rapport.

It is a matter of letting oneself be known in order to help other people to improve and in order to enable oneself to improve. If the 'improvement' one seeks has nothing to do with one's intimacy, simplicity is of secondary importance. A teacher can show a young man how to drive a car without any need to enter his intimacy. However, in every relationship, although initially it may not aim at intimacy, it is always possible, to some degree, to make oneself known in order to try to share whatever one feels is important – happiness, joy, work well done, serenity, etc.

The simplicity of small children

Many small children have a kind of grace which lets them act so naturally that they cause others to be open and simple. They say what they think and that is good, although they have to be taught to choose the right time and the right thing to talk about. The problem the educator has is to be able to help the young person to keep on acting in this natural way without being over-spontaneous, and at the same time to express his intimate intentions and not cloud them in a sophisticated or two-faced way. We will concentrate on the subject of training the child to discover his intimacy and to appreciate it correctly.

In looking at the behaviour of children of different ages, we will see how a moment comes when particular things they do lose their grace – their 'naturalness' no longer justifies their existence. And educators find they need to correct the child and get him to behave in a way which is more generally acceptable to others. For example, a very small child who comes into the sitting-room with no clothes on or who belches in public: in both cases, the time comes when it ceases to be funny and becomes something which should be corrected, and the reason for this is that no one grasps values just by himself. He needs help to recognise what is the right way to behave in keeping with certain objective standards. For example, good table manners may seem to lack a certain naturalness, yet they do make for a certain elegance and efficiency. Doing things with simplicity does not mean, therefore, doing things spontaneously, if this spontaneity goes against truth, beauty, goodness or order. To have the virtue of simplicity a person needs to use his mind and his will in the right way.

From what we have said, we can deduce that, as far as small children are concerned, they need to gain experience about what best fits in with objective standards, and they need to learn to relate their behaviour to what they know to be right.

The experience of being natural

On thinking about education one can get the impression that it consists of a series of 'artificial' methods aimed at getting the young person to achieve some sort of pre-established level of improvement. However, we should not forget the very great influence which experience of all sorts of different situations brings: through this the child really makes his own a whole series of values. Sometimes experience itself teaches him what the norm is; sometimes it is possible to conform to the norm, the rules, and then later on discover their real value. Both ways are complementary.

From a very early age, a child can grasp the value of beauty by living amid beautiful things: he sees colours, shapes etc. He can also come to recognise harmony in sounds – the wind, bird-song or simple music – when his mother sings, for example – or more complex music, on a record. He can grasp other values, such as order, for example, by seeing it in the home or when he takes a part in some organised activity. And so on. By experiences like this he meets up with different feelings which he does not objectively recognise: but he does experience them subjectively. For example, the feeling of security, knowing that someone loves him, that everything is in its place, knowing what is important, knowing that other people take him into account. Through this experience he will open up more to these influences and become imbued with things which it is worthwhile to share with others.

This same attitude will help him in his religious life. 'Naturalness and simplicity are two marvellous human virtues which enable men to take in the message of Christ. On the other hand, all that is tangled and complicated, the twisting and turning about one's own problems, all this builds up a barrier which often prevents people from hearing our Lord's voice.'[75]

As we have said, these experiences bring him to recognise values. And yet this is not the only way to grasp natural values. The rules of the game, in all the various aspects of living, ways to behave in the company of other people, rules for composing a picture or mixing colours, rules about how to do different jobs, etc.: these can all seem rather unnatural, yet if they are compatible with a value-orientated approach to life, by following them faithfully a person can come to understand their real purpose and value.

From all we have said so far, it seems clear that the basic job of educators of small children is to introduce them to experiences through which they can grasp and 'respond' to what is genuine. This can be by way of reacting to personal experience or by conforming to pre-established rules. However, both routes can also lead them to discover the dangers this process involves.

If young people's intimate intentions are based on experience of counter-values or impoverished values, simplicity will make no sense. In fact, if the rules they learn have to do with secondary aspects of human life, the danger is that they will interiorize something which leads them towards a barren, superficial sort of existence.

Simplicity and teenagers

We do not want to make an artificial division based on different ages. But we shall look at children who have reached the stage where they are aware of their own intimacy. We will examine some of the problems that can arise when interior aspects of one's personality blossom and the young person, now making more use of his mind and will power, has an opportunity of acting with simplicity, because he thinks it is good to do so (rather than out of spontaneity), based on experience and guided by his educators. Of course, there is no rigid step between these two stages. From an early age the child should be shown ways *to be simple* and the reasons for being simple, but it is in adolescence that greater problems arise.

Simplicity is a matter of allowing oneself to be known, achieving continuity between what goes on inside you and how you usually behave, in speech, dress, and general behaviour. This virtue is intimately connected with the virtue of truthfulness, which inclines a person always to tell the truth, and with the virtue of loyalty, which inclines one's will to keep to what one has committed oneself to do, to keep one's promises.

We might ask the question: why would someone express himself in a way that does not reflect his real intentions? Among the reasons why, in the case of teenagers – due partly to their sense of insecurity – are these:

- wanting to be like someone else and therefore trying to imitate that person, tossing one's own convictions aside;
- seeing the way one expresses oneself as an end in itself and therefore, expressing oneself in some chosen style without worrying about whether this means one is being genuine;
- thinking one is superior, inferior or simply different to what one really is, and acting in keeping with this false image;
- spending all one's time in superficial environments where there is very little chance one can express one's true self, due to the barriers which others' life-style imposes;
- wanting to hide one's real intentions.

We will go on to look at these problems, but first it will be useful to think a little about the motives which a person ought to have if he wants to acquire the good habit of simplicity.

If a person cultivates simplicity he will gain access to permanent values which will enhance his life. He won't try to dodge or find excuses for not accepting his true self. In this way he will become a well-integrated, noble person, growing in effectiveness because he is true to himself.

Secondly, he will be able to establish simple, easy relationships with others and from this will grow the friendships everyone needs. This also makes for good relationships between marriage partners and between parents and children for it enables everyone to share his uniqueness, his intimacy, with others. And, as we said earlier, the ground is prepared for receiving God into one's heart.

A third motive for being simple is the realisation that simplicity leads a person to strive to acquire all the human virtues, to acquire greater maturity. 'Such behaviour may be difficult to achieve, but it can never be strange. If some people find it surprising, it is because their eyes have grown dim and they are clouded by a hidden cowardice and a lack of determination."[76]

Finally, another reason for being simple is 'not to look silly'. Anyone who tries to be what he is not, becomes odd or eccentric and can only cause others' amusement.

Obstacles to simplicity

Here we will bear in mind the way the virtue of simplicity expresses itself in speech, dress and general behaviour.

Slavish imitation of someone else or of some way of doing things can be remedied by helping the young person to think the thing through. Often it is a matter of showing him that he is not acting genuinely – genuineness is a quality which young people usually go for – and helping him to adjust his behaviour. Obviously, if the problem basically is that he wants to hide his real intentions, because, quite consciously, he wants to obtain certain results by using some preconceived tactic, we are up against the vice of astuteness – and that is not easily countered. But this is true for any problem where the young person just does not have the necessary good will. Here we will concentrate our attention on young people who, even though they make mistakes like anyone else, still have a basically positive attitude.

In connection with this question of getting them to think, there is a series of typical situations which it is useful to bear in mind in order to be of help to them and also to make sure that we ourselves do not fall into the temptation of a certain duplicity in the way we operate:

- As regards dress: wanting to seem better off, poorer, younger, older or, simply, different. This is the case if the person who knowing that everyone who is going to some function is going to wear a tie, dresses on purpose in the least conventional way possible. Of course, I am not referring to excesses which tend to undermine a person's very self.
- As regards speech: wanting to appear more intelligent by using complicated words: pretending that one does not have qualities which one obviously does have; quoting writers one has not read, in order to appear well read; appearing to be better off or better educated through one's tone of voice or the 'experiences' one tells about; pretending to be revolted when one is not; making oneself out to have abilities one does not have; etc.
- As regards behaviour: trying to project a false image of oneself: pretending one has a lot of work to do when that is not so; organizing one's life in such a complex way that one has no time for the things that really matter; reading everything, looking at everything, listening to everything on the excuse of wanting to be up to date, instead of trying to get a better grasp of the more important things; spending one's time, money, effort in a frivolous way, in order to show off, etc.

We should also bear in mind another area which can lead to a lack of simplicity, though it is not easy for an outside observer to notice it. I refer to what goes on in someone's mind. In one's own intimate life a whole series of scruples can develop which prevent a person from recognising the things that really matter. In so far as possible, parents should help their children to distinguish between important things and secondary things: this makes them have more simplicity in their dealings with others. It is worth remembering that a person can act in a falsely simple way in relationships with others, doing so as a tactic to cover up their private problems.

Finally, let us look at social life as one of the things that causes lack of simplicity. Our relationships with others can operate at a deep level, when we want to know others and to prudently let ourselves be known because that is helpful to both parties. Or they can operate at a superficial level, when one talks and listens only pretending to be interested or concerned. This can happen when one performs social duties as a mere obligation, and when one looks on others as mere objects with no right to be respected as the human beings they are.

There is, of course, the question of how far one should go to 'pretend' to be interested in order to open the way to a deeper relationship with someone. Obviously it is a matter of finding some balance between the tactic of taking an interest in something which I really am not interested in, and the quite legitimate objective of being interested in the other person as person and therefore in anything that interests him. The latter desire can lead someone to incorporate into his social behaviour and his thoughts, subjects which initially he would have no personal liking for: he incorporates them in order to communicate with and be interested in others. Obviously, this implies making an effort.

The way simplicity expresses itself

Simplicity expresses itself in different ways depending on a person's intentions. If he pursues a series of goals which include improving as a son of God, as a son of his parents, as a parent, as a spouse, friend, companion, worker etc., and helping others to do the same, his simplicity will be noticed in his everyday behaviour. Simplicity can be detected in the refined way someone deals with others, in his obvious joy at meeting someone he knows, in his patience in a difficult situation, in his habit of looking on the positive side of things, in a tendency to avoid being argumentative, in a capacity to do things without attracting attention, in the warm praise he expresses without going too far, in enthusiastic gratitude, in an ability to correct his mistakes, in dressing well or in having a trusting and respectful relationship with God.

Therefore, simplicity is not a virtue with only a limited field of action. It affects all the other virtues and makes them enormously attractive and genuine.

Parents should watch their children in order to note which aspects of simplicity they need to improve on. Where does each child find difficulty? It may be in his ability to express himself in speech, or in writing, or in relations with others or perhaps in his own mind.

To be able to look after children in this regard parents themselves need to be simple and to have a capacity to show their trust and affection. It is not enough to trust one's children and love them: this trust and love needs to be expressed. Simplicity will bring parents to act in a warmhearted way and, if they are Christians, they will draw continuous inspiration from the Holy Family of Nazareth.

SELF-ASSESSMENT

Briefing Note: see pages 29-30, above.

Do I practise simplicity?

1. *I try to act transparently in my close relationships with others and with God.* (There are two major problems in living simplicity. First of all one needs to know what one's aims in life are, and secondly one has to avoid having one thing in one's heart and another in one's actions.)

2. *I think about what my aims in life are and I have a clear answer.* (Simplicity will be impossible in one's behaviour if one has not ordered one's ideas.)

3. *I realise that simplicity is necessary for discovering truth, for having authentic relationships, and even so as not to make a fool of myself.* (Trying to be what one is not, or cheating or acting with duplicity, are sure ways to being pitied or even ridiculed by others.)

4. *I try to establish a consistency between my actions and what I think and say.* (To be consistent the whole time is not easy, but if one manages it, it establishes a personal style which is recognised as such by others. In this way one can be trusted by others and feel comfortable in relationships.)

5. *I try to dress elegantly, in keeping with who I am. I try to avoid dressing in ways which could lead other people to think I am something that I am not.* (Someone said that elegance is making the garment fit the body, and the two to suit the situation. We are not suggesting that one should not dress up for a special occasion, for example, but one should try to avoid excesses.)

6. *I express myself in language that suits the subject and the people I am talking to.* (Irony, pedantry, and hypocrisy all militate against simplicity. But so does using language which does not match one's own principles or one's personality.)

7. *I try to let myself be known intimately at home and even more so in my relations with God. However, I share my intimate self prudently with others.* (Turn one's own intimate self into public property is not what simplicity is about. Simplicity is not naivety.)

8. *When relating to other people, I try to show real interest in the things they are interested in.* (One can notice when people are only pretending to be interested. They say, 'How interesting!' in a half-hearted way. Their minds are somewhere else.)

9. *My simplicity can be recognised by: being refined towards others; a sincere expression of joy on meeting someone on the street; patience shown in some difficult situation; the fact I try to find positive things in other people; avoiding unnecessarily complicated conversations; congratulating others without exaggerating; giving enthusiastic thanks; apologising when necessary; dressing elegantly; a confident and respectful relationship with God.* (These are not the only ways to practise simplicity, but they may be useful as a first checklist.)

10. *I normally show trust and affection in my relations with others.* (People who distrust others or who are selfish cannot practise the virtue of simplicity. Deceit and duplicity are their fate.)

Teaching others to practise simplicity

11. *I try to create and take advantage of situations which will enable the smaller children to grasp what is genuine and to develop worthwhile values.* (Simplicity has to do with being natural and experiencing goodness, beauty, truth and order. It helps the children internalise values in a natural way. This can happen on trips into the country, visiting an exhibition, spending time with someone who is ill, or through a joyful family life.)

12. *I help the smaller children learn to keep rules which are inspired by these values.* (Once again, we want children to experience values through actions.)

13. *I try to have a spontaneous and natural atmosphere in the home, although I insist on children learning to control their basic tendencies.* (Uncontrolled spontaneity has no value in itself. It must be controlled by the will. The smaller children will find this difficult but, little by little, they will discover how they should behave in each circumstance.)

14. *I help the children think about their actions so that they can see if they are related to family or school values.* (Getting the children to conform should change to getting them to think before making their own decisions. Simplicity does not exclude thinking. On the contrary, it requires it.)

15. *I try to get the children to be straightforward in their relationships in the family and with God so that they can hear his voice.* (People with mixed-up ideas, with interior worries or who don't want to be what they really are, are rarely going to be able to live a truly Christian life.)

16. *I help the adolescents detect any tendency they may have to think they are richer or poorer than what they really are; that they are older or younger than what they really are; or a tendency to try to be just like everyone else rather than wanting to be themselves.* (Thirteen- or fourteen-year-old girls often put on make-up as though they were eighteen-years-old. Many children want to dress like their peer-group even if it does not go with their personal style, or they invent stories to make out that they are more interesting than they really are.)

17. *I help the adolescents not to deceive themselves as regards their intelligence or their competence in some matter.* (There are other ways of living duplicity and which may carry on for the rest of their lives. For example, quoting from books they have never read, using a tone of voice which is not their own.)

18. *I help the youngsters think about all the activities they engage so as to distinguish between those that are vital, others that are important, others secondary, others unnecessary and finally those that are negative in themselves. This means I try*

to help them make their lives less complicated. (Some youngsters want to read everything under the pretext of being up to date, they want to see every film that's on, because their friends do, or they spend excessive sums of money or time on listening to music, or talking on the telephone. They go out just for the sake of going out and they sleep far more than they need.)

19. *I help the youngsters get to know themselves so that they can set up small objectives to aim at.* (With certain kinds of very sensitive youngsters one should be careful because they can develop scruples.)

20. *I put the youngsters into situations which will stimulate them to think about the connection between what they usually do and their intimate goals in life.* (It is easy to cheat oneself. And this applies not only to youngsters. We need other people – spouse, mother or father, child, friend, teacher or priest – to help us in our process of personal development.)

21 Sociability

Sociable people make good use of and discover ways of getting together with others; they manage to communicate with them through the genuine interest they show in them, in what they say and do, in what they think and feel.

Sociability's true meaning emerges when we consider the human person as a social being. A person needs other people if he is to improve, and he has a duty to help others to develop as fully as possible. If there is no communication between the different members of a society or group, neither will more profound relationships come about, such as friendship or marriage. Indeed even the possibility of acting in favour of others depends on their first having made their needs known.

On the one hand, sociability is a virtue which helps many other virtues to develop at the level of relationships between individuals, but on the other it leads to specific acts in favour of different groups of similar people, without one ever becoming very close to them. In this sense, sociability has to do with a kind of unselfish solidarity based on the supreme principles of charity and love of one's neighbour, much more than merely utilitarian motives.

We will look at four aspects of the development of this virtue:

- how to educate children so that they learn to get on well with a group of people and be interested in them,
- how to develop the child's ability to communicate with others,
- how to make best use of and create good ways of being sociable,
- how to connect sociability with solidarity.

Getting on well with and being interested in others

The small child's first contacts with the other members of the family occur in an intimate atmosphere and only after some time does he begin to have contact with other children outside the family setting. Also, during these first stages the child does not usually take into account the existence of other children: he can play in the same place as they but he will not play with them. Contact is limited to affective reactions whenever his living-space is invaded, or he may watch some of the things they do. At first it might seem that these activities are not geared to train small children to get on well and be interested in others. But that is not true. In the first place, the child has to learn to be physically in the same place as other children of his age, even though there is no conscious communication going on. Then, children begin to learn that they need other children for doing certain attractive things – playing a game or attaining some common objective – and then communication becomes quite necessary. We can notice how children begin to accept the rules of the game and to realise that, within the general similarity of the group, each child is different, has different qualities. Therefore, the child will seek out different companions for different activities, depending on the qualities he has discovered or the sympathy the other child has aroused. Thus, the captain of a team will chose people who are able to play best, or the person he likes most. From quite early on small children can notice two aspects in others: whether they are good at things and whether they are likeable. When he notices that someone is likeable the child takes the first steps towards friendship; when he sees that someone is good at something this leads more to sociability. For sociability does not involve having to share intimacy: it means learning to take an interest in others, to learn from and to help them.

Small children will get on well with others if the rules of the game are imposed by their educators. Therefore, one of the most important stimuli for getting a child to accept, without any difficulty, being in contact with a group of strangers (the first day at school, for example) is if someone he trusts introduces him to the group in an affectionate way, showing him who is the new person in charge – in this case, the teacher – and if he is told, immediately, some rules of the game which he can easily keep. For example, telling him where his seat is, showing him clearly how to take part in some activity, etc.

This problem of adapting to a new group of people can arise at all ages. It may be due to natural shyness or to the 'frustrations' of realising that now that one is in a new group one is less important than before.

A child's shyness can largely be counteracted by helping him to have more confidence in his own ability. To do this you have to identify what things he is good at and, then, perhaps without other people noticing, encourage him to do these things and show affection to him, making him see that he has done the thing well: this is the point when the attention of others can be called, for them to see how good he is. Others will notice what he does well, not what he does badly. An older person, however, has to use his own will-power to overcome his shyness. It is quite normal for many people to feel nervous or ill at ease in new situations, with new people – in some cases this shyness increases as they get older. The first step in overcoming shyness is to help the person to recognise it for what it is; it also helps to realise that other people in the group may feel the same way. Sometimes, people's facial gestures or the way they walk or speak would lead you to think that they have no difficulty in communicating with others – but this behaviour may only be a cover-up for their sense of insecurity.

A person who has too high an opinion of himself meets other difficulties. He may want to be the leader of the group: he may seek in the group a chance to throw his weight around. This is a form of pride which obstructs communication because it fails to grasp the real value other people have. Therefore, it is good to get the small child to learn early on that he is not the only one in the world. If parents can involve their child in the family of friends of theirs this might help him: not only will he see that he is not the most important person there, but he will find that there are different rules of the game in the other home. Getting on well with people means you have to learn the rules of the game of that particular group.

We have been speaking particularly about small children, but problems also arise among older children: they too need to be helped to take a positive interest in others.

Before he becomes conscious of his own intimacy, a child can have difficulty in being sociable because he is isolated from the group or has tried to break the rules of the game which allow the life of the group to run smoothly. He can still have these problems in pre-adolescence or he may try to limit the extent of his close relationships and shut the group out of his mind.

The reasons for this 'exclusivist' approach are, in part, quite good. He wants to share intimate things with just a few chosen people who are his friends. He needs to talk about his experiences, his feelings etc., to people who are not going to sit in judgment on him. However, sociability implies that he should not break off his relations with other people. It is good for him to talk to different people, to be involved in different groups – in sports, hobbies and so forth; but these activities are not ends in themselves. I mean, they can be used not just for the purpose of the activity itself: they can help him be concerned about and interested in other people. Children will learn to take an interest in others if they realise these others have something interesting to contribute. And this means they need to learn how to ask questions. Specifically, many people are tempted to classify others as 'bores', for example, simply because they have never bothered to ask them about their opinions or experiences. There are always things we can learn from others, and children can grasp this if their parents try to show them the advantages of taking an interest in other people by asking questions.

To sum up, what we have said so far is that to develop this virtue parents have to:

- introduce their children, from an early age, to groups outside the family where they will get an opportunity to learn the rules of the game;
- help them to overcome any sort of shyness they may have, giving them affectionate support and explaining to them the rules of the game for getting on well with others;

- help them to recognise that everyone, by definition, is interesting: they should try to 'draw out' of every person his best qualities, parallel with developing closer friendships.

But sociability depends largely on one's capacity to strike up good relationships. And this means one has to be able to communicate.

Communicating with other people

In describing this virtue at the start, we said it was a matter of communicating with others on the basis of the interest in and concern one shows for them, interest in what they say, in what they do, in what they think and feel. However, you cannot show this interest unless you learn to express it verbally and through gestures. Nor can you offer others your own thinking etc., in any way which attracts them, unless you have these abilities. It is a matter of *knowing how to ask questions and having the knack of telling other people interesting things in a nice way.* I think in fact that it is more important to learn how to ask questions than how to tell things oneself – though, obviously, there has to be a balance.

In order to ask questions, you have to know the other person to some extent. For, if we do not know some basic things about their job, where they come from, their interests, their hobbies, etc., we will not be able to ask questions on which they have interesting information to contribute. For example, if you begin by asking some stranger about his opinion on the advantages and disadvantages of trade tariffs, he may have no opinion or know nothing about the subject. That is why conversations between strangers usually begin with an exchange of basic information or else they deal with things which everyone knows something about, even if it is not very much: subjects like education, politics, or local affairs. If the conversation has to do with something which people generally know little about, it is not usually very satisfactory. On the other hand, if it deals with one person's speciality, there is the danger that he ends up 'lecturing' others.

Some consequences follow from this. Sociability means that you have to be able to combine personal attention (allowing the other person to share what he knows) what he personally feels is important, with attention to the group, getting people to express opinions on subjects of interest to all.

The ability to ask questions implies, perhaps, thinking out some questions or subjects before meeting and then listening to the answers, asking more questions in order to develop the discussion, and expressing one's own opinion, now and again, briefly. In this sense, being sociable means being someone with broad general interests.

On the other hand, one should not forget other people's feelings. It is not easy to detect how each person is reacting to the way a subject is developing. But sociability does mean having concern for the way people feel.

These abilities can be nurtured in family settings, by encouraging the children to ask each other questions after a television programme, or about any event everyone knows about. Or, when some guest comes by, explaining to the teenagers who he is and suggesting things they could ask him. This way a young person gains in self-confidence and takes an interest in others through getting them to say interesting things.

On the other hand, we have said that it is also a matter of learning to express oneself. This is not something that schools pay much attention to, usually. Pupils are not normally very good at expressing themselves. There are a number of reasons why this is so: too much insistence on memorizing facts without encouraging the pupils to think on their own account; a tendency for young people to use 'slogans' rather than try to express shades of meaning; frequent use of swear words or slang expressions and therefore a tendency to beat people down by being loudmouthed rather than convince them by force of argument.

Bearing in mind this kind of thing, parents should encourage their children to learn to express themselves. From an early age they can tell stories to their brothers and sisters, organise some game in which each participant has to speak for a limited amount of time or some subject drawn out of a hat, ask them to tell about what happened in some TV programme; let them read the newspaper and then talk about the more important items etc. We should never forget that the great thing about reading is that it is the best way for them to increase their vocabulary and powers of expression. Naturally they should get guidance not only as regards the content of what they read but also about even the author's style.

We have already dealt with problems of shyness in the company of others but there is also the problem of children being anti-social through never keeping quiet, talking all the time. They should be spoken to privately and every effort made to get them to think more. And their friends should be given the same advice, as far as possible.

Summing up, the most important problems to do with ability to communicate are: talking too much or too little, through lack of vocabulary or not thinking enough; always talking about one's own interests without taking other people's interests into account; keeping quiet out of shyness or pride; not knowing how to ask questions; not knowing how to keep conversation going; and not knowing how to bring up subjects which are interesting in themselves.

Making good use of and creating ways of being sociable

We have referred, in passing, to various situations which are natural channels for the development of the virtue of sociability, such as for example one's own family, the families of friends, and school. However, sociability can be promoted by creating other channels or exploiting those which other people create.

Small children get used to mixing with others through experience in groups created by their parents and educators, but the time will come when they develop a social life of their own. This usually begins with birthday parties where the child invites their companions home, or on outings. This is not very difficult for the child – his parents do most of the work! – because he knows these other children already. Sociability is really tested when strangers or near strangers are invited as may happen when the whole family is away somewhere on holidays; or even, when children are in their teens, when they begin to meet others who come from a different school or locality. Organising these social activities, or helping the children to organise them, is good, provided that parents retain the right to be present or near-by in order to take a hand if the 'tone' of the party goes off in the wrong direction. There are some parents who think that they should never be around when the older children bring their friends home. But I don't agree; obviously it is not a matter of being there all the time; but if the parents are sometimes chatting with the young people, asking them what they think, getting them to think etc., this can help the teenagers in their own relationships.

Additionally, it is good to keep an eye out for other good ideas, club activities, parish outings, sports activities, suitable for the young people, in order to encourgage them to take part in groups of people they do not know so well, but where there is a good atmosphere. They same applies to parties organised by the children's friends. It would not be wise to let teenagers go

to a party if one knew that none of the parents or no other responsible person was going to be there. It is not a question of trusting or not trusting one's own children, but of being sensible enough to make sure, as far as possible, that the scene is wholesome. Exactly the same concern can and should apply to parents' own social activities.

Sociability and solidarity

At this point it might be good to look a little further at the connection between sociability and solidarity. Solidarity is a very fashionable idea these days; it normally means support which different people with common interests give each other in order to maintain or obtain their rights. In this sense, the solidarity of a group of people automatically is in confrontation with the solidarity of another group: the whole concept is rather exclusivist and impermanent. Once the common objective has been obtained, there is no further need for solidarity: it has only the role of a means to attain some limited end. However, solidarity can be taken in a much higher sense. For people who believe in man's transcendence and his orientation to God, solidarity is a question of human brotherhood. Having one and the same origin, nature and destiny as everyone else, a person can recognise an unlimited field for joining in with others. And, in terms of education, solidarity will lead the human person to relate to everyone in order to render them service as best he can. In this sense, we can say that 'solidarity is, at least logically, prior to man's sociability. People are not in solidarity with others because they are sociable by nature; they are sociable because solidarity already exists.'[77]

From what we have said it can be seen that sociability must be based on a deep respect for others. And this respect means not only that one should be careful how one acts so as not to harm people but also one should try positively to help them.[78]

SELF-ASSESSMENT

Briefing Note: see pages 29–30, above.

Am I sociable myself?

1. *I realise that I need others in order to grow as a person and that I have a duty to help others grow, too.* (This is what a 'social being' is. Sociability, understood as a virtue, will not make any sense if one doesn't try to improve.)

2. *I make an effort in my own life to establish relationships with different people and groups.* (These contacts also offer opportunities for practising other virtues, for example, friendship, social responsibility, or understanding. Usually, as life goes by, people tend to be restrictive as regards new contacts, often because of the effort involved in having to adapt to people we don't know.)

3. *When I come into contact with strangers or with people I scarcely know, I make an effort to show interest in what they do, who they are, what they say and what they feel.* (If this interest in knowing other people doesn't exist, or if we don't show it, no kind of communicative process will start.)

4. *I take advantage of different kinds of situations in everyday life in order to establish these kinds of relationships.* (There are a lot of opportunities; some people grasp them and others don't. For example, in a parents' meeting at school there are always some who only talk to people they already know, whereas there are others who make an effort to broaden their range of friends. The same thing happens at a conference or at other kinds of meetings. Some people take advantage of trips they have to make in order to meet new people, and others prefer to stay in their shell.)

5. *I try to create new situations on purpose in order to get to know more people.* (One thing is to take advantage of the situations which crop up, and another is to organise some activity on purpose. I refer to inviting people whom we scarcely know home for a meal, inviting someone to take part in some sporting activity, organising some group activity, an outing, for example.)

6. *I make an effort to overcome my shyness or lack of self-assurance in order to relate to others better.* (There are many causes of unsociable behaviour. Some have already been mentioned, but laziness and/or self-sufficiency can be factors, too.)

7. *I usually make an effort to ask other people questions and then I listen carefully to their replies.* (This could even mean thinking up questions to ask prior to a particular special gathering, until one has developed the technique of knowing how to ask questions.)

8. *I try to express myself in an attractive way in order to awaken interest in the listener.* (Obviously sociability requires communication between at least two people. If other people have little initiative, I need to help them. If they have initiative, there won't be much difficulty in developing a relationship inspired by sociability.)

9. *I try to be a cultured person who has wide interests.* (Communication requires having interests that we share with others. If we have very limited interests, we can be sociable only with those people who share the same limited interests – a surgeon with another surgeon, for example.)

10. *I notice other people's reactions in order to find the right theme for conversation and to check if I am talking too much or too little.* (One problem in connection with sociability is not knowing how to express oneself; but another, perhaps more common, is trying to dominate the conversation, talking too much.)

Teaching others to be sociable

11. *I teach the small children how to obey the rules necessary for getting on with other people.* (It is the first step on the road to sociability – knowing how to get on with people.)

12. *I organise activities for the smaller children where they have to learn to count on others.* (Small children will start off playing on their own, but for team games they need each other. Here educators have to play a part.)

13. *I help the children get to know their classmates and friends, to some extent.* (For example, when they choose people to form part of a team they are

learning about criteria for knowing and for relating to others. In this case the criterion may be the other child's skill at the game or simply because one likes him/her.)

14. *I help shy children to develop some abilities which will make them more acceptable to the group.* (If lack of sociability is due to shyness, it is not wise to try to force the child be more sociable. If they are forced, they will probably fail. The important thing is that they should know how to do something that the others need.)

15. *I help only-children and self-sufficient children to recognise the need to adapt to the group, and I explain to them that the group will not adapt to them.* (Only-children have little experience of adapting to others, and those who are self-sufficient have never needed others. That is why being sociable is difficult for many children of this sort.)

16. *I help the adolescent children have close friends – which is all very natural – but I also encourage them to be open to others.* (Each stage of development has its own problems as regards sociability. In adolescence this kind of 'exclusive' friend is probably one of the greatest because sometimes it leads the youngsters to pay little attention to others and even come to despise them.)

17. *I teach the youngsters to ask questions, to help them get to know other people.* (When they ask questions, they discover that other people are interesting, that they have something to say for themselves.)

18. *I teach the youngsters to express themselves in public.* (The youngsters need to have interesting things to tell, and need to know how to tell them.)

19. *I teach the youngsters to look for subjects which everyone can talk about when they are in a group.* (The integration of the group depends on the members having common interests. Frequently some sub-group will start talking about some subject which interests only them, and the rest cannot participate. This is not only 'bad manners' but also a lack of sociability.)

20. *I teach the youngsters to create or use situations where they can develop their sociability.* (For example: get-togethers to celebrate something, trips to some cultural or sporting event, activities in the parish, activities in a club, games or outings.)

22 Friendship

By means of friendship, a person, who already knows other people through shared interests in work or leisure, develops regular personal contract with them. Friendship involves mutual rapport – each taking an interest in the other and in her or his improvement.

It can be difficult to see friendship as a virtue. In what sense is it a good operative habit? Saint Thomas Aquinas says that friendship is a kind of virtue because it is a *habitus electivus* which comes under the general heading of justice in the sense that it is a sign of sharing. However, it differs from justice in that justice looks at friendship from the point of view of legal indebtedness, whereas friendship is based, rather, on moral indebtedness or, better, on gratuitous benefit. We are discussing, then, disinterested mutual affection.

Before looking at how to teach friendship, one further thing should be clarified. In our description at the beginning of the chapter, we referred to regular personal contacts arising out of mutual rapport. But it was not clear whether these contacts are the only basis of friendship or whether a person who engages in these contacts does not need to have some other special quality. In other words, is it possible for friendship to exist between two people who act in a morally wrong way? Friendship arises out of virtue and it grows as virtue grows. This growth, in turn, makes the person more loveable and more capable of loving. Therefore, bad people are pleasing to each other not in so far as they are bad, or indifferent, but because everyone has some good in him and people respond to this. There is no friendship where there is no virtue.'[79]

A third point to bear in mind is that friendship means a very close relationship. Therefore, a person cannot have deep friendship until he has reached the point of discovering his own intimacy and of learning how to share it with others. In this sense, it is useful to distinguish friendship from other acts related to it. 'Sociability extends to everyone; love, to one's neighbour, to the people about; friendship, to one's intimates.[80] But, in real life, it is difficult for friendships to arise unless one gets involved with people in general. It is a question of having lots of social relationships and practising the Christian virtue of charity with everyone, because only in that way can mutual sympathy and rapport arise and friendships develop.

Friendship: conditions and characteristics

In everyday life adults find themselves in all sorts of human relationships, (based on work or leisure activities) out of which friendships may or may not grow. A typical situation is where we invite to our home a couple who have recently come to live near us: in the conversation we automatically look for subjects which everyone is familiar with, and we get an exchange of impressions: we discuss children, schools, different parts of the country, etc. And it is also normal to find out what interests the other people have and what they work at (though some people, through shyness or pride, take no interest in others and do nothing to try to get to know them). This knowledge is necessary if the people concerned are to get any further involved with each other. If, in conversation, no common interest or experience is discovered, then it is very unlikely that any friendship will develop. Therefore, we can say that these are the conditions necessary for friendship to arise: there should be some common interests and a minimum of homogeneity in the types of people involved and their grasp of the subjects discussed. If these common interests include being interested in each other, and if as a result of being together they each develop a greater personal maturity, a friendship begins which can be detected in a mutual desire to share experiences, feelings, thoughts and plans.

Our children also get into situations of this kind – at home, in school, in clubs for young people. Not all their companions will be friends, even though they engage in lots of activities together. Depending on age, the relationship will vary in tone and we should bear in mind the way these relationships arise, when it comes to looking at the subject of friendship. For example, can friendship be said to apply between parents and children, or between young boys and young girls?

It should be that friendship is not the same as sharing some activities or knowing someone for a long time. Friendship implies some sort of connection which can be the result of a long process or a half-hour meeting. 'Friendship is a free spiritual union of mutual, expansive and creative human love; it is a connection different from sex or the instincts of the flesh.'[81]

Within this context it is obvious that there can be friendship between parents and children, but it is even clearer that the parent-child relationship is not limited to friendship. As soon as there are regular contacts between parents and children where each tries to help the other to improve, there can be friendship. However, the parent who takes an interest in what his child is doing, who talks to him, who gives him real support, but who does not seek – or does not find – a reciprocal response in this relationship: this parent is developing a relationship different from friendship. Usually, people say that it is good for parents to be friends of their children in the sense that they ought to take an interest in these things in order to create an atmosphere of acceptance and open communication in which the children can tell their parents intimate things. However, as I see it, parents can give their children friendship only in so far as the parent manages to get his child to respond in some way: the child has to seek the parent's good. When a son really takes an active interest in his father, he can do so as a son or as a friend. The two roles are complementary, but it is worth emphasising that the son continues to be a son of his father even if he does not become his friend.

The relationship between a boy and a girl presents a different type of problem. Following the description of friendship we gave at the beginning, we can see how a friendship can arise very naturally between a boy and a girl. They can see each other regularly, there can be mutual sympathy and rapport, and each can take an interest in the other and in the other's improvement. However, between people of the opposite sex another factor comes in: the basic attraction or the radical possibility that the male-female relationship may eventually lead to the mutual surrender of their bodies. For the young person who acts in an upright way this means marriage, whose character as a natural contract between a man and a woman, 'differentiates it totally from the unions which animals form among themselves under the impetus of blind natural instinct, and in which reason and deliberation have no part; it also distinguishes marriage entirely from those irregular unions of human beings in which there is nothing of a true and honourable bond of wills, and which are devoid of any legitimate domestic status.'[82]

The whole *raison d'etre* of man and woman is obvious from Gen 1:27-28: 'God created man in the image of himself, in the image of God he created him, male and female. And God blessed them and God said unto them, Be fruitful and multiply and replenish the earth.'

Therefore, in a personal relationship with someone of the opposite sex a young person will be in a situation in which there exists the possibility, created by God, of committing himself completely, body and soul.

A young person with the right principles might think that he is quite capable of differentiating between these two dimensions, but he ought to realise that at the very least he is taking an unnecessary risk. When he finds someone whom he thinks he could marry, he should think of her as his future wife and treat her with the respect which a person merits who could be his partner in an enterprise blessed by God. If he does not realise that the physical aspect is implicit in this personal involvement, he may try to separate the two aspects and this will encourage such aberrations as pre-marital sex, for example.

On the other hand, it is perfectly correct for people of opposite sexes to come together in connection with some activity, if they realise that the object of the exercise is precisely that: to study for exams, for example. This is not friendship, but companionship, and all they have to do is bear in mind the proper limits of the relationship.

Children learn the rules of the game where activities involving participation by people of the same sex are concerned – sports, etc; but often parents and other educators do not teach them the rules of the game for situations where people of both sexes take part. A man who does not use his will-power is rather like an animal, and children have to be trained to use their will in that very often badly understood area of relationships between man and woman.

Friends at different ages

I do not propose to look at the psychology of human relationships at different stages in life, but just to deal with some basic factors from the point of view of what parents can do.

When a couple go to the school and ask the teacher whether their children have any friends, they often don't really know what they mean. It is good for the child to have friends, but let us see what this means in the case of small children.

Clearly, we are not speaking here of a friendship based on personal commitment. It is more a matter of knowing if the child plays with other children, if he talks to them, if he shares his interests with others, if he is generous to others, and then whether he spends more time with some particular children.

This interaction with other children enables the child to develop two important facets of his personality. On the one hand, he begins to recognise his role within the group; he realises that he has something to contribute to the group and something to get from it; he begins to obey the rules of the game and will be called to order by his companions if he fails to keep them. In other words, he is learning to be a social being. In this learning process, he sees that other children are stronger, cleverer or more influential – or that he in fact is influential. At this stage, the most important thing is that he learn to get involved in the group, mainly through positively accepting his role in this group and the parts the others play.

A child who takes part in one of these activities or interests (football, talking, playing marbles) is called, at this stage, a 'friend', and the children who prefer other activities are companions. The most problematic children in this stage are shy ones, who are afraid to take part in a group, and spoilt children, who often have a very bad time because suddenly they discover that others are not inclined to indulge their whims.

Some years later, 'friends' who are members of a group with common interests change, and there is a tendency to look for more intimate friends, people in whom the pre-adolescent can confide. The group continues to have importance, but the child can already distinguish companions from friends. He has not yet learned to contribute positively to the relationships, and sometimes the only use he has for friendship is the chance it gives him to express his feelings.

Later, when he wants to be independent of his parents, the young person tries to know many people whom he can call his 'friends', though they are still only companions with interests in common, who meet to study, to go on excursions, etc. The more he matures, the more selective he becomes in these relationships, distinguishing between a general sort of relationship and one which calls for commitment on his part. It is not very usual for a person to have many friends. Of course, he will know quite a few people and establish relationships with them, in which there is a sharing of particular aspects of life.

Friendship and the other human virtues

We have said already that there is no friendship where there is no virtue. Therefore, the development of the whole range of human virtues is essential for friendship. A few examples should show this. Loyalty is a virtue which helps a person to accept the bonds implicit in his attachment to his friend; as time goes on, it strengthens and protects the series of values that go to make up friendship. Generosity makes it easier for a friend to help another, taking into account what is useful and necessary for his improvement. Modesty will control the extent to which he surrenders certain aspects of his intimacy. Understanding will help him to recognise the various factors which affect his situation. Trust and respect lead a person to show interest in his friend: to show that he believes in him and in his ability to improve. We could say, therefore, that a good friend is someone who tries to surpass himself in a whole series of virtues. The problem is: how to get our children to choose this kind of person as a friend, and to keep up the friendship?

From another point of view it is also the problem of what is usually called 'bad influence'. What does 'bad influence' mean?

On the one hand, we should be realistic and recognise that there is not much point protecting a child from outside influences on a continuous basis, because at some stage he is going to meet them and if he is not prepared to deal with them they may be much more harmful. However, it is not a matter, either, of abandoning our children, thinking that we should not or cannot help them.

Someone or something is a bad influence who brings about such a change in a person that his usual behaviour is at variance with right values. The worst effect of bad influence is when there is a radical change in the person's principles, implying destruction or abandonment of the truth.

In other words, bad influence tends to form the development of vices rather than virtues.

If we agree on this, we will see that occasional influence is not very important, provided the effect on the child's behaviour is only temporary. That is to say, if some companion has told the child why he is in favour of abortion and our child accepts the reasons he gives, because he is not clear in his own mind on this subject, it is not very important if he announces he is in favour of abortion; in fact, it gives us a chance to discuss the subject with him.

However, if this idea is backed up by others which lead to a new style of behaviour and of approach, then the situation is serious.

Therefore, we can say that the most dangerous 'friendship' a person can have is a relationship based on dependence of one person on another where the young person allows this influence to be exerted on him and makes no use of his own principles. Parents should keep a careful eye on the so-called 'friendships' between their as yet immature children, and people who are very sure of themselves but whose principles are all wrong.

Secondly, you have to keep an eye on the friendship a child may have with someone else which is based not on that person's personality but on the attraction of activities he brings the child into. For example, the attraction of a powerful motor-bike, something in itself quite reasonable, could be bad if it were a sign of complete lack of moderation in its owner or his parents.

Finally, parents should look after their teenage children who don't know how to commit themselves in a relationship, who change companions continually for no particular reason, who don't think about what they want or expect of others. Friend-ship implies service. A child who has not learned to serve others will only with difficulty develop a friendship based on mutual improvement.

But we have not yet answered the question we posed earlier: how to get our children to choose 'good' friends?

A child will choose someone he finds attractive. And this 'attractiveness' depends largely on what the parents have taught their children from an early age. If the children have had a soft life, going always after superficial pleasures, it is quite likely that the child will look for 'friends' among people who can give him the same sort of pleasure. If, on the other hand, the parents have tried to practise generosity, being concerned about others, it is more likely that their children will grasp this value and assimilate it themselves.

Therefore, parents should try to guide their children as regards the sort of activities they get involved in, aware that in any group a majority of people will be either suitable or unsuitable. It seems reasonable to expect that they will find more scope for good friendship in a club for secondary schoolboys than in a group which meets to smoke cigarettes, drink and talk disrespectfully about girls, for example. However, the group which stands a better chance of providing good friendships may seem boring and staid. Here is a challenge for the parents: organise or promote activities which are really interesting, which appeal to the young people's sense of adventure or to their artistic interests or their concern for others.

In better settings of this sort, the young person can begin to choose his friends, and parents should try to give him some guidance showing him how to be a good friend, visiting the other person when he is sick, cheering him up when he is a bit gloomy, going with him when he has some job to do, sharing his intimacy as far as makes sense. And making an effort to keep in regular contact not only during normal times, such as term time, but also during holidays, by sending postcards or ringing him up. It is this effort to keep in touch that enables some people to stay friends, even to the end of their life, with someone they knew in childhood.

The family's role

Sometimes it almost looks as if family life prevents one from keeping up friendship. For example, when the parents want to take the whole family on an outing and one of the children prefers to go off with some friend. It is good to organise activities where the family can feel united, but it is also good to respect the children's personal tastes. If we accept that our children should have friends, and companions, and family life, a little common sense will solve the problems.

However, there is another role of the family – it is a role of the parents, mainly – which is worth mentioning. Parents want their children to have friends, but they also want to be sure that the friendships are the right ones. It is their job to present the family they have to their children not as a castle where only members of the family are allowed but as a grouping which is ready and more than ready to receive other people into it. Parents have no right to enter into their children's intimacy (and part of this intimacy is their relationship with their friends) but they do have a duty to create an environment and to create attractive situations where they can get to know their children's friends. When they do come to know them they should be careful not to judge or prejudge these people simply on their external behaviour or the way they dress. In some cases there may be no problem: in others, our child may be able to do the other child a lot of good, and we can let the friendship develop after we have made things clear to our child, who already is rather mature; but on other occasions we will have to tell him that this other person is a dangerous influence and explain why. We cannot say 'no' continually, and in fact there will be no need to if we have managed to get across to our children what true friendship is.

On the other hand, the home is the place where children can feel secure. They begin to develop relationships with outsiders and they experience disappointment and are let down. They will develop more readily in society mainly through knowing that they are accepted in their own home.

Summing up, the family should serve its children by allowing them to invite others into their home, where they can see their life-style, and be influenced for the better by it. And, also, the family should always have its arms wide open so that its child, when he begins to forge his own future in all sorts of relationships with others, can return whenever he likes, knowing that his relationship with his parents is more than friendship: it is a relationship of son or daughter.

In this connection, it should be pointed out that parents cannot and should not try to be a substitute for the children's friends. Children expect their parents to be just that, parents.

The parents' example

Most of us, when we relate to others, tend to do so on very personal criteria. Some married couples concentrate their social life on the extended family; others, gravitate round a club; others don't even think they have time to have friends; and others meet people only in the context of work.

A married couple also have a problem which an individual does not have. For example, one wife may get on very well with another, but the two husbands may not be friends at all. But, as we said earlier, we should differentiate between 'friends' with whom we share some hobby or activity, and people whom we are personally committed to.

Children should see in their parents people who are ready to commit themselves, to help, to give, even if it costs an effort, because that is what makes friendship such a great thing. Parents who concentrate their 'friendships' on superficial social activities lead their children to think that friends are tools for making life pleasant for oneself. Inviting people home, behaving nicely towards them, and then criticising them behind their backs gives a child a totally wrong idea of his duties to his companions.

In other words, we are asking parents to have great respect for the people they have contact with; to weigh up opinions and events rather than criticise the people involved, and to really commit themselves to many of these people so that they become genuine friends whose presence enriches both the individual and the family.

Conclusion

Friendship presupposes a certain togetherness, a meeting of minds and feelings and desires. It follows from this that most of one's friends will share one's basic principles, though some may have a radically different outlook. If there is respect, flexibility and a real desire on the part of both to help each other, to find the truth, then a deep friendship can develop. If that is not the case, the relationship will meet lots of obstacles and mutual affection can easily disappear and turn into a desire to dominate the other party. In other words, it will be a fragile friendship. Friendship will be cemented through the effort of both to develop, at least, in human virtues. A good friend makes demands on his friend, is understanding with him, is an example to him, gives him what he needs – neither more nor less – and finds time to spend with him. Nowadays we are very mean with the time we devote to friends and that makes no sense; it is inhuman.

SELF-ASSESSMENT

Briefing Note: see pages 29-30, above.

Do I practise friendship?

1. *In my contact with people at work or in a social context, I am conscious that they may become my friends in the future.* (Friendship means choosing among people one knows. If we know few people, we will have less freedom of choice. But one should also be conscious of the possibility of meeting new people in those situations.)
2. *I know that for friendship to develop with someone, there must be some degree of homogeneity and common interest.* (It is possible to establish friendship with someone who is very different, but there must always be some common interests.)
3. *I am interested in my friends as people. I am not just interested in the things we have in common.* (If we are only interested in others as companions for doing something together, but are not interested in them as people, it would not be correct to talk about having friends. We would just be companions.)
4. *I make sure that I have regular contact with those I have selected as friends and who have selected me as their friend. I find time to keep in touch with my friends.* (Friendship is reciprocal. I cannot call someone my 'friend' if they do not want to call me their 'friend'. On the other hand, friendship means establishing regular contacts. For example: meeting each other, phoning each other, writing to each other, thinking or praying for them.)
5. *I understand that the quality of the friendship will increase to the degree that there are more exchanges related to intimate questions and to the degree that there is more mutual interest in the other as a person.* (If this kind of exchange related to intimate questions does not exist, the relationship cannot develop. But it is not a question of discussing all intimate questions, even those which are more appropriate for other kinds of relationships.)
6. *I am conscious that my friendship with people of the opposite sex should have its limits.* (Natural friendship leads people to want to share intimate things. A relationship between a man and a woman could involve intimate sharing of the body; therefore the limits of the relationship need to be established prudently.)
7. *Although I do relate well to all my children as a parent, I realise that a friendship may develop with one rather than another.* (It is logical that one will have more in common with one child than with another, but this is not important as the parent-child relationship must have priority.)

8. *I understand that to be a good friend to my friends, and for them to be good friends with me, we should be striving to improve in a number of human virtues.* (For example: loyalty, understanding, generosity, modesty, sincerity.)

9. *I try to pay attention to my personal friends, but I realise that married couples should also try to find couples with whom to be close friends.* (This isn't usually easy: often our friend's spouse may not become our spouse's friend. All the same, it is worthwhile trying to develop friendship as a couple.)

10. *I give good example to the rest of the family by the way I look after my friends.* (I visit my friends when they are ill, I don't talk badly about them behind their backs, I make an effort to keep in contact, I remember their birthdays, I invite them home, I write to them when I am on holiday.)

Teaching others to develop friendship

11. I teach the small children to know how to associate with others, to play with them, to talk to them and to share their interests. (At this early age the real concept of friendship does not exist. It is rather a question of introducing them to situations where they have to learn to relate to others. It is later on when they start choosing their friends.)

12. *Once the child is about eight years old I try to get them to play and work in teams, by committing themselves to the rules, and to the team.* (It is still not the age for the children to chose intimate friends. At this age, it is important for them to learn to commit themselves to a group or a team, recognising what they are contributing to the team personally, and recognising what each of the other children is contributing, too.)

13. *I try to create or use situations where the children can mix with others whose parents share the same values as my own family.* (If the children have this opportunity when they are young, some of these other children will probably come to be their friends in the future.)

14. *I try to get the children to develop a number of human virtues to foster the possibility of their being good friends in the future.* (One cannot be a good friend without being virtuous. Some people don't realise this; they are satisfied when their children have superficial relationships with others based only on common interests.)

15. *When they reach adolescence I explain to them what friendship is, and how to be a good friend.* (We should never forget the importance of reasoning with the children. As the subject of friendship has a strong emotional side to it, it is wise to clear up their ideas about what friendship is as early as possible.)

16. *I try to look after my own friends, not only because I know that we all need friends, but also because I realise that the best thing would be for my friends'*

children to be my children's friends. (This is the best preventive medicine when it comes to dealing with bad influences.)

17. *I accept that the adolescents are going to spend a lot of time with their friends and that that is natural and necessary.* (One will have to insist on adolescents paying attention to their family, but without 'getting at them' too much.)

18. *I try to link the youngsters up with new groups to give them more scope to choose friends.* (For example, parish activities, youth clubs, sporting associations.)

19. *We encourage our children to invite their friends home.* (It is not a matter of inviting everyone and anyone home, irrespective of their values or lifestyle. A good criterion for the children to apply is that they should not invite anyone home whom they would not accept as a future spouse of one of their siblings.)

20. *I explain what the limits of a relationship with a person of the opposite sex are.* (As we have mentioned earlier, it is a question of giving clear, concise information. Probably one will have to return to the subject on several occasions.)

23 Understanding

People who are understanding recognise the various factors that influence feelings or behaviour; they study each of these factors and how they relate to one another (and encourage others to do the same), and in their behaviour they take these factors into account.

We will now look at the subject of understanding in the context of personal relationships. The description we have given makes no reference to the consequences of understanding another person. But it is clear that if one grasps the various factors which influence a person's mood or behaviour it will be much easier to help that person improve in all kinds of ways. Indeed, just to feel understood can be a great help at times.

Thus, one reason for developing this virtue is a desire to help other people in the way that suits them best, bearing in mind the key factors in each case.

Someone might ask whether this is a virtue for young children or whether it need only be thought about when children are older. To answer this, we have to bear in mind what we said about the reason for wanting to understand. A desire to help someone, to meet their needs, does not usually arise until a person becomes aware of his own intimacy, although it can begin earlier in a more superficial way. I am referring to situations where small children become aware of someone else's mood or notice, from the way he is behaving, that he needs something. For example, if a child notices that his mother is very tired he can try not to make noise or he can try to help in some job in the house. If he notices that his brother or sister is unhappy, he can give him a present or lend him something of his in order to cheer him up. But these are usually spontaneous reactions which stem from the affection he feels for others. He is trying to put things right, he wants his mother to get a rest or his brother to be happy. In other words he 'understands' that something is missing, something is preventing these relationships from being what they ought to be. The causes of these unusual situations do not concern him. He does not usually try to understand deeply.

At these ages it would seem that the parents' job is: to help their children recognise the characteristics of each member of the family; to realise that there are good times and bad times for talking, for asking for something etc.; to be aware of the different moods of others; and to raise questions like: What can have happened that he is acting like that? Why is she so sad, happy, etc? In this way the small child gradually grasps the different factors which can influence a person; but understanding at a deeper level only comes with recognising in himself feelings similar to those he sees in others.

And this brings us to an important question: is it possible to understand someone else if you yourself have never experienced what he is experiencing? If 'understanding' means recognising the factors which influence a person's feelings or behaviour, the answer will be 'yes', because all one needs is one's own experience and to have found other people in the same or a similar situation in the past. At least one can come to understand enough to help that person cope with some difficulty or to help him do better, Of course, one has to be aware of the danger of transferring one's own feelings and reactions to another person just because his situation looks like a situation one has experienced oneself. Understanding is not just feeling for someone, that is to say, sympathy; it is also a matter of seeing things from the other's point of view: empathy. This degree of understanding will develop only if someone realises the importance of being understanding and recognises that he has a responsibility to help others.

Empathy

It seems clear that parents, in the context of educating their children, should concern themselves to some degree with each of the following problems:

- How to help children to be well equipped to understand others?
- How to get them to learn to see the other person in an empathetic way, recognising the various factors which influence his feelings and behaviour?
- How to teach them to communicate their understanding in such a way that they help the other person?

Conditions for being understanding

We can learn a lot by observing our everyday dealings with other people. For example, we can discover the right conditions for a person to be able to receive information. If one tries to communicate some piece of information when someone is worried about a personal problem, it is more than likely that he will not listen or will not take in what is being said to him. Thus, if a parent gives a series of instructions to a child just after the child has seen an accident and wants to tell his parents about it, he probably will not listen. The same thing happens in understanding others. If the children are focussing on their own problems, they naturally will not open up enough to be concerned about others. This is easy enough to understand, but it is not so easy to put into practice. If we want our children to be in a position to understand others, we must help them first to forget their own problems. But perhaps the word 'forget' is not the right one. Rather, they have to see their problems in the proper perspective:

assessing whether they are important or not very important, and beginning to try to get over them. Observation shows, also, that if you use the resources to get over a problem, interior stress largely disappears. Therefore, the problems which can most get in the way of the virtue of understanding are those which seem to have no solution. These produce a mood in which a person goes round and round, worrying the thing over, incapable of noticing or focussing on the need to help others.

Thus, we can see that a child who has learned to have reasonable confidence in his own abilities, in his parents' help and other people's help, and especially to believe in the help of God, is in the best position to try to understand others.

It is also a question of helping children not to have prejudices. We have dealt with this matter earlier, but here it would be useful to reflect on some of the typical problems children have in this connection. Understanding is an act of eliciting information without judging the other person. Therefore, if one rejects the other person's behaviour from the word 'go', there is very little chance of one's paying due attention to the factors which led to that behaviour. For example, a father could get angry with his son because he has been rude to him. All he sees is the rudeness; he does not even try to understand the boy and find out why he has been rude. Does the boy really mean to insult and annoy his father? Or is the insult an expression of some intense pain the boy feels, which he does not want to or cannot express?

What enables one to have a good attitude towards others is serenity, a sense of security, flexibility and good humour.

Teaching people to be perceptive

It would be absurd to think that in these few lines we could produce an answer to the problem of how to train people to have empathy when so many experts have been trying for years to agree on this subject. Most psychologists agree that empathy, positive appreciation and lots of affection are needed in our approach to other people. But it is not so clear how one can practise empathy or teach it to someone else. Some people are born with it, others are not. What we are trying to do here is help parents educate their children: not to give a programme, but rather some points where they can begin to try to do better.

To begin with, it is worth pointing out some things a teenager should get clear in his mind:

- People are not all the same. Each person reacts differently to stimuli. Therefore, one should not think that the other person is going to feel the same as oneself in a given situation. Adults, too, make this mistake. For example, some people say: That doesn't annoy me, why should it annoy him?
- What people say or what they do is not necessarily a true reflection of their intimate intentions or feelings. Before trying to find out what are the

real causes of someone's behaviour, one should try to see what the facts of the situation really are, not what the person's external behaviour suggests that they are.

- It is very easy to be simplistic, thinking that there is only one cause for any given problem. Normally there is a series of causes. It is not a matter of taking the first cause and seeing it as the only real cause.
- In normal situations – not in atypical situations – perhaps the most important thing for the other person is to know that someone is concerned about him and that that person also respects his privacy.
- Finally, it is not a matter of being able to understand someone completely. That is never possible. This difficulty is reflected in the reply of a father to his teenage daughter after she says that he does not understand her: My dear girl, how can I understand you when you do not even understand yourself?

We can sum up by saying that the understanding we are aiming at should express itself in a form of help whereby the other person is enabled to understand himself enough to be able to use the means available to him to get over his difficulty or make an effort to improve.

However, in an effort to diagnose a person's difficulty, we should bear in mind various kinds of factors which can influence his feelings or behaviour. In this connection, there is the temptation to ask the person directly: what is wrong with you? And, of course, in most cases the answer will be: Nothing.

The situation may be influenced by:

- something which happened previously. There could be a close connection between a child's gloominess and the fact that she has copied in an exam ination;
- something which he has left undone. For example, the connection between gloominess and the fact that he has not studied for an exam,
- something someone else has done. The connection between the punishment a teacher has given and the child's gloominess;
- something the other person has not done;
- something the child has thought, seen, felt or heard.

We have given some examples here to show how difficult it can be to discover what the real problem is or what are its real causes. For example, when we noticed that the child was depressed, we might have asked him directly what the reason was. Perhaps he replied that it was because the teacher punished him. But is that really it? It could have been because the teacher found out that he had been copying, or because he realised he had not been studying enough, or because some other pupil in the class had jeered at him for copying etc.

The person who wants to help will do something different in each case. If the child realises that he ought not to have copied, he should be helped to get over his annoyance and study better. But if he is depressed because the teacher found him out, the understanding he is given should not encourage this feeling. Therefore, understanding does not necessarily lead one to go along with the feelings or behaviour of the other person. Understanding implies that once one has found what is really worrying the other person, then, looking at things from his point of view – that is, accepting him as he is – one looks for some way to get him to improve.

And, how can we develop in children this capacity to be understanding? By helping them recognise the different ways other people feel, and why they behave in different ways. In other words, by teaching them to be sensitive. In practice, this means a series of questions such as: Have you noticed that your brother is very happy, angry, sad, etc? I wonder why that is? Are you sure? What other reasons might there be? Why do you think he did that? etc. Moreover, it is not only a matter of helping children to understand their brothers and sisters, but also their companions, their teachers, and even their parents. A lot has been said about how parents have to understand their children. But the children, too, have to understand their parents. And this is an important job for each of the parents: that is to say, the mother can help the children to understand their father, and vice versa.

Showing that one understands

Depending on the type of problem the other person has, what is needed is: understanding him and showing him understanding; understanding him and taking no action; showing that one is concerned about him and not making an effort to understand him too much. It is a matter of understanding and taking no action where the child is able to overcome the difficulty on his own. For example, the case of a small child who has become annoyed over something unimportant and who is quite well aware that he is being silly. If he is given too much attention it could be counterproductive, because that means exaggerating something which he wants to forget about quickly. In other cases, the child may be able to get over the problem himself, but he needs affectionate help; he needs to know that someone is on his side. Here, too, it is better not to investigate the thing too deeply. So, we can distinguish between understanding a person, his feelings and his behaviour, and understanding what he needs.

We will concentrate here on the need to feel understood. Many studies have been done on techniques of communication. But it is not a matter of turning our children into expert counsellors of their brothers and sisters and companions. We prefer, now, to discuss briefly some approaches which can make the job easier, without going into too much detail.

- It is a matter of showing that you have understood the other person, that you have not judged him. Therefore, you have to be careful even about the way you express yourself. You must try to avoid words which imply value-judgments and try to use descriptive language. A person feels understood when the person who is listening to him repeats, sometimes using the very same words, what the other has told him, without making value-judgements.
- It involves helping the other person to solve a problem. Therefore, you have to avoid pre-determined approaches. You should be saying: Let's see what we can do; not: Here is what you have to do.
- In order to show that you understand you need time and the right conditions. It is a question of showing affection and attention. You cannot do this properly if there are interruptions, such as telephone calls, etc. If a child wants to help a younger brother or sister it may be better for them to go out for a walk or at least look for some place where there will be no interruptions.
- Finally, it involves showing a person that one is not 'above' his problem: in other words, not giving him the impression that, although you understand his problem, the same sort of thing could never happen to you: this superior attitude would show, among other things, a lack of capacity to understand, on your part.

From what we have said, it is clear that the virtue of understanding is particularly important for parents, but children, especially teenagers, need it also. For children can be a very real help to their parents as regards their younger brothers and sisters. Sometimes it is difficult for parents to understand what is happening with their children; whereas they understand each other really well. Recognition of this fact is also a form of understanding.

Understanding other people begins when a person makes an effort to understand himself. We need to strive to get over our own prejudices, in order to avoid unworthy and unnecessary feelings which get in the way of our own improvement. If we know our own shortcomings we will try to avoid situations which encourage them or, at least, it will help us not to get trapped again by the same feeling or the same kind of behaviour. We usually talk about rectifying, making amends, in reference to unjust things we do to other people; but we also need to think about ourselves. Once we recognise the main causes of our moods or odd behaviour, that very understanding should be what spurs us to try to get whatever help is necessary and to start again. However, we will never ever come to understand ourselves completely (never mind other people) because every human being is a mystery.

SELF-ASSESSMENT

Briefing Note: see pages 29-30, above.

Am I an understanding person?

1. *I realise that I should educate each child in a different way because each one is different. Therefore I need to know and understand each of them.* (If one thinks that all children should be treated in the same way, then understanding makes no sense. Sometimes educators act in this undiscriminating way without realising they are doing so.)
2. *I myself try to be in the best possible position to understand others.* (For example, if an educator is very worried about some personal problem, he/she will find it difficult to look after someone else.)
3. *I listen to, observe and speak to others in order to understand my children/pupils.* (Understanding means knowing; and not just knowing what the children have done but also going behind their behaviour to discover what their real motives are.)
4. *I exchange points of view with my spouse or with the teacher in order to get a better grasp of the situation and avoid having prejudices.* (Understanding requires keeping abreast of information concerning the children. If we don't do this we may end up having an fixed and unfair view of a child.)
5. *I have thought about how to assess the youngsters – to distinguish what is important and what is secondary.* (We would not understand a child if we focused only on some aspects. For example, we might only notice whether they are tidy or not, without paying attention to the degree to which they are living generosity or friendship.)
6. *I try to put myself in the children's shoes, to see things from their point of view.* (This is what is called 'empathic' understanding. Some people manage to do this better than others, but it is always worth trying.)
7. *In general, I show my interest in the children so that they can see that they are important to me.* (The manifestation of understanding is important for the other person to feel understood. It will be easier to get this result if we show that we really do understand.)
8. *I show my understanding with gestures – smiling, with my eyes – and explaining what I think the situation is, so that the youngsters can see that they have been understood.* (Mere understanding is not enough. We need to show that we have understood.)

9. *I show my respect for the youngsters by not prying into their intimacy and by waiting for them to come out in their own time.* (The process of understanding cannot be rushed. Knowing how to wait until the youngster is ready is, in itself, a sign of understanding.)

10. *I look for the right moment to do what I think best for the youngster, knowing that 'understanding' can be expressed in many different ways.* (For example, after failing an exam, 'understanding' can mean different things according to the circumstances. It could mean keeping quiet, telling them off, encouraging them, listening to them or just being with them.)

Teaching others to be understanding

11. *I help the youngsters get to know themselves to some degree, so that they can come to trust in their own capacities.* (A youngster who is not sure of himself will never be able to pay attention to the needs of others and understand them.)

12. *I help the youngsters develop their capacity to listen to people, to observe them and to look after them.* (These are the basic capacities one needs for knowing others. Once we know them, we can pass on to trying to understand them.)

13. *I help the youngsters think through their own problems so that they can then forget about them and turn their attention to others. I also help them discover what prejudices they have as regards others.* (Adolescents are often very affected by emotional problems. When this is so, they tend to have an extremely negative perception of others.)

14. *I help the adolescents discover how other people feel and think.* (In fact one can start developing this capacity from an early age. It will be sufficient to ask questions like: 'If you do that, how will your mother feel?' or 'Have you thought about how your friend may feel now that their father has died?')

15. *I help the youngsters identify differences of character, intelligence, sensitivity, etc. in their brothers and sisters and in their friends at school.* (To understand means to recognise differences. Because people are different, one needs to make the effort to understand them and act accordingly.)

16. *When someone has done something or when something has happened, I help the youngsters try to understand why.* (It is just a question of asking oneself, 'Why did they say that?' or 'Why did they do that?)

17. *I try to get the youngsters to put themselves in the other person's shoes and see things from their point of view.* (This isn't easy, even for an adult. But suggesting, reasoning, calling the child's attention to the situation, are worthwhile: it helps keep them see that other people have different points of view.)

18. *I tell the youngsters that they should try to adapt to each person and to each situation.* (What they did for one friend yesterday is not necessarily what they should do today for another.)

19. *In general, I give good example by trying to understand others without being prejudiced or too rigid, to help the youngsters learn how this can be done.* (We want the children to help others in all sorts of little ways.)

20. *I try to help the youngsters understand their parents and their teachers better and better everyday.* (The parents can help the youngsters understand why the teachers act in specific ways, and vice versa.)

24 Patriotism

Patriotic people recognise what their country has given and is giving them. They pay it due honour and service, by supporting and defending the values it stands for; they also make their own the noble aspirations of every country in the world.

Before discussing how to teach this virtue, I should like to say something about the description I have just given of it. One's country gives a person the indispensable conditions he needs for his intellectual, moral, social and economic life. Therefore, he needs to recognise what his country has given him and is still giving him, if he is to act justly towards it. Initially, patriotism has to do with the personal relationship between each individual and his country. Only later on does this mean defending and protecting the values which it represents, against harmful external influences. It is interesting to note that Saint Thomas Aquinas includes this duty towards one's country within the virtue of piety, which also regulates a person's relations with his parents and with his entire family. He says: 'on the basis of birth and upbringing, parents and country are the closest sources of all our existence and development; as a consequence everyone is indebted first of all under God to his parents and fatherland.'[83]

In a still broader sense, the idea of piety can be applied to the respect and love which one renders the Church, as mother and teacher of all men and women and all nations, as regards supernatural life, and as the lifeforce of human society. It is curious to note how the customs of certain countries in the past have given real support to this triple duty – toward Church, family and nation – guiding its children towards professions and responsibilities connected with these duties. For example, in the eighteenth century the eldest son inherited the family property and had the duty of managing it for the benefit of the family. The other sons would enter the Church or the army.

On the one hand, patriotism also means recognising what one's country has given one and still gives one. On the other, it means rendering it the honour and service it deserves, supporting and defending the values it stands for. One of the vices which undermines patriotism is 'cosmopolitanism' which implies indifference – attitudinal or concrete – towards things that have to do with one's country: this can lead a person to be unconcerned about the common good and just look for personal satisfaction at the expense of his fellow-countrymen.

The last part of the description refers to respect for all other countries. In this connection, point 75 of Vatican II's *Gaudium et spes* says: 'Citizens should develop a generous and loyal devotion to their country, but without any narrow-mindedness. In other words, they must always look simultaneously to the welfare of the whole human family, which is tied together by the manifold bonds linking races, peoples and nations.'

A person's duty is not limited to concern for his own country. This exclusivist approach leads to our exaggerated nationalism where one despises other people – by words and actions. National life should be regarded as something non-political. 'National life became a principle of decomposition of the community of nations when it began to be used as an instrument for political ends, that is, when the organised central power of a State made national life the base of its own expansionism, its own desire for dominion. Therefore, we regard nationalistic politics as the germ of rivalries and the torch which enflames discord.'[84]

We shall now move on to concentrate on the teaching of this virtue.

Patriotic feeling

The virtue of patriotism, in the sense of a good active habit, means developing one's mind in order to act justly, in keeping with certain values which one has identified and assimilated. But this habit, to start with, needs to be based on feelings which can develop throughout one's life, but especially during childhood. Patriotic feeling stems from a feeling of attraction for the place one spent the early years of one's life, a feeling which gradually extends to broader and more complex structures – town, region, the country as a whole.

The parents' duty here is to find ways of teaching the child the values specific to his environment. This will help him to feel at one with his companions who share these experiences – in the mountains, on the river banks, on the roads etc. – in the different seasons of the year. Don't we all have childhood memories of this sort?

But this sense of oneness, which comes from shared experience, should also extend to appreciation of other cultural aspects less connected with nature. Children should be taught aspects of local history, stories about local heroes, famous people from the locality, and typical customs, dances etc., in such a way that they feel part of a common historical tradition. But this should go further than their immediate locality: there will be values they can share with everyone in a region or even in the whole country or in the whole world. The main idea is to get children to feel very linked to their environment and, without weakening those links, to open up to values shared by people further afield.

We have been speaking about a patriotic feeling which is necessary to the development of this virtue. But, if it were no more than a feeling, patriotism would have no value and no effects. It has to do with sharing values with one's fellow-countrymen in an effort to improve conditions generally or protect what the country has already achieved. If we look, we can see that often a country has a well developed patriotism in war-time, with everyone striving to defend its rights or what it stands for, but what happens when there is no war: how can people share common values in a pluralist society?

Supporting and defending values

The term 'common good' can be used to cover all the values one can practise at a country-wide level. And this 'common good' calls on all the members of society to work responsibly and well, to strive to achieve a just society and peace and respect for one's country, its institutions, customs, history and attainments.

We have seen earlier how a child can learn about his country by reference to its history, language, culture etc. Feeling part of this common patrimony means that first one must know it and then be able to explain it and pass it on to others. It seems obvious that it is up to parents to find ways and means of showing their children this heritage – bringing them to museums, buying suitable books, talking about its history, underlining its achievements and also its mistakes. Children should also be taught to express this knowledge: for example, when guests come to the house from farther away the children might be invited to tell them things about the locality. If they are foreigners, the children could talk about the country.

Children can also be taught to look after the place they live in. Keeping the environment tidy and clean – not throwing litter or writing on walls – is usually called being civic. But if children realise that it is their duty to look after the common good of everyone, this type of thing can also be considered as very much part of patriotism. Some children, if they get proper training, can come to work professionally in the area of environmental care – the prevention of pollution, for example. Others will organise activities in their spare time to look after public property. This can also be considered patriotism if the person acts out of a sense of responsibility for what belongs to everyone in the country. And they can come to feel proud of their country's attainments or, maybe, notice some of its shortcomings and try to correct them. A person who complains about his country is no patriot. A patriot will criticise his country but he will try to do something to correct what he has been critical of.

Children should also be shown the customs and institutions of the whole country because if they concentrate completely on their own region they can lose sight of the country as a whole and the effect would be that they would be developing this virtue in a rather exclusivist sort of way, unaware of the needs of all their fellow-countrymen.

We must remember that all of us – adults as well as children need to perform, with some regularity, acts which make us feel part of our country. The sort of things which make for this could be: a national day, the success abroad of someone from our country, television programmes which deal with the different regions, military parades, meetings of nation-wide organisations etc. Nor should we underestimate the value of respecting the National Anthem or the national flag. If parents teach their children to respect the National Anthem, if their parents take pride in their history, if they tell them things about different aspects of the country, if they introduce them to the heritage of the country, the children will realise what they owe their country. They will respect their country and they will be in a position to make a personal contribution to make it as good as it can be.

Earlier we said that the common good means that everyone must work responsibly and strive to bring about a more just society, one which is at peace and which can therefore develop. In practice, this is not so easy, because it seems that people are divided into different factions, each seeking its own advantage at the expense of the others. A policy of claiming rights tends to sectionalise rather than unify community efforts. Therefore, we should try to teach our children to realise the importance of their personal contribution to the country. We have dealt elsewhere with the virtues of justice and hard work, but we did not mention the connection between those virtues and the virtue of patriotism. The job of educators, in this regard, means that they themselves should fulfil their duties to others and then explain to children how necessary this effort on everyone's part is.

Here we will simply suggest a few points it would be worth making to children:

- A country can only get into a good economic position if everyone works responsibly, thinking not only about his legitimate rights but also about his duties and about the common good.
- Justice requires that everyone obey the laws provided they are just in themselves – and, therefore, they should pay their taxes, do military service (if there is any), exercise the franchise, etc.
- Justice also requires that everyone use the channels available for installing a greater degree of justice at all levels. Therefore, for there to be a strong, united country, a person should take an active part in association with parents, neighbourhood associations, local government, etc., in accordance with his abilities.
- Peace is the result of charity being practised by the members of a society. Therefore, people should seek out the best way to be charitable towards their neighbour and towards everyone, respecting diversity of opinions, joining forces to bring about improvements, and protect-ing themselves against any form of violence which endangers peace.

Recognising the noble aspirations of all other countries

We have adverted on a number of occasions to the danger of being interested only in one's own little region: this is the basis of patriotic feeling, but it should broaden out to one's entire country. This means that we should not only have a patriotic feeling but also an intellectual appreciation of the ethos of one's country. Now, we must go further still and show that patriotism should not be restricted to concern for one's own country. Every man and woman has a responsibility for all his fellows, and therefore for everyone, worldwide. This means that he should know, as well as he can, the attainments of all countries: the values they enshrine. For children, this means having a healthy curiosity to learn about other people, to think about what they can learn from them and about what they themselves can offer those people.

This virtue of patriotism can be especially well understood by a Christian. Among the gifts of the Holy Spirit, which he receives in baptism, is the gift of piety; and piety awakens a filial affection towards God, who is seen as a Father, and a sense of universal brotherhood towards everyone, in that they are our brothers and children of the same Father.

On this basis, patriotism will be a basis for having understand-ing for everyone: 'To be "Catholic" means to love your country and to be second to no one in that love. And at the same time, to hold as your own the noble aspirations of other lands – so many glories of France are glories of mine! And in the same way, much that makes Germans proud, and the peoples of Italy and of England..., and Americans and Asians and Africans, is a source of pride to me also.'[85]

SELF-ASSESSMENT

Briefing Note: see pages 29-30, above.

Am I myself patriotic?

1. *I realise that, 'after God, parents and country are sources of our being and governance, because our parents have nurtured us and we have been nurtured in our country'.* (These words of St Thomas Aquinas may call our attention to the importance of patriotism - not a very popular virtue nowadays.)

2. *I try to avoid thoughts and actions which could lead to a too cosmopolitan or too narrow an outlook, as is the case with exaggerated nationalism.* (In patriotism we look for the golden mean, as we do in all virtues. Everyone has their own country, but the good of that country should not oppose that of others.)

3. *I recognise the values have to do with the common good and that underpin and justify patriotism.* (Sometimes one only notices a 'general feeling' of

patriotism in time of war or when a country feels that it is being harassed in some way. However, patriotism should be based on the common good of those who make up the society in which we live.)

4. *I realise that one important value for a country is a stable economy and I do my work well to benefit others as best I can.* (Patriotism calls on each citizen to look for the good of others. At the present there is a tendency to separate things in life: 'I work for myself and then give the needy whatever is left over.')

5. *I try to exercise social justice, realising that it is part of patriotism.* (This means doing such things as keeping the law, paying taxes or exercising one's right to vote.)

6. *I accept my personal responsibility in society, looking for the good of others.* (This means participating in parent-school associations, in local government, in NGOs etc.)

7. *I realise that peace is a prerequisite for patriotism - peace among the members of society, peace in each social organisation, peace in each family.* (This peace will exist when each member is at peace with themselves because they know that what they are doing, they are doing well. It requires tolerance, charity and respect for others.)

8. *I try to look after what is common to all, that is what belongs to everyone.* (This is why one should look after the countryside, the environment, national or local traditions and customs.)

9. *I know that it is good to do things that symbolise national unity because that helps to unite the people of a country.* (For example, celebrating national holidays, supporting a national sports team, getting to know the different parts of the country and their history, attending national professional meetings.)

10. *I know that patriotism underpins universal amity. 'To be "Catholic" means to love our country, and to let nobody surpass us in that love. And at the same time, it means to hold as our own the noble aspirations of all the other lands.'* (This idea comes from Blessed J. Escrivá's book The Way; the passage goes on to say: 'How many glories of France are glories of mine! And in the same way, many things that make Germans proud – and Italians, British, Americans and Asians and Africans – are also sources of pride to me. Catholic! A great heart, an open mind'.)

Teaching others to be patriotic

11. *I try to get the small children to know their birthplaces, where they live, their municipality, their county, province or state, their region and their country.*

(Patriotism usually begins with one's immediate surroundings, because from these childhood experiences come common memories which unite people.)

12. *I try to see that the children to learn about local history, local heroes and important people.* (This kind of information is needed in order to be able to identify oneself with a place. People and their feats make the purely material environment come alive.)

13. *I teach the children local customs, traditions, sports, games, dances.* (They are ways of becoming a person with roots.)

14. *I try to help the children feel part of the course of history.* (Knowing where we come from gives us a sense of security and it helps us face up to the unknown future.)

15. *I teach the children what the local and national values are so that they can live them and support them.* (These values may be honesty, loyalty, happiness, compassion or hard work, for example.)

16. *I teach the children to share these values with others and to be proud of them.* (If they manage to share these values, everyone will benefit. It is not a question of looking down on others because they are different, but rather of recognising that people complement each other.)

17. *I encourage the youngsters to talk about their country to foreigners so that they too can appreciate it.* (Patriotism transcends self-interest and looks for everyone's enrichment.)

18. *I encourage the youngsters to take part in activities which support local or national values.* (These can be state holidays; sporting, dancing or singing competitions; etc.)

19. *I do what I can to see that the youngsters travel abroad and learn what other countries have to offer and what their problems are.* (Some knowledge of other countries is vital for patriotism to have a universal dimension. Living with foreigners in their own country is probably the best way, but it is also good to read books, watch documentaries, or listen to people who have lived abroad.)

20. *I help the children think about what their country has given them and, therefore, discover what they owe it.* (Many people only think about themselves and forget about others. They have no sense of solidarity or patriotism.)

Appendix I: Character building in schools

Some difficulties met with in schools

One of the difficulties a school can encounter when it decides to pay attention to education in virtues, is that it feeds a need to have some sort of plan or programme.

An overall plan may not be the best idea. On the one hand, we should remember that the idea of virtue refers to the golden mean and, on the other, that each student has more or less difficulty in developing each virtue. That is, each student, from birth, has a natural tendency to practise some virtues well and others not. Some people find it easy to be responsible or orderly but, at the same time, they have difficulty in being sincere or flexible.

That is why it is necessary (as far as possible) to personalise education in virtues, taking account of the individual traits of each child.

We also need to remember that some virtues are more suited to specific times in a child's psychological development. For example, it would not be sensible to insist on a small child's being prudent, as this virtue requires a well developed mind. However, this does not mean that we should not insist on specific habits related to that virtue from early age.

Nor would it seem reasonable to insist on modesty at an early age, because this virtue requires awareness of one's own intimate self (something which occurs in adolescence). Again, it would not seem appropriate to insist on the virtue of orderliness with older students, who should now be able to focus on virtues which require more intelligence. If we do have to insist on this virtue with an older child, it will be a case of remedial education.

The needs created by the students' environment must also be taken into account. For example, living in a holiday resort beside the sea it is not the same as living in a village lost in the mountains. Each situation will determine which virtue(s) should be stressed.

Finally, we should take into consideration the values present in the school's ethos.

This all means that when we are trying to work out what virtue or virtues should be priorities for any particular child, we should take into account:

- the personal characteristics of each student,
- the psychological traits of each age group,

- the nature of each virtue,
- needs created by the environment,
- priorities related to the school's ethos.

There are further, 'institutional', limitations. I refer to the teachers' readiness to regard the virtues as educational objectives. Teachers are used to setting objectives and evaluating the degree to which they have been achieved. In the case of virtues, however, achievement is more difficult to assess – especially because motivation is such an important factor.

The problem is, how can we assess why a student acts in one way or another? Evidently, it is just not possible. Therefore we cannot know what degree of development a student has achieved in relation to a particular virtue. Or at least we cannot know enough to give the student a grade or a mark. It is, of course, possible to evaluate the frequency with which the student practises specific acts related a virtue. This can be useful, but it is not the same as evaluating the student's development in the virtue. Students may 'perform' out of fear of failure, or because they are offered attractive rewards, or because they want to get ahead of others, or out of a Kantian sense of duty, or whatever. If teachers manage to achieve behavioral results which have that sort of motivation behind them, they will not be helping the children achieve personal maturity or be leading them towards that happiness we mentioned before, or helping them learn to be responsible citizens or responsible workers.

Organisational aspects of character building in schools

In view of what we have just said, some readers may feel it is not wise to try to 'institutionalise' education in virtues. But that is not completely true. Certainly the process should be personalised as far as possible. Moreover, attention should be paid to the teachers' own process of improvement: this is very important, because how they act in everyday contact with the students can influence the latter decisively in their way of thinking and in their behaviour. The students should be able to appreciate how attractive the virtues are through seeing them being practised by their teachers. (If the virtues are not practised in an attractive way by the teachers, most probably their virtues are not authentic. They may even have fallen into a vice through giving excessive attention to a particular virtue.) We are not trying to suggest that the teachers should give a perfect example. This would be impossible. But the students need to observe and think about actions carried out by others and which evidence a constant desire to improve. It is the teacher's own effort to improve as a person that will have a decisive influence on students.

Let us accept, then, as initial necessary principles:

- PERSONALISATION
- EXEMPLARY BEHAVIOUR

Now we can go a little deeper into some ways of 'organising' education in virtues. Specifically, we can stimulate the development of virtues by:

- Taking advantage of existing activities and programmes in the school.
- Organising teaching activities which promote the development of virtues.
- Organising complementary activities which one knows from experience will favour the development of virtues in general or of one particular virtue.

Availing of existing activities and programmes

Through the activities they organise in class and through the academic subject itself, a teacher should be able to promote some virtues. Further opportunities are offered by other school situations - the breaks, complementary activities, in the dining hall or on the school bus. Here, we are not talking about devising new activities, but availing of ones that already exist.

To take advantage of these opportunities, teachers need to be aware of what virtues should be considered priorities for each age group, or aware of aspects of virtues they should give more attention to.

While bearing in mind what was said previously about the principle of personalisation, it is possible to develop a general plan of priorities for the development of virtues, one which will be useful to the majority of the students.

For example, up to the age of seven it would make sense to stress the virtues of orderliness and obedience, and aspects of sincerity, respect for others and sociability. From eight to twelve years old, if we take into account the fact that the child will now have more will-power and is entering a difficult time from both the physical and psychological point of view, it could be sensible to focus on virtues such as fortitude, industriousness, perseverance, responsibility, or on virtues which help people relate better to others, for example, generosity, companionship or social responsibility.

From thirteen to fifteen years old (earlier, in the case of the girls) it is time to stress virtues related to children's private selves: modesty, friendship, and some aspects of moderation. From sixteen to eighteen years old, now that their reasoning powers are better developed, more attention should be paid to virtues which require more capacity for thinking, for example, prudence, loyalty, understanding or flexibility.

Provided one has this sort of list of priorities there is no need for detailed programming for the development of each virtue. Rather, procedures should be put in place to help teachers keep those priorities in mind in their everyday endeavours.

For example, there could be periodical meetings where teachers can exchange experiences about how they have managed to get the children to develop a part of some virtue. This kind of activity should heighten teachers' awareness of education in virtues.

Certain necessary rules of behaviour can also be translated into specific goals for a period of time. These goals should refer to observable behaviour; they should not try to cover all the virtues.

Experience shows that any kind of prioritising makes demands on teachers. Therefore these priorities should not be modified too frequently; perhaps a class should focus on just one virtue, or on a part of that virtue, for a whole term.

Although we have suggested that it is not useful to develop a detailed programme for the development of virtues, it would be advisable for the teachers to incorporate into their programmes those virtues considered to be priorities for each age group. This will allow them to take advantage of some learning situations to develop those virtues; they should be able to see when the subject content allows them to stress particular virtues.

Organising specific teaching activities suitable for virtues development

Teachers will probably want to reinforce the development of virtues, especially as regards the gradual process of internalising the values that they reflect. And, also, even if we try to increase the degree of focus that teachers have as regards the development of virtues, it will probably be difficult to achieve complete consistency in their efforts.

So, it will probably be useful to think about specific content to be introduced into some subject or to develop a new subject designed to reinforce the virtues.

The main aim of this kind of subject content, in my opinion, is to help the students discover a number of values, so that they can learn to appreciate them and thus be interested in trying to incorporate them into their own lives. We are not talking about activities which help the students clarify values. In fact, in the values clarification movement, those involved concentrate more on needs than on values. Sometimes the two, but not always.

In this field a lot of work has been done. In recent times Kohlberg's 'dilemmas' approach has been very influential.

Also, different kinds of activities have been tried out for all age groups. These include: games, stories, clarifying dialogues, role-playing; and group techniques such as the symposium, the round table, the debate, the workshop etc.

From the organisational point of view it would be useful for there to be a coordinator whose job it is to get feedback from all the teachers involved with a view to passing it on to others who are interested.

Also, if the students' interest is roused in these subjects, some way of channelling it, and letting them turn their knowledge into action, should be established. This will probably entail personalised attention to each student.

Organising complementary activities

When complementary and optional activities are organised at school, little thought tends to be given to the connection between them and the whole idea of development of virtues. Two criteria given priority are usually that the cost should not be high and that some parent or teacher needs to be ready to look after the activity. That is eminently sensible. However, one can also take account of the extent to which the possible activity can promote the development of virtues.

For example, one school priority might be the development of the virtue of social responsibility. To this end, the school organises activities that can help develop this virtue in children of all ages. With the smaller children it establishes activities whereby the children can do something for their classmates, and for their grandparents. Later on, other kinds of activities are introduced so that the students can cooperate with local organisations dedicated to social needs. The older children can be given the chance to spend their holidays or weekends helping meet real social needs.

In fact these kinds of activities can create what is usually called a "culture" of virtue in the school. Also, when the students carry out these actions related to social responsibility, they develop other virtues at the same time, for example, perseverance, generosity or sincerity.

Other kinds of activities will be especially suitable for developing other virtues. For example, camping, trekking, and mountain climbing require perseverance or fortitude.

Some schools organise groups within the class whose job it is to think about how to improve the class itself, making suggestions to the teachers, helping their classmates or helping to organise class activities. This develops prudence and responsibility, to mention just two virtues.

A theatre club can offer opportunities not only to develop oral expression, to feel more self-assured or to learn play a role, but also to learn to be companionable, orderly, courageous, etc. if the person in charge knows what they're is doing.

I hope there is no need to give further examples of how special activities can be introduced with the idea of offering opportunities for the development of virtues. But we must remember that the efficiency of such activities will depend on the example given by the person who organises them, and their determination to take advantage of them for this end.

And this idea leads us into our last commentary on this subject.

Virtues in educators themselves

School managers will need to spend time and effort helping teachers improve as regards human virtues. This may mean: work groups, suitable reading material, personal interviews, organising meetings with guest speakers. As we have mentioned before, giving good example is a vital motivational force for the development of virtues in the students.

I don't believe that one should consider the development of virtues in school as just one more objective. All activities in school should be imbued with virtue. Then we can add on other activities if we think it necessary.

This is a challenge for any school. However, if the challenge is taken up, the teachers will almost certainly get more satisfaction and their students too.

Appendix II: Short descriptions of virtues

AUDACITY
Audacious people set out on and complete courses of action which may appear imprudent, convinced that – after calm assessment of the facts and taking account of possible risks – they can achieve a genuine good.

FLEXIBILITY
People who are flexible adapt their behaviour readily to the particular circumstances of each person or situation, but without abandoning their own principles of behaviour.

FORTITUDE
In situations which make it difficult to improve, courageous people resist harmful influences, withstand difficulties and strive to act positively to overcome obstacles and undertake great deeds.

FRIENDSHIP
By means of friendship a person, who already knows other people through shared interests in work or leisure, develops regular personal contact with them. Friendship involves mutual rapport – each taking an interest in the other and in her or his improvement.

GENEROSITY
Generous people act unselfishly and cheerfully for the benefit of others, conscious of the value of their help and despite the fact that it may cost them an effort.

HUMILITY
Humble people recognise their own inadequacy, qualities and abilities, and press them into service, doing good without attracting attention or expecting the applause of others.

INDUSTRIOUSNESS
Industrious people are diligent at things essential to supernatural and natural maturity, and help others to be industrious too, in everyday work and other duties.

JUSTICE

People who are just strive constantly to give others what is their due, so that they can exercise their rights and responsibilities (the right to life, to own property, to political freedom, etc.), as parents, as children, as citizens, as workers, as rulers, etc. – and they also try to see that others do likewise.

LOYALTY

Loyal people accept the ties implicit in their relationship with others – friends, relatives, superiors, their country, its institutions, etc. and they defend and reinforce the system of values which these represent.

MODERATION

People who are moderate distinguish between what is reason-able and what is self-indulgent; and they make reasonable use of their senses, their time, their money, their efforts and so on, in accordance with true and upright principles.

MODESTY

Modest people recognise the value of their own privacy and respect that of others. They protect their privacy from the gaze of others; they reject anything which might encroach upon it and relax this practice only in circumstances which can be of benefit to themselves or others.

OBEDIENCE

Obedient people accept as their own, instructions which come from authority, provided they do not go against justice, and they act promptly to comply with them, striving faithfully to interpret the will of the person in authority.

ORDERLINESS

Orderly people follow a logical procedure (essential for the achievement of any goal) when organising their things, using their time, carrying out activities on their own initiative, without having to be constantly reminded.

OPTIMISM

Optimists have confidence (based on reason) in their own abilities, in the help which they can get from others and in the ability of others; thus in every situation, they can identify, first of all, positive elements and opportunities for improvement and, secondly, difficulties and obstacles in the way of such improvement; they take advantage of everything favourable and face up to the rest in a sportsman-like and cheerful manner.

PATIENCE

Patient people keep calm in situations where they experience some difficulty.

PATRIOTISM

Patriotic people recognise what their country has given and is giving them. They pay it due honour and service, by supporting and defending the values it stands for; they also make their own the noble aspirations of every country in the world.

PERSEVERANCE

Once a decision is made, a persevering person takes the steps necessary to achieve his or her goal, in spite of internal or external difficulties, and despite anything which might weaken their resolve in the course of time.

PRUDENCE

In work and in dealings with other people, prudent people assess in the light of right standards: they weigh the favourable and unfavourable consequences for themselves and others prior to taking a decision and then they act or refrain from acting, in keeping with the decisions they have made.

RESPECT FOR OTHERS

People who have respect for others act or refrain from acting so as not to harm, and indeed to benefit themselves and others, in line with their rights, status and circumstances.

RESPONSIBILITY

Responsible people accept the consequences of their actions, be they intentional or unintentional, so that others benefit as much as possible or, at least, do not suffer. They are also concerned that those over whom they have any influence should act similarly.

SIMPLICITY

Simple people ensures that their normal way of acting – their speech, the way they dress, the way they behave – is consistent with what their real intentions are; they allow other people to know them accurately: they are what they seem.

SINCERITY

Sincere people make full disclosure, where appropriate, to the right person and at the right time, of anything they have done, seen, thought or felt with regard to their own or another's situation.

SOCIABILITY

Sociable people make good use of and discover ways of getting together with others; they manage to com-municate with them through the genuine interest they show in them, in what they say and do, in what they think and feel.

UNDERSTANDING

People who are understanding recognise the various factors that influence feelings or behaviour; they study each of these factors and how they relate to one another (and encourage others to do the same), and in their behaviour they take these factors into account.

Notes

1 I. Celaya y Urrutia, 'Virtudes' in *Gran Enciclopedia Rialp* (Madrid), Vol. 23, 607.
2 St Augustine, *Apost.* 167, p. 8.
3 J. Hervada, 'Amor conyugal y matrimonio' in *Nuestro Tiempo* (Pamplona), No. 237, March 1974, p. 13.
4 J.A. Galera, *Sinceridad y fortaleza* (Madrid 1974).
5 R. Royo Marín, *Teología de la Perfección Cristiana* (Madrid 1968) 589.
6 J. Urteaga, *Man the Saint* (Dublin 1959).
7 Royo Marín, op. cit., p. 592.
8 Royo Marín, op. cit., p. 589.
9 Royo Marín, op. cit., p. 589.
9a Galera, op. cit., p. 164.
9b O. Durr, *La obediencia del niño* (Barcelona 1968)37-38.
10 O.F. Otero, *Autoridad y autonomía en la familia* (Pamplona 1975) 20-21.
11 O.F. Otero, op.cit., 71.
12 J. Mausbach and C. Ermecke, *Teología Moral Católica* (Pamplona 1974), Vol. III, 74f.
14 Mausbach & Ermecke, op. cit., p. 75.
15 *Fe y Vida de Fe* (Pamplona 1975) p. 55.
16 Op. cit., p. 56.
17 Cf. J.R. Gibb, 'Defensive Communication' in the *Journal of Communication*, XI, 3 (September 1961), p. 141-8.
18 Op. cit., p. 47.
19 J. Choza, 'La Supresión del pudor' in *Nuestro Tiempo* (Pamplona), No. 205,11.
20 J. Pieper, *Prudencia y Templanza* (Madrid 1969) 121.
21 J. Pieper, op. cit., 147.
22 Art. cit., p. 8-14.
23. Art. cit., p. 11-12.
24 Art.cit., p. 18.
25 *Conversations with Monsignor Escrivá de Balaguer*, 3rd ed. (Dublin 1980), No. 100.
25a V. García Hoz, 'Contestación a una pregunta en una entrevista' in *Palabra* (Madrid), March 1972, p. 11.
26 M. Scheler quoted by García Hoz, art. cit., p. 12. 260
27 Mausbach & Ermecke, op. cit., p. 198.
28 C. Llano Cifuentes, 'Libertad y Compromiso' in *Istmo* (Mexico City), No. 61, March-April 1969, p. 16.
29 O.F. Otero, *Educación y Manipulación* (Pamplona 1975) 91-92.
30 I deal with the subject of children's friends in *Reunión familiar* (Barcelona 1975).
31 J. Escrivá de Balaguer, *Friends of God* (*Dublin* 1980), No. 51.

32. Industriousness has to do with natural and supernatural maturity. A person without supernatural faith can strive towards gradual achievement of natural maturity.
33 J. Escrivá, *Christ Is Passing By* (Dublin 1983), No. 48.
34 As for moral aims, the educator will try to see that children have a good grasp of the criteria which lie behind good behaviour, and at times he will have to give them explicit instructions as to what to do. It is not a matter of requiring them to behave in a particular way, detail by detail, but of getting them to grasp why they should act in the right way. The kind and amount of information the parents give will depend on their prudence. We will look at this later.
35 O.F. Otero, op. cit., p. 31.
36 Escrivá, *Friends of God*, No. 79.
37 F. Ponz, *Address* on the occasion of the opening of the 1978-79 academic year at the University of Navarre.
38 Cf. *Sum. Th.* II-II, q. 136, a. 12.
39 Royo Marín, op. cit., 592f.
40 Escrivá, op. cit., No. 79.
41 Cf. St Thomas Aquinas, *Sum. Th.* II-II, a. 29, a. 3.
42 Diogenes Laertius, *Life and Opinions*, I, p.69.
43 Quoted in J. Pieper, *Las Virtudes Fundamentales* (Madrid 1976) 101.
44 J. Rest, *Development in Judging Moral Issues* (Minneapolis 1979), 22.
45 Pieper, op. cit., 153.
46 Durr, op. cit., 342.
47 Durr, op. cit., 70.
48 O.F. Otero, *Autonomía y autoridad en la familia* (Pamplona 1975) 21.
49 D. Isaacs, *Como evaluar los centros educativos* (Pamplona 1977), 236.
50 St Thomas Aquinas, *In III Sententiarum*, dist. 33, a. 2, a. 5.
51 St Bernard, *Sermons on the Song of Songs*, 49, 5 (PL 183, 1018).
52 Escrivá, op. cit., No. 164.
53 Pieper, op. cit., p. 44.
54 Escrivá, op. cit., No. 85.
55 All these capacities can be developed in teenagers by means of the case-method used as a basis for discussion with groups of young people. It is encouraging to see how, with proper guidance, they can deal with subjects connected with justice, love, freedom, etc.
56 Op. cit., p. 75.
57 Escrivá, op. cit., No. 88.
58 Cf. K. Rogers in *Task and Organisation* (New York 1976) 351.
59 Horace, *Odes*, 3, p. 25.
60 Pieper, op. cit., p. 194.
61 Cf. D. Krathwohl, 'Dominio Afectivo' in *Taxonomía des los Objectivos de la Educación* (Buenos Aires 1971).
62 I. Celaya y Urrutia, 'Audacia' in *Gran Enciclopedia Rialp* (Madrid 1971), Vol. 3, p. 348.
63 Escrivá, *The Way* (Dublin 1982), No. 401.
64 *Celaya y Urrutia*, art. cit., p. 349.

65 Escrivá, *Friends of God*, No. 96.
66 P. Rodriguez, *Fe y Vida de Fe* (Pamplona 1974), p. 56.
67 St Teresa of Avila, *Interior Castle*, Sixth Mansion 10: cf. Peers (trs.) *Complete Works*, Vol. III, p. 323.
68 Rodriguez, op. cit., p.. 51.
69 *Sententiae*, No. 37, PL 183, 755.
70 Escrivá, op. cit., No. 101.
71 W. Cowper, *The Winter Walk at Noon*, Bk VI, line 96.
72 J.J. Gutierrez Comas, 'Humilidad' in *Gran Enciclopedia Rialp*, Vol. 12 (Madrid 1973), p. 245.
73 2 Cor 12: 9–10.
74 Cf. St Thomas Aquinas, *Sum. Th.* II-II, q. 4, a. 7 ad 2.
75 Escrivá, op. cit., No. 90.
76 Escrivá, op. cit., No. 90.
77 J.L. Gutierrez Garcia, 'Solidaridad' in *Gran Enciclopedia Rialp*, Vol. 21 (Madrid 1975), p. 597.
78 Cf. Chapter 7 above.
79 A. Vazquez de Prada, *Estudio sobre la amistad* (Madrid 1975), 203.
80 Op. cit., p. 162.
81 Op. cit., p. 188.
82 Pius XI, Encyclical *Casti Connubii*, 31 December 1930, No. 4.
83 *Sum. Th.* II-II, q. 101, a.1.
84 Pius XII, *Christmas Message* 1954.
85 Cf. Escrivá, *The Way*, No. 545.